Critical acclaim for *Authentically Black*:

"Another conversation starter from the author of *Losing the Race*." —Rosemary Herbert, *Boston Herald*

"McWhorter has delivered some powerfully compelling criticisms of many White liberals, Black leaders and Black intellectuals." —Alex P. Kellogg, *BET.com*

"This collection of nine articles . . . extends the arguments McWhorter made in *Losing the Race*: African-Americans must give up the 'seductive drug' of holding whites accountable for every perceived problem in the community; avoid welfare and demand opportunities for self-realization, not charity and handouts; fight their unacknowledged 'sense that at the end of the day, black people are inferior to whites . . . an internalization of the contempt that the dominant class once held for us.'" —*Kirkus Reviews*

"McWhorter's siren call for dynamic self and societal transformation . . . deserves to be heard."
—Thomas Davis, *Library Journal*

"McWhorter takes on a lot of hot button issues and with each one he makes his case without flinching. What makes his book of value is his forthright analysis of the self-defeating attitudes and behavior that continue to hobble a great many blacks. His inside knowledge and candor make this a necessary book to add to the growing library of works that deal with this particular aspect of America's enduring entanglement with race."
—Elizabeth Wright, *The American Conservative*

"For the good of us all, one hopes that the sensible views McWhorter promotes will prevail . . . McWhorter is right."
—Preston Jones, *Christianity Today*

"A worthy book."
—*Booklist*

ALSO BY JOHN McWHORTER

Towards a New Model of Creole Genesis

*The Missing Spanish Creoles: Recovering the Birth of
Plantation Creole Languages*

*Word on the Street: Debunking the Myth of a
Pure Standard English*

Spreading the Word: Language and Dialect in America

Losing the Race: Self-Sabotage in Black America

The Power of Babel: A Natural History of Language

*Doing Our Own Thing: The Degradation of Language
and Music and Why We Should, Like, Care*

Authentically Black

Essays for the Black Silent Majority

...

JOHN McWHORTER

GOTHAM BOOKS

GOTHAM BOOKS
Published by Penguin Group (USA) Inc.
375 Hudson Street, New York, New York 10014, U.S.A.
Penguin Books Ltd, Registered Offices: 80 Strand, London WC2R 0RL, England
Penguin Books Australia Ltd, 250 Camberwell Road,Camberwell, Victoria 3124,Australia
Penguin Books Canada Ltd, 10 Alcorn Avenue, Toronto, Ontario, Canada M4V 3B2
Penguin Books (NZ) Ltd, Cnr Rosedale and Airborne Roads,
  Albany, Auckland 1310, New Zealand

Published by Gotham Books, a division of Penguin Group (USA) Inc. Previously
published as a Gotham Books hardcover edition.

First Gotham Books trade paperback printing, January 2004
10 9 8 7 6 5 4 3 2 1

Acknowledgment is made to the following, in which various forms of this book's
pieces first appeared:

The Harvard Journal of African American Policy, "Profiling and 'Getting Past Race'."
The New Republic, "Against Reparations," "Gimme a Break!" and "Uses of Ugliness."
City Journal, "The Campus Diversity Fraud," "A Usable Black History," "The Mau
Mauing at Harvard," and "Why Blacks Don't Need Leaders."

Copyright © John McWhorter, 2003
All rights reserved

Gotham Books and the skyscraper logo are trademarks of PenguinGroup (USA) Inc.

The Library of Congress has cataloged the Gotham Books hardcover edition as follows:
McWhorter, John H.
Authentically Black : essays for the Black Silent Majority / John McWhorter.
p. cm.
ISBN 1-592-40001-9 (hc.)
ISBN 1-592-40046-9 (pb.)
1. African Americans—Social conditions—21st century.   2. African Americans—Race
identity.   3. African Americans—Intellectual life—21st century.   4. United States—
Race relations.   5. United States—Social conditions—21st century.   6. African
Americans in popular culture.   7. Popular culture—United States.   8. United
States—Intellectual life—21st century.   I. Title.

E185.615 .M354 2003
305.896'073—dc21   2002026073

Printed in the United States of America
Set in Giovanni Book
Designed by Carla Bolte

Without limiting the rights under copyright reserved above, no part of this publication
may be reproduced, stored in or introduced into a retrieval system, or transmitted, in
any form, or by any means (electronic, mechanical, photocopying, recording, or
otherwise), without the prior written permission of both the copyright owner and the
above publisher of this book.

The scanning, uploading, and distribution of this book via the Internet or via any
other means without the permission of the publisher is illegal and punishable by law.
Please purchase only authorized electronic editions, and do not participate in or
encourage electronic piracy of copyrighted materials. Your support of the author's
rights is appreciated.

This book is printed on acid-free paper. ♾

I dedicate this book to the over one thousand African-Americans who have given me their support for my public writings and statements on race since the publication of *Losing the Race* in the fall of 2000.

In letters, e-mails, phone calls, reviews, and public encounters, from black businesspeople, teachers, schoolchildren, undergraduates, police officers, public officials, working people, authors, actors, mothers, fathers, seniors, and even prisoners, I have been confirmed in my opinion that there is a Black Silent Majority in America, committed to real progress but too seldom heard from.

We Will Rise, folks. For that matter, we already have.

Contents

Preface

This book collects various pieces I have written in the wake of the publication of *Losing the Race: Self-Sabotage in Black America*.

That book has often been misunderstood as a statement about education. Understandably so, as since I am a college professor, many of the demonstration cases I chose were from the educational arena (the "acting white" syndrome among black students, Affirmative Action, Ebonics). However, my actual goal in *Losing the Race* was to explore general currents in racial ideology that are predictable, given blacks' history in this country, but which have become more harmful than helpful.

The educational issues my life has brought me close to usefully illustrate these phenomena. But if I happened to be a criminologist, I would have written a similar book drawing from sentencing issues and racial profiling; if I were a businessman I would have concentrated on the corporate world, small business development, and Affirmative Action in hiring and contracting.

All of which is to say that my interest is in the general fact that almost four decades after the Civil Rights Act, African-Americans remain the country's "race apart," an eternal problem case. Many facets of this problem did not happen to fit the specific argumentational trajectory that I built *Losing the Race* upon. Since then, I have had the opportunity to address many of these other aspects in print. *Authentically Black* gathers a sample of those pieces between two covers, with the first two essays written especially for this book.

I am not one for long introductions. This book will stand on its meat, the pieces that follow. It is up to the reader what general conclusions he or she draws from them. As a summary statement, I will offer only the following, which I hope the reader will concur with after finishing the book, despite inevitable disagreements with specifics.

———

On the topic of blacks in America, among thinking people over the past few decades *common consensus has drifted away from common sense.* By this I do not mean just my common sense, but everyone's. The left tells us that black people's job is to insist that short of ideal conditions, only the occasional shooting star among us can do much better than show up. We are taught that as good people, we must pretend to believe that unequal outcomes are always due to unequal opportunity, that it is impossible that culture-internal ideologies can hobble a group from taking advantage of pathways to success. This ideology is taught in universities, assumed on many newspaper editorial pages, and preached by all too many of those anointed as black "leaders." In fact, we are too often told that this is less ideology than truth, and that it is only those who question it who have "an ideology."

Yet I firmly believe that most of us deep down no longer truly believe in this supposed "truth." Whites have learned that they are best off pretending to, on the pain of being tarred as "racists" in public. More importantly, as I will argue in the first chapter, even most blacks no longer believe in this purported Common Consensus (if they ever did), despite all evidence to the contrary. Certainly there is a vocal contingent of black leftists who will insist on professional victimhood to their graves. Their prevalence in the academy and among black leaders of a certain age gives the misleading impression that this is *the* "black" way of thinking.

But it isn't. As they say, you can't fool all of the people all of the time. A people on the rise with the world open to them cannot be convinced forever that their watchcry must be "I cannot surmount obstacles." This is clear to any sane human being, and as such, in private, most black Americans operate according to the same Common Sense that whites espouse behind closed doors on "the race problem." Most Americans *black and white* know that life is not perfect for anyone, and is perhaps even less perfect for most blacks, but hardly to the extent that we could not make our way up the last few steps to the mountaintop by pulling in our stomachs and forging ahead. And most Americans *black and white* know that as often as not these days, what is holding blacks back is more the impression otherwise than "white supremacy."

Yet it is always "in the air" that the Common Consensus is somehow a larger truth. This idea hangs so thick, and is argued with such blazing indignation, that blacks end up wangling a way of splitting the difference between this and Common Sense. It has become a kind of fragile mental poise: while keeping Common Sense close to the heart, one wields the Common Consensus as a skin, as it were—in how one views one's race as a group, in ticklish conversations with whites when "the black thing" comes up, in who one votes for hell or high water. This variation on the "double consciousness" that W. E. B. Du Bois wrote of is the subject of Chapter One, grounds all of the pieces in this book, and is the source of the book's title. Since the late 1960s, blacks have been taught that presenting ourselves and our people as victims when whites are watching is the essence of being "authentically black."

―――――

That is what this book is. But before proceeding to the main course, I feel it charitable and necessary to make clear what this book is not.

―――――

Most of the criticisms leveled against *Losing the Race* were predictable. But the one that initially took me by surprise was that the book is "not scholarly." I have since realized the source of this charge: apparently many are under an impression, quite reasonable, that a book written by someone with a Ph.D. will necessarily be an academic one.

Thus I must make it clear that I never intended *Losing the Race* as a work of scholarship, nor do I present this one as such. My academic work is in linguistics. I have written two academic books and about twenty-five academic articles on linguistics, written in tapeworm phraseology, their every point argued by close engagement with several other academic texts and articles. This is the accepted standard in academic discourse, and I have deeply enjoyed my participation in this realm of discussion.

Yet I would not wish any of these books and articles on anyone outside of my field; they are written to communicate only with a few hundred academic linguists. In my writings on race, I have no intention whatsoever of couching my opinions in that format. I firmly believe that our race dilemma is too urgent for writings on it to serve as fodder for a few hundred graduate students and scholars and then be stashed away on university library shelves, making no difference in the thinking of anyone beyond the ivory tower. It might bear mentioning that my race writings have no connection to my reputation and career path in linguistics, nor does my linguistics work have anything to do with race issues in America. When I write on race I am wearing a completely different "hat."

When wearing that hat, I intend my writings as what we might call informed editorials. I certainly consider myself responsible for the factual accuracy of anything I present to the public. I furthermore attempt to found my opinions upon open eyes, wide reading, and careful reflection, although I can hardly claim that this renders my contributions the last word on any subject. However, I intend the results not as academic cogitation, but as an attempt at informed Common Sense that might touch the everyday thinking of readers interested in hearing me out.

One often sees writers in this genre designated "public intellectuals." I have no problem with being classed in that group, but it must be clear that as such, my intended audience is not people with Ph.D.s (although I welcome their engagement and feedback). *Authentically Black* is written for the public, more specifically the reflective citizen who is interested in extended thoughts on race presented in accessible fashion.

Therefore, one will search this book in vain for sustained engagement with the valuable scholarly contributions on race of the likes of Alain Locke. I have little to offer the reader seeking philosophical engagement with, say, Frantz Fanon or Audre Lorde. I am not given to flagging my essays with nods to assorted philosophers, novelists, and littérateurs largely familiar only to academics. If the reader is by chance sampling this preface at a bookstore and would prefer a study of that kind, I in all sincerity beseech them not to buy this book. *Authentically Black* will refer in passing to a range of writings, facts, and figures. But it is most certainly not an academic or "scholarly" book. I would feel that I had failed in my goal if it was.

––––––

This book is written to Americans of all races and political persuasions.

I cherish my black readership, and offer a heartfelt thanks to each one of the African-Americans who have e-mailed, written, or called me or approached me on the street and in cafés since *Losing the Race* was published. At publication time, this totaled well over a thousand black Americans in two years. Many people have a hard time believing this when I say it, but I never expected this from a book about what some linguist thinks about race in America. But I cannot help being happy that what I wrote makes some sense to so many people.

But if I may, *Authentically Black* is not written only as an in-group conversation between me and other African-Americans. I have two imperatives in writing about race. One is certainly to urge black people to reconsider the version of "blackness" that has been foisted upon us so passionately and distractingly since the late 1960s. However, an equally important one is to explain to whites the roots of a race discourse that so many of them today find, to put it politely, frustrating—or to put it less politely, appalling.

Losing the Race was occasionally called a "black-bashing" book, of course. But many white readers have gleaned that one of my main intents was simply to explain what looks so counterintuitive and self-defeating to them, and I have continued in this goal in my subsequent writings. I am firmly convinced that the problems often seen in America as "black" are actually just human. Any ethnic group confronted with the same sociohistorical variables would fall under the exact same self-defeating ideologies.

Many blacks are alarmed that whites may not understand that racism can be systemic as well as overt. But, folks, most whites got this message long ago. Today, what many whites do not understand is why so many blacks have concluded that systemic racism is a sentence to failure rather than a surmountable obstacle. Both whites and blacks are responsible for the prevalence of this illusion in America. I hope to outline in my race work just how we have gotten to that point and how we might get beyond it.

As such, white readership is as important to me as black readership, and Latinos, Asians, and everybody else are equally welcome in the conversation. This book is for anybody interested.

Finally, some interpret my writings on race as aimed at white conservatives. And the truth is that most of what white conservatives believe on race in America is much more constructive for black people than what the white left has bamboozled us with over the past forty years. However, I must assure the reader that I would consider it a waste of time to spend so much energy composing text designed simply to tell a certain contingent of whites what they already believe. Furthermore, some of my views rankle white conservatives and would never pass muster in any of their journals of opinion. For example, an op-ed condensation of Chapter Two of this book, on racial profiling, elicited its first wave of testy mail from whites rather than blacks. More than a few whites have written me in the wake of *Losing the Race* asking me to reconsider views I express in that book incompatible with the conservative agenda, such as my espousal of Affirmative Action in the business world.

On the contrary, I write with my eye on the white left as much as the white right. The white left see their enshrinement of racial preferences and open-ended welfare and their recasting of the black criminal as a "rebel" as proof that they are not "racists." But these positions, superficially humane, deny African-Americans the incentive to strive for the best within us, and even have a way of teaching us through the back door that being an also-ran is the heart of being "authentically black." As such, what passes for enlightenment becomes, in its way, racist all over again.

A common wishful canard tells us that the truth on any issue is in the middle, that humankind would advance to a new level of awareness if only everybody would learn to incorporate all viewpoints. But this is not true for all issues. For example, the planets revolve around the sun, period. They do not "in certain senses" revolve around the earth; any "middle ground" here would be intellectually bankrupt.

Yet I believe, on the basis of all indications known to me, that when it comes to how black people will cease being America's poster children, the truth is indeed in the middle of the political spectrum. The right's sentiment "Black people need to just get real and put up or shut up" will not do by itself. Maybe it's true in a purely intellectual sense, but for too many, four decades of a different ideology in the air have made it impossible for this alone to be a useful spur for change. But on the other hand, that ideology in the air—the leftist conviction that "black people can only achieve when society is perfect and until then they are all heroes for just getting out of bed"—is equally unsuitable. This ideology describes children, not a race of strong people living in, warts and all, the most glorious country on the planet.

I am obsessed with a quest to help chart a path between these two positions. Thus where white readers are concerned, I write for all political persuasions. I am not seeking anyone's patronage, and would feel naked without my other career in linguistics. Like *Losing the Race*, *Authentically Black* is not a ploy. It is, simply, a book.

———

And with that, let's get to it.

Oakland, California

1

The New Black
Double Consciousness

. . .

In his landmark book The Souls of Black Folk in 1903, W. E. B.
Du Bois famously analyzed the black American as possessing what he
called a double consciousness, caught between a self-conception as
an American and as a person of African descent. As Du Bois put it:

> The Negro ever feels his two-ness—an American, a Negro; two souls,
> two thoughts, two unreconciled strivings . . . two warring ideals
> in one dark body, whose dogged strength alone keeps it from being
> torn asunder.

As so often, Du Bois's teachings apply as well to black Americans
over a century later. In that vein, the double consciousness he referred to is often claimed to apply equally well to today's black
Americans. But this observation is typically made with an implication that "after all this time, nothing has really changed," that whites
remain implacably opposed to including blacks in the American
fabric, leaving black people eternally "torn asunder."

But that analysis stems from the common impulse to resist ac-knowledging that race relations in America have undergone seismic changes since 1903. Du Bois's conception remains relevant indeed, but only in an evolved reflex of the one that he described. ∎

Black America today is permeated by a new kind of double consciousness that has strayed far beyond the one Du Bois examined in 1903. To wit, a tacit sense reigns among a great many black Americans today that the "authentic" black person stresses personal initiative and strength in private, but dutifully takes on the mantle of victimhood as a public face.

For many non-blacks, the private orientation toward personal empowerment will sound unfamiliar. Naturally so, because most of us only experience black discourse from the outside, and thus see the enshrinement of victimhood as a standard modus operandi. At the head of 2001, so-called black leaders Jesse Jackson and Al Sharpton promised that black Americans would "resist" the Bush presidency given allegations that racism held down the black vote in Florida. That year, the hottest issue on the race landscape was the notion that black America's main task is to agitate for financial compensation for the work of slaves none of us ever knew. We could even see this sense of victimhood as our "Sunday best" in all but a sliver of blacks voting for Al Gore, whose party has championed identity politics for decades, reveling in the self-congratulatory smugness of treating blacks as helpless.

But these affairs are only one part of the true story about black Americans in our moment, and much of the more colorful headline escapades are, in essence, a kind of histrionic smoke screen. Nothing came of Jackson and Sharpton's chest-beating regarding "resisting" the Bush presidency—and may history record that this theatrical threat had evaporated several months before the September 11 terrorist attacks temporarily pushed race issues off the table. Indeed, both "leaders" beat their chests on the issue anew eleven months later, at a "State of the Black World" conference in Atlanta that November. But this conference was poorly organized—translation: there was little genuine commitment behind the ideology it represented. And even with these rock stars on the bill, it was sparsely attended, and many of the invited speakers did not even show up. This was no accident: it showed that these mechanical attempts to replay the March on Washington in a different America are no longer moving most black people enough to get them out of their houses.

Meanwhile, Jackson's main political vaudeville act that year had been to propose himself as an envoy to the Taliban. And then, take it, Al—the Reverend Sharpton, despite urgent issues facing blacks in his constituency, had chosen a hunger strike protesting the military occupation of distant Vieques as his next song-and-dance. After authoring the most influential book ever written on reparations, *The Debt*, Randall Robinson was difficult to even reach for requests to debate his position. The book itself, containing a mere few pages out of hundreds on just what "reparations" would consist of, was ultimately a dramatic gesture, not a brief for concrete engagement. And so it went. All of this was, to take a page from the lit-crit crowd, "performative," a kind of symbolic playacting.

We gain a perspective on the true black America from polls over the past ten years, such as that done by the *New York Times* of roughly a thousand blacks from around the country. In the year 2000, a mere 7 percent of blacks thought racism was the most important problem for the next generation of Americans to solve. That same year, 51 percent of blacks thought race relations were generally good, whereas ten years before, only 33 percent did. In 1992, 29 percent of blacks thought progress had been made in race relations since the 1960s; by 2000, twice as many (58 percent) did.

Nor are these numbers mere statistical curiosities hard to connect with life as we live it day to day. Results like this square easily with a black person's ordinary experience. All of the positions commonly deemed "black conservative" are easy topics at a black barbecue today. Bring these things up and you are almost sure to have at least half the room agreeing and the professional victimologist or two among the group coming away feeling on the defensive. Most blacks understand that "the white man keeps me down" has become more a routine than an earnest statement.

But often, when asked about race issues when whites are present, the same people who sound a lot like Shelby Steele among "their own" will pause for a moment and then carefully dredge up episodes of possible racism they may have encountered in their lives, claim that there aren't enough positive images of blacks in the media, etc. In the black community today, there is a tacit rule that black responsibility and self-empowerment are not to be discussed at any length where whites can hear.

Why are most black Americans so uncomfortable acknowledging the successes of their race in public—beyond athletes, entertainers, and Blacks in Wax frozen in old photos as distant icons rather than flesh-and-blood figures? To the outside observer, nothing could look more counterproductive.

But the discomfort is based on a guiding conviction:

Black people cannot rise without whites' assistance. Therefore, in public we must downplay the improving conditions in black America, to make sure that whites do not decide that all is well and abandon us to misery.

In daily life this assumption is encapsulated in the often heard phrase "We can't let whites off the hook." Black Americans roughly sixty and younger have spent their mature lives where this phrase is as much a part of the scenery as the "one in three young black men are in jail or involved with the criminal justice system" mantra that I will discuss in the next chapter. Many ideological tendencies in the black community are based neatly in this "whites on the hook" idea, virtually unquestioned and spiritually resonant.

▪ ▪ ▪

Like many cultural hallmarks, the new double consciousness is not usually consciously felt. Few blacks actually go around saying "When white people are around, don't make us sound like we can take care of ourselves." The ideology often plays its hand as much in what is not said as in what is.

Black politics post-1964 is a good example here, and history provides revealing contrasts. Let's go back to the inspiration for this essay, W. E. B. Du Bois. Here he is seeking to get the Progressive Party to include a race program in its platform in 1912. This is no classic passage from one of his great works. It's just a passing statement in a long and remarkable life:

> The Progressive party recognizes that distinctions of race or class in political life have no place in a democracy. Especially does the party realize that a group of 10,000,000 people who have in a generation changed from a slave to a free labor system, reestablished family life, accumulated $1,000,000,000 [in] property, including 20,000,000 acres of land, and reduced their illiteracy from 80 to 30 per cent, deserve and must have justice, opportunity and a voice in their own government.

On its face this is a rather faceless recitation of statistics. But here is how it is crucial: note how unthinkable it would be to hear a black leader chronicle black successes in this way today. Our Kweisi Mfumes see their job as to list black miseries. They would see a statement like Du Bois's as risking that whites might lose sight of their culpability regarding our condition.

Du Bois's strategy was to show whites that blacks had proven that they were worth bringing into the fold. Jesse Jackson's strategy is to show whites that to not bring blacks into the fold makes them immoral, and that this means that whether or not blacks present ability, diligence, or moral solidity beforehand is beside the point. This has been the leitmotif of Civil Rights discourse for over three decades now. Politics meets the New Double Consciousness: blacks under about forty-five have known little else.

Of course, Du Bois's quest was a vain one: in his day opposition to blacks' inclusion in society was too deep-seated and prevalent to yield to logical argument. But this is ninety years later. Ours is an America with welfare, Affirmative Action, a dazzling array of scholarships, loans, and funding programs targeted at minority education, and Community Development Corporations run by whites to help inner city blacks buy the buildings in their neighborhood. In our America, racial discrimination is illegal, and even the mere expression of racist sentiments is socially condemned and often legally actionable. Even in his long life, Du Bois never knew any of these things. Sure, some problems remain for us nevertheless. But is this a society suggesting such implacable opposition to blacks that we cannot afford to sell ourselves just a little?

Yet many blacks today are distinctly uncomfortable hearing it said too loudly where whites can hear it that, for example, *most black people are not poor.* Let a white or black writer say this and many black thinkers—as well as white allies—are alarmed. Suddenly the same people who are indignant that whites think most blacks *are* poor furiously define the poverty line as far upward as possible. Whole monographs appear warning that black families tend not to have as much accumulated capital in the form of savings and investments as white ones. Again, we cannot take this as working in the spirit of Du Bois. He was hardly unaware of black poverty, and spent decades gathering painstaking reports on it. However, he would have been perplexed at the modern requirement to stress the bad news over the good.

In his landmark survey of 1899, *The Philadelphia Negro*, Du Bois discusses what we would call the black underclass, describing a layer of society strikingly like the one familiar to us. But he emphasizes that these people constitute only about a tenth of the black population in Philadelphia (and has no leaning toward celebrating their moral pitfalls as noble rebellion). To the modern reader, *The Philadelphia Negro* can be an almost odd read, as Du Bois devotes most of the space to blacks who were successful or at least hardworking and financially self-sufficient. Today we spontaneously expect a book called *The Philadelphia Negro* written by a black man to be a chronicle of black misery and failure—isn't that, after all, what a statement on black people that whites read is supposed to be about?

For Du Bois and his comrades, no. Du Bois's double consciousness did not require that blacks only discuss their successes behind closed doors, leaving restaurateur B. Smith to be thought of as "pushing the envelope" in celebrating affluence as "the black Martha Stewart." It is the New Double Consciousness that implants this tendency today.

———

And it is why the black community only embraces Colin Powell as a black hero in a fainthearted way. "Ongoing black genocide" growls star black radical academic bell hooks in highly sought-after speaking gigs nationwide. But somehow it means nothing to people like her and her fans that *the Secretary of State is black*! When Du Bois wrote *The Philadelphia Negro*, the prospect of this would have sounded like science fiction. But this victory means nothing to many blacks. Why? One is not supposed to say this too loud, but really, to a great many black people Powell is not, well, "really" black.

"What's *that* all about?" I often hear whites say in reference to certain blacks, as brown-skinned and full-lipped as one could wish, being called "not black." The answer comes from a contrast: let's go back to Jesse and place him next to Powell. It is difficult to perceive just what gains for the black community Jesse Jackson has been responsible for over the past twenty-five years. He's certainly a "symbol," and okay, he ran for president, but that did not put more clothes on any child's back. Yet quibble though we may with this or that about him, his "blackness" is unquestioned. He is readily considered a "black leader"—even *the* black leader—because he is committed to keeping whitey on his toes.

On the other hand, Powell, serving in a Republican administration, obviously is not. The New Double Consciousness teaches us that playing the blame game—in public—is the very essence of being authentically black. "Really?" one might ask. But think about it: it is precisely because of his failure to indulge in this sport that Powell is not considered truly "black" at all. "Black" people resist whitey—one's only choice is in how graciously one chooses to do it. Here is the verdict on Powell from a black man who once served as a Congressional aide:

> He's really just a slickly packaged white guy who has just enough melanin and makes just enough references to his past as a black kid in New York to seem empathetic to black people. He's like an Ed Brooke, but without the white wife. Instead, Powell's son has the white wife.

It's not the melanin issue that is behind that statement. No one questions the "blackness" of Redd Foxx or Vanessa Williams, while plenty question the "blackness" of, for example, Clarence Thomas. Jesse Jackson is a "black leader" who has done nothing whatsoever to improve the lot of the people he represents, but he remains "black" because he likes trying to keep whites guilty, and is a "leader" because he does it in the national spotlight. And the minute Powell popped up in the headlines threatening to resign unless the Bush administration pumped more block grants into the ghettos and stuck up for Affirmative Action, he would suddenly be a "real black man" and "one of our leaders."

————

Thomas leads to another example of the New Double Consciousness in operation. If black authenticity means not letting whites off the hook, then blacks who suggest—in anything but the most parenthetical of fashions—that enshrining victimhood is not exactly the most progressive of notions are regularly excoriated as "traitors."

This is often misanalyzed as a matter of blacks trying to hold on to power or patronage. But this cannot account for the prevalence of the perspective even among ordinary blacks with no interest in such things. What one is considered to be a traitor against is the unwritten agreement that our job is to keep whites feeling guilty, lest they slide off of that hook.

A review of *Losing the Race* on Amazon.com is useful here. It sums up the New Double Consciousness so perfectly that I will quote it almost in full:

I'm hesitant to write this review. On the one hand, I absolutely loved the book, despite having started it hating McWhorter from what I had heard about him. As I read it, I found it harder and harder to disagree with him. However, I'm worried that

McWhorter's argumentation will be picked up by truly anti-black people . . . I'm troubled by the fact that white people who already harbor prejudices against African-Americans now have yet another weapon.

This man is no black nationalist zealot. He is a sober, concerned individual who is imprinted with the zeitgeist of our moment. Hundreds of black people have expressed the same reservations about the book to me. For a few, my breaking the unspoken rule elicits sharp contempt, but in most, just a looming discomfort. That particular discomfort is a keystone of modern black identity: a sense that whites are always just on the verge of taking us back to the past, meaning that we must maintain an aggrieved public presence to remind them of their "duty."

"Why can't people just have different opinions?" many whites wonder on seeing hostile responses to "black conservatives" from black writers and activists. But it's not that black people do not understand that opinions will differ. It's that when it comes to race, the sense that black success requires white guilt leads to an assumption that anyone who strays beyond a narrow range of leftist perspectives on race is either naïve or inhumane.

The blacks denouncing the Ward Connerlys as Uncle Toms are neither planning to run for office nor too dumb to understand that everybody is not always going to agree with them. The New Double Consciousness is the rub, leading them to mistake their views as morality rather than opinions.

―――

Amazon.com provides another illustration, in the reader response to Lawrence Otis Graham's book *Our Kind of People*, published in 2000. All Graham did was write a quiet, genial survey of the accomplishments of well-to-do blacks since the Civil War. There is not a hint of disparagement of less successful blacks in it. The closest the book comes to this is a few quotations from rich blacks who say that they do not socialize with blacks below them in class because they do not have enough in common with them to sustain deep relationships. But one of Graham's main focuses in depicting these very people is their black charity efforts, which he chronicles with almost excessive thoroughness.

Yet Graham's book has been savaged by many black readers. His Amazon reviews are almost chilling to read through. One reader's response is a cold-eyed ad hominem tale: she apparently watched Graham day by day on a commuter train years ago and saw him as frustrated in his attempts to "be white." For her, his book is merely a back-door strategy of asserting his self-worth, by showing that if he has to be "black," then America damned well better know that there exists a black elite and that Graham—who grew up with at least one foot in that world—is part of it.

One might think that the black community would take such a book as inspiring. When my best friend, a black man, and I discussed the book, our main observation was that we had never known of people like this growing up, and were happy to see that even in the old days there had been a few of us who had gotten that far. But the book cannot make that kind of impression on blacks taught that black authenticity means "keeping whites on their toes."

For many black readers, it's okay for a magazine to run a feature on this black CEO or that black television superstar. But Graham wrote a whole book, extensively publicized, about thousands of successful blacks no one has ever heard of, few of whom give much indication of being supernaturally talented. In other words, *Our Kind of People* implies that black success is almost, well, ordinary. Graham broke a tacit rule: where whites can hear us, we are not to imply that black heroism could ever be a *group* trait.

▪ ▪ ▪

Where has this new Janus-faced double consciousness come from? Just why would a people who privately emphasize their inner strength feel so deeply that they must keep this so quiet once they step outside?

The reason is a particular outgrowth of the New Double Consciousness, another guiding notion so deeply entrenched in modern black thought as to rarely be explicitly declared. Few black Americans have ever had occasion to consider it an opinion rather than a truth. The idea:

> Until all racism is extinct in the United States, there remains a devastating obstacle to success for all blacks except those who are lucky or extraordinarily gifted. Such people are rare, and thus most blacks remain barred by racism from realizing themselves.

Of course no one walks around saying this. Many blacks may have trouble even recognizing it as a keystone of modern black thought. But again, it reveals itself at the wheel in opinions otherwise perplexing.

———

In a 1991 Gallup poll, almost half of the blacks polled thought that three out of four blacks lived in the inner city. Even many black American scholars labor under this misimpression. In 1998,

Columbia African-American Studies department chair Manning Marable's depiction of black America in the *New York Times* was that "a segment of the minority population moves into the corporate and political establishment at the same time that most are pushed even further down the economic ladder."

But not only is the "black is poor" idea refuted by statistics, but it does not even square with ordinary experience in the early 2000s. Today, middle-class black people, as quiet as it's kept, are not engaged in a constant quest to smoke out the rare fellow black who grew up like them. Graham's book chronicles clubs like Jack and Jill that the old black bourgeoisie founded to bring well-heeled black children together, in an era when such people were rare enough to need formal associations to find one another in. But part of the reason my friend and I received this as new information is that by the 1970s, there were so many blacks of, at least, middle-class heritage like us that we could as easily run into each other by accident in school or just out in the driveway. Nor does a walk down the street of an American downtown give any suggestion that most of the blacks one sees are living hand-to-mouth. Indeed, when whites suggest otherwise, most blacks bristle. At such times blacks often indignantly point out that "there's great diversity in the black community," that all black people do not live in the ghetto.

But why, then, did those Gallup poll results come out that way? How could Manning Marable so casually deem "most" blacks as poor or on their way to it?

The cognitive dissonance here comes from that idea of "racism" alone as a decisive check upon black advancement. If racism still exists, and only superstars can get beyond it, then it follows logically that black America must be a group of poor people. One will have this sense quite regardless of what one actually sees. The sense will persist even if one knows *intellectually* that most black people are not poor, and is well posed to dress down whites surprised to find out that you did not grow up on welfare.

Naturally, then, poll after poll shows that blacks tend to assume that even if conditions for themselves and their immediate communities are good, they are less so for most other blacks. In the *New York Times* poll, in 2000 72 percent of blacks thought race relations were good in their communities, but only 57 percent thought they were good in America. The black person may know that the white man is not keeping *them* down, but tends to assume that he *is* keeping *other* blacks down.

———

There is nothing inherently "black" about this. It's what happens when any human being is steeped in a guiding *paradigm*, the term popularized in the 1960s by Thomas Kuhn in his analysis of how scientific inquiry proceeds. For centuries, astronomers assuming that the earth was the center of the universe could not help noticing that many stars' orbits did not conform to the paths one would expect if they were actually revolving around us. Astronomy texts were full of lists of stars that were "exceptional" for some reason. No matter how many such cases piled up over the years, no astronomer considered revising the basic assumption that the earth was the middle of everything. It was all they knew, and most people have too much to do to make a habit of questioning foundational assumptions. Besides, if you never hear any alternatives, it's all too easy to assume that the assumptions are truth incarnate. Thus those stars that keep trekking off their expected paths must just be hairs in the projector lens, static, distractions from the "real deal."

But under a conception where the sun was considered the center of the universe, the paths that those "exceptional" stars followed were predictable. There was no more need for lists of the stars that didn't fit the paradigm. The new conception accurately reflected reality where the old one had been a distortion of it. But previously, even the brilliant had subscribed to the old paradigm because it seemed so plausible on its face—after all, even to us today, it sure looks like stars are revolving around the earth when we look up at night.

The sad fact is that the "racism is what we really need to be talking about" idea leaves blacks today in the position of the pre-Copernican astronomers. Most young blacks cannot help seeing this misconstruing of the role of racism in advancement as natural. After all, those people spraying black protesters to the ground with fire hoses in those old newsreels were certainly racists, weren't they? And even if there are no more signs on the water fountains and we can stay at the Holiday Inn and work in law firms, if whites still do not love us, if there are still "racists" about, then aren't most of us blocked from making our way just like the people in the newsreels were?

———

But the answer here is no. In the trajectory of a race, legalized discrimination is one thing, but mere residual racist sentiment is quite another. The conflation of the two as equally insurmountable scourges is a modern development, not a timeless legacy of "blackness." We know this because untold numbers of oppressed groups throughout world history have risen to the top through their own efforts *despite* not only residual racism, but even legalized discrimination.

Many tell us that white opposition to blacks is so uniquely fierce that it is useless to compare us to others. But how useless is it to compare us to ourselves?

From the late nineteenth century onward, American cities typically had thriving black business districts reproducing white America down to the last detail, including excellent schools— Bronzeville, Chicago; the Auburn Avenue district in Atlanta; the Shaw district in Washington, DC; even Harlem before the 1940s. (In Chapter Eight I dwell further on the Bronzeville example.) These people were no strangers to racism, which was overt and hostile across America. They could not shop in many white stores or stay in most white hotels; they were barred from most prestigious positions in the mainstream world; they read regularly of lynchings; and interracial relationships and marriages were all but unheard of and condemned anyone who dared them to acrid social ostracization. And yet the very people who lived in that world would be baffled at the consensus among their descendants that whites' biases render us powerless to shape our destinies for the better.

Now, one could argue that even if a group *can* eventually rise despite legalized discrimination, that to remove this barrier is a moral advance, like environmentalism or democracy. In that light, the value of Martin Luther King's Civil Rights victory was that he convinced white America of a higher form of being human. Yet the fact remains that even before the Civil Rights Act and its progeny, such as Affirmative Action and expanded welfare, black incomes and employment were on the rise—we were on our way to realizing ourselves even *without* a leg up, although without King it may have taken longer. But be this as it may, *the outlawing of discrimination left just residual racism as our obstacle.* And that's hardly a picnic. But what our ancestors had already pulled off even under *Plessy v. Ferguson* shows that today, yes, there is "racism"—but it is not a sentence to failure.

Yet again, the man considered the bard of the black condition knew this. In 1905 Du Bois convened a group of black movers and shakers at the Niagara Conference to pen a manifesto for black uplift. Within our modern context, one of its most bizarre sentences is Du Bois's grousing charge that "Black America needs justice and is given charity." Du Bois wrote this just days after the members of the conference had had to meet on the Canadian side of Niagara Falls because no hotel in Buffalo—not Birmingham, Buffalo—would house them. We today think "Racism!"—and it was. But Du Bois was not waiting for whites to start loving black people, for them to give us the "charity" of "feeling our pain" with handouts and gestures. He just wanted opportunity to make the best of himself through his own efforts.

This even determined his politics. In 1912 Du Bois flirted with backing Theodore Roosevelt despite his being an obvious racist, and shifted his support to Woodrow Wilson despite being equally aware that Wilson did not "admire," as he put it, black people. "Like writing history with lightning," Wilson (erudite former professor and Princeton president) said about the searingly racist film *The Birth of a Nation* in 1915—and less well known is his

follow-up, that it was "all so terribly true." But for Du Bois the issue was not whether either of these men thought black people
were cool. It was which one of them would be more amenable to
allowing blacks to realize themselves. "Racism"—e.g., whether
Roosevelt or Wilson referred to blacks as "niggers" in private or
thought blacks were their mental equals—wasn't the issue.

———

That kind of racism is *our* obsession, even when none of us have
to endure the bluntly overt bigotry that was a daily experience for
so many of our ancestors just several decades ago. Fewer and
fewer of us black Americans are now old enough to remember a
time when "racism" was not a pungent, manipulative buzzword,
when a revelation that such-and-such white person might be a
"racist" was not a dramatic high point in a black conversation,
when black leaders smoking out purported "racism" in contexts
no one black or white suspected it existed was not a staple of the
evening news.

"Why do we have to keep dredging it up like this?" many whites
often wonder. "Stirring all that stuff up" is another way whites often put it. Both metaphors reveal a sense that racism is now something down below, which would just burn itself out if people
weren't always poking around in the embers down there. Whites
wonder why blacks, too, do not see racism as something largely
trampled underfoot, better left to just decompose while we up
here move on to a better day.

But there is a concrete reason why many blacks insist on stirring
it up, and it's not political patronage. The reason is that second
tacit assumption, that even in its subtler forms, racism prevents

blacks from succeeding in any substantial way. Historically, this is the product of blacks learning the lessons of the Kerner Commission Report of 1968 perhaps too well. Once thinking folk in the 1960s were electrified by the realization that racism could be systemic as well as deliberate, the scene was set for the "psychologization" of the race debate. It was here that we passed from "Are blacks barred from entry into that profession?" to "Does that white person like black people?" Elisabeth Lasch-Quinn deftly pegged this transformation in her *Race Experts*, which never got the coverage it deserved partly because she isn't black, and partly because it was released just a few weeks before the September 11 tragedy.

And the reason black America fell so hard for the line that residual racism spells defeat is one that must elicit sympathy, not blame. Black Americans have been so uniquely susceptible to this ideology because it offers a balm for something sitting at the heart of the African-American consciousness: a sense that at the end of the day, black people are inferior to whites. Certainly on the surface we hear incessantly about black pride. But lying below this is a sad historical legacy: an internalization of the contempt that the dominant class once held us in, and sometimes still does.

Too many black leaders have addressed this and worked against it for me to need to defend that position here: if this were not sitting at the core of the African-American soul, then Malcolm X would not have needed to create a "Black Man" archetype; "Afrocentrist historians" like Mofefi Kete Asante would not be on a mission to create a black history we can be proud of; teachers nationwide would not need to forge a mission to teach their students to be "proud to be black." Anyone who objects that black people do not have a self-image problem has centuries of tower-ing black thinkers to defend their belief against.

And what this problem means is that when we are told that the oppressor is at fault, it is a seductive drug. What better way to get past that nagging sense that whites are better than to always have an articulate indictment at hand, namely that whites are socially unfit "racists" bent on "oppressing" us? Now, in 1967, the charge obviously made a lot of sense. But the problem is that as conditions for black Americans have gotten better and better, the convenient reflex to prefer condemnation of whites over looking within our-selves has hardened into a routine. Today, more often than not, we are quick to smoke out the latest thing "whitey" did less be-cause whites are standing against us than because it feels good. Playing the underdog is a pleasure for any human being—he's evil, I'm goodly. African-Americans, haunted by a sense that whites are better, have innocently overindulged in playing the un-derdog for thirty-five years.

This is a tragedy. Whenever I read one more commentator grip-ing that blacks "play the victim" as a political ploy, I am dismayed that the person is unaware of a grisly psychological stain on a race. All the black Americans out there grousing about "white su-premacy" and smugly dismissing "black conservatives" as naïve sellouts are speaking from this private sense of inadequacy. *No one who misses this can fully understand the race problem in mod-ern America.*

But the fact remains that this tendency has deeply perverted Civil Rights activism and thought. Before the 1960s, Civil Rights leaders were focused on eliminating discriminatory practices. The idea was that with these concrete barriers eliminated, black Americans would make their way to the mountaintop *even in a less than ideal world*. Since then, however, the new assumption has been that our job is to eradicate not discrimination but "racism"—how whites feel about us—regardless of whether or not there are discriminatory laws on the books. You know, that "racism" we can tar whites for and leave them with nothing to say. While we walk away feeling triumphant—sweet solace for a people with our history.

But like geocentric astronomy, this focus on "racism" is not truth. It is an opinion that would have baffled Frederick Douglass, Du Bois, Ida B. Wells, and Adam Clayton Powell, Jr. And increasing numbers of blacks are realizing this. To return to Colin Powell, Charles Moskos and John Sibley Butler, a black sociologist, have written a primer on how the military has achieved so much in creating interracial harmony called *All That We Can Be*, which cites Powell's autobiography approvingly. These authors are dedicated to getting us beyond the race problem, and are quite aware that racism is not dead in America. But here is one piece of advice they offer:

> Lamentable as the presence of white racists may be, it is not the core issue. Indeed, Afro-American history testifies eloquently that black accomplishment can occur despite pervasive white racism. It would be foolhardy to consider the absence of white racists as a precondition for black achievement.

■ ■ ■

Racism, then, is not "What we really need to be talking about." The impression otherwise is founded upon the New Double Consciousness: a tacit notion that our fate depends on whites being guilty that they do not see us as true equals, even if in private we know that we are as capable of achieving under imperfect conditions as any other people. To insist on this as the "authentically black" manifesto is to render the African-American race the most resourceless, passive people in the history of *Homo sapiens sapiens*. We are not a strong people, Black is not Beautiful, until we get out of the habit of thinking that we will not be free until white people like us.

We besmirch the legacy of Du Bois to distort his conception of the double consciousness into a call to dress up indignant passivity as progressive thought. For Du Bois, the double consciousness was not a static badge of pride, but a problem to be gotten beyond. As he put it, it was "the longing to attain self-conscious manhood, to merge his double self into a better and truer self."

Okay, "self-conscious manhood," "a better and truer self"— how do we translate this into real-life, meat-and-potatoes terms? Like this.

———

First of all, does this mean "letting whites off the hook"? Not necessarily. Whites do have some responsibility in compensating for the horrors of the past. Blacks built the great black business districts in young cities that were still wide open, with acres of virgin land and service industries in their infancy. The segment of blacks left behind today are faced with making their way in cities already up and running. Besides this, four decades of defeatist common wisdom have left all too many blacks with a psychological barrier to success. This is often leveled as a mere potshot or complaint, but here I intend it as a constructive observation. Whether or not that defeatism is appropriate or healthy, it's there, and simple calls to "knock it off" will serve no purpose. And this means that like it or not, black America will require more "goosing" than, say, most immigrant groups.

However, we must be able to recognize the goosing when we see it. The "racism is destiny" paradigm often blinds us to seeing that certain policies typically tarred as "anti-black" are precisely what we must require of those "on the hook." The geocentrist astronomer saw a star's peculiar orbit as an exception where the heliocentrist one saw just what the doctor ordered. The modern black person often sees "more racism" in policies that actually offer us the sole thing that will bring us to parity with whites: opportunities to thrive *on our own efforts.*

If whites offer an open-ended welfare program that pays black women to have illegitimate children, then they remain "on the hook." If they offer a time-limited welfare program that acknowledges the obstacles poor black women face but teaches them how to fend for themselves, then they are not "racists." In encouraging black self-sufficiency, they are "off the hook." If whites patronizingly dragoon underqualified blacks into positions beyond their abilities, then in denying blacks the opportunity to learn how to compete, they remain "on the hook." If they identify as many qualified blacks for a position as they can, support them in their efforts, but require the same standards they consider beyond question when applied to their own children, even if this means that blacks constitute less than 12 percent of the staff or student body for the time being, then they are "off the hook." And so it goes.

And what this means is that we must shed another deep-seated assumption that may once have been true but is now obsolete: that the Republican Party and Civil Rights are antithetical concepts. Congressmen John Conyers, Jr., and Jerrold Nadler revealed this assumption in a letter supporting Mary Frances Berry, chairwoman of the United States Civil Rights Commission, in her refusal to seat Republican nominee Peter Kirsanow on the commission. In late 2001, a controversy arose over whether the member who had been appointed to fill out Judge Leon Higginbotham's term upon his death had the right to remain on the commission for a full six-year term. This member, Victoria Wilson, was a Democrat, and Kirsanow's replacing her would have split the commission four to four between Democrats and Republicans, breaking Berry's traditional stronghold over the commission's opinions.

Conyers and Nadler in their letter charged that Kirsanow's appointment would "neutralize" the commission "as an independent voice for Civil Rights." To them this surely seemed an obvious point. But note their assumption: that members who have the ear of a Republican administration compromise, by definition, the ideological purity of Civil Rights itself. Certainly Berry and her pals did not consider their commission "neutralized" when there were six Democrats to two Republicans under the Clinton administration. To Conyers and Nadler, then, to be Republican is to disqualify oneself as sincerely committed to Civil Rights at all.

But no. The party that wants to pay black women to have illegitimate children, denies black students the incentive to do their best in school, does the bidding of teachers' unions more interested in patronage than teaching black children to read beyond the fourth-grade level, and pays court to a mendacious, self-aggrandizing, rabble-rousing cartoon character like Al Sharpton as one of the best among us, is most certainly not, ladies and gentlemen, the embodiment of any Civil Rights that black leaders of the 1950s and 1960s would have recognized.

In sum, then, we follow Du Bois's teaching on attaining "self-conscious manhood" in realizing that whites who seduce us with handouts and set-asides in order to atone for the past remain on the hook, while *whites who give us the opportunity to stand on our own two feet are off the hook.* There is nothing more one group of humans can do for another.

———

And if we understand this, then we are prepared for the second way to follow Du Bois's counsel: we must resist the sincere but misguided black Americans who warn us that if we do not engage in the game of exaggerating black victimhood, then whites may "turn back the clock." To be "authentically black" in a way that yields concrete fruits rather than the same old idle histrionics, we modern blacks must have deeply felt responses to this idea, ever at the ready.

We must ask such people: precisely what are you afraid whites are going to do? What evidence can you present that whites have ever "turned back the clock" since the mid-1960s? I have lost count of how many times black people I have asked this question have been caught without an answer. Ideology does not require empirical confirmation to thrive; we know this regarding, for example, bigotry or religious conviction. Blacks bound by the reflex to assume that whites are ever poised to turn the hoses on us again are similarly driven by a received wisdom: the New Double Consciousness.

But then some blacks *will* have an answer: welfare reform and the impending threat to Affirmative Action suggest a "racist backlash." And here, we must ask ourselves if being "authentically black" means being dedicated to uplift or to idle rage.

If we choose uplift, then we must inform our interlocutor that old-style welfare left millions of black people penned into inner cities. "But welfare was instituted for white people," our interlocutor says. And we will say, "But it was vastly expanded especially for unwed black mothers in the late 1960s, such that its earlier version would be all but unrecognizable to welfare recipients today."

Then we must note that Affirmative Action made others into the very "token blacks" that were considered such an injustice into the 1970s. (Notice that the "token black" term is now virtually obsolete—this is no accident; the modern idea is that black tokenism is permissible "collateral damage" in the imperative to keep the oppressor feeling culpable.) "But in universities, Affirmative Action just means admitting the black candidate over an equally qualified white one to make up for the inequities of the past," our interlocutor might object. Whereupon we must tell them that actually, for decades now universities have regularly admitted black students with much lower grades and test scores than others, that this has been revealed in one university system after another, and has proven to be a national tendency. (If the interlocutor proposes that "diversity" is an overriding imperative, then our response will be informed by Chapter Five.)

We must also remind our interlocutor that while some whites support welfare reform and diluting Affirmative Action, just as many ardently believe that the policies of the 1970s and 1980s were preferable, including innumerable government bureaucrats and all university presidents. And we must add that today, as often as not, revelations of residual racism are aired or prominently defended by whites, such as the claim that blacks are given less generous Nissan car loans regardless of financial status or credit rating; loan discrimination against black farmers in the South; racial discrepancies in medical care, etc.

And here, usually, comes "One out of three young black men are in jail or involved with the criminal justice system." Which is true. Blacks and the criminal justice system is the most urgent race issue in our moment, and is the last locus where serious racism still plays some part. However, even it does not legitimate the New Double Consciousness.

Yes, there are racist policemen, and some of them overdo profiling as a result. As we all know, racism is not dead in America. But remember, the question is whether racism prevails as blacks' main obstacle to success. In that light, the idea that profiling itself and the number of black men in prison shows that "racism" has swooped down upon black America like a hawk and seized "our men" is, once again, ideology, not truth.

Profiling is a tough issue, and I will address it in the next chapter. But for now, the questions we must here ask our interlocutor—and ourselves—are these two:

1. What would *you* do if confronted with a young black teen who was dedicated to selling drugs to people in his neighborhood and recruiting his little brothers and cousins to join him, other than removing him from general circulation?

2. If you feel that taking him off of the streets is not the right solution, then what would you say to the inner-city residents and
   black leaders who call it "racism" when whites *stop* taking such
   young men off of the streets?

I write this a year-and-change after *Losing the Race* was published. Not once have any of the myriad people I have since con-
versed or corresponded with on the profiling issue had a coherent
answer to those two questions.

Profiling is not evidence of whitey pummeling us any way he
can. It is an awkward outgrowth of the effort to rid inner-city neighborhoods of a violent drug trade and the rampant addictions it led
to. Yes, it brings out the worst in some policemen. But then politics
and ideology bring out the worst in the black school board administrators leaving millions of black children functionally illiterate.
Life is never perfect, and there are always some bad apples regardless of race. But most policemen—quite a few of them black—focusing on young black men in searching for drugs are simply following
orders. And we all know that if they did not, then they would risk
one more little black girl shot through the head on the sidewalk,
caught in the cross fire of a turf war between drug peddlers. The
stringent drug laws instituted in the late 1980s were heartily supported by the Congressional Black Caucus, most of whom are virtual poster children for the New Double Consciousness. To wit:
focusing on young black men in working against the drug trade in
ghettos is not, in itself, a racist act.

This does not mean that all is well between blacks and the law.
But it does mean that we cannot defend the New Double Con-

sciousness on the basis of racial profiling. We sabotage ourselves to assume that we must keep whitey on his toes because of Rodney King, because if there were no profiling at all, Rodney King's aunt might get shot while out buying groceries.

And finally, we must ask, "While we are keeping quiet about how strong we are, what is your alternative program for black uplift in the meantime, and"—and this part is crucial—"what evidence can you present, from (1) the American past or (2) another country, that indicates that the program you present will bear fruit?"

Let's make no mistake: it is not fair that any people have to start from a place of disadvantage. But many blacks translate this into supposing that black progress means grimly waiting for white "payback." The emotional payoff here is obvious. But at the end of the day, it is a human universal that achievement only comes from within. It would be nice if there was another way, but there simply is not. If anyone says otherwise, their ideology is bankrupt *unless they identify a single people in American or even world history who have risen from anything but their own efforts.*

––––––

Which brings us to the final point. If we truly believe that we are the agents of our own fate, then we must wean ourselves of taking certain habits of thought as ordinary. Like the astronomers who accepted heliocentrism, we must change our lens.

For one, we must become utterly at ease proclaiming our victories where whites can hear. We must not flinch, for example, when a black or white writer proclaims the simple fact that *most black people are not poor.* There is not the slightest evidence that whites hearing this are going to eliminate welfare completely, bar black students from universities, and take to dragging black people from their homes and hanging them from trees. Arrant discrimination is now illegal—white people regularly lose their jobs for even calling us dirty names. The rest is up to us to accomplish *despite life's imperfections.* There is not a single country on this planet where "racism" in at least its subtler forms does not exist. Black Americans have been through too much over the past four hundred years to waste their time chasing rainbows. To insist that nothing can be expected of us until life is perfect is to make a joke of any pretense that we are a strong people.

And that means: whatever remaining "anti-black sentiment" is out there must concern us no more than it did the people who built Bronzeville, Chicago, or the millions of black families who worked their way into comfortable houses in the suburbs after the *real* obstacle, legalized discrimination, was eliminated. "Anti-black sentiment" must concern us no more than, well, it truly does concern most of us *privately.* We must not let the New Double Consciousness teach us that in public we must don the costume of the underdog. What ethnic group has ever risen on the basis of such a defeatist, self-loathing ideology?

To beat the New Double Consciousness will mean letting go of other routines now taken as ordinary. For example, we must divest ourselves of the impulse to treat passing episodes of "stereotyping"—e.g., evidence of residual racism—as a cosmic injury on the level of lynching. A black education professor at UC Berkeley, driven by a sense of duty to work against the "danger" that *Losing the Race* will distract whites from the hook they ought to remain upon, wrote an op-ed in the *San Francisco Chronicle* listing his and other blacks' various encounters with "racism." In one anecdote he presented, a white man dropped a quarter into the empty coffee cup a black student of his was holding while standing on a corner, mistaking her for a homeless person. The student came into the professor's office crying at the indignity of this brush with "racism."

One might see the white man's impulse as the very pity and guilt that so many seek. But in any case, what we must shed is the sense that this episode has anything to do with this student's earning a Ph.D. and living a life of grace and accomplishment. If this one little episode compromises her ability to develop a sense of, in Du Bois's terms, "self-conscious manhood," then prospects are dire for the African-American race.

The impulse to build one's self-conception around this white man's act is not a matter of timeless "black identity." It is a symptom local to our times, and it is a mistake. One searches the works of Du Bois in vain for any extended concern with petty indignities of this kind—he was about making sure blacks could make their own gardens grow, period. His contemporary Ida B. Wells was a fierce critic of lynching; she would thoroughly understand our crusade against the more abusive outgrowths of profiling. But she would not have known quite what to make of a black professor devoting public ink to the likes of having a quarter dropped into one's empty coffee cup.

And that was because Ida B. Wells was possessed of a true inner pride that slogans like "Black By Popular Demand" only fake. Maybe we wonder where she got it. She, in step with the Victorian ideology of her era, would not have jibed with the Mother Africa concept that so many have pointed us to since the 1960s. And though this notion has its good points, after thirty years it has had little genuine impact on most of us beyond sartorial statements and Kwanzaa. We are centuries beyond Africa; Nigerians and Botswanans are foreign to us—we are at heart a distinctly American people.

Are we haunted by a sense that our tragic history right here in this country doesn't offer much to be proud of? In Chapter Seven I will show that this is understandable, but that in fact black American history offers quite a bit that we can stick our chests out about. And we must attend to this. Look around—other ethnic groups' self-regard is based on their accomplishments, their culture. Indians, Chinese, and Jews have not built their sense of identity upon how articulately they keep white Americans guilty. They are ahead of us. Let's learn from them.

———

In closing, one question looms. Just why *should* we work against the New Double Consciousness? More than a few black academics and leaders and their non-black comrades tell us that when we adopt a staged sense of victimhood, we are philosophically advanced, purveying a higher form of consciousness by seeking uplift through "performativity."

Don't believe this for a minute. Sometimes all the world is *not* a stage, and the last thing black Americans need is to be "stereotyped" further as entertainers. We are not acting; this is our lives here.

First, brass-tacks pragmatism beckons. When we let the "strong at home, victims in public" routine pass as "authentically black," it channels our political allegiance to whites who concur with us that we are helpless objects of pity. And as long as black America pulls the lever robotlike for the candidates that offer us white guilt instead of concrete pathways to self-empowerment, we are as politically impotent as blacks were when Du Bois wrote.

And second, dare I propose: if we remain concerned about how whites feel about us—and maybe we always will—then the only way to eradicate residual racism is to make our own way and show what we are made of. Since the 1960s, many have told us that this is unfair because we were brought here as slaves and treated like animals for centuries. We are taught that for African-Americans alone, the cart must be put before the horse and we must teach whites not to be racist *first*, even when seeing us at our worst. I will never forget, if I may, one more Amazon review of *Losing the Race* where a black woman wrote, "I insist on my right to be mediocre."

Nimble, but Du Bois would turn in his grave. History records no race rising to the top on the basis of so dismal a watchcry, and unsurprisingly, it has not worked for us. We've been pretending it would for almost forty years and yet residual racism persists. Whites responded to Dr. King's moral call to eliminate legalized segregation, and have come a long way in recasting their vision of blacks as humans rather than chattel. For most whites today, to be called a racist is as horrifying a prospect as being pegged as a witch was in Colonial America. But whites have gone about as far as they will; the rest of the job is ours. What will make whites truly see blacks as equals, as they now do Jews, the Chinese, and the Irish, is our matching them in self-sufficiency. We will not earn whites' admiration by blackmailing them into pretending to respect us by screaming that we are "Faces at the Bottom of the Well" until racism does not exist in America.

A race does not make its mark by how successful it has been at exacting charity, but by how much it achieves without charity. Fair? No. But it's true. Du Bois, writing "Black America needs justice and is given charity," knew that justice and charity were not the same thing. If we really see him as a guide, we must take him at his word, and check our tendency to think that being authentically black is to seek white charity by scripted indignation.

————

We must keep front and center that human beings can achieve beyond all measure even amid residual racism. To insist that black Americans alone are incapable of this makes a mockery of all proclamations of black pride. It is spit in the eye to the Civil Rights leaders who dedicated their lives to making our existence possible. And it condemns us to status as America's eternal also-rans.

Our job is to disseminate the message as widely as possible that the race that reaches the mountaintop is one that embraces with vigor its achievements, trumpets them to all who will listen, and teaches its children that doing so in the face of obstacles only makes the victory sweeter.

2

Profiling and "Getting Past Race"

...

"One out of three young black men is in jail or involved with the criminal justice system." This factoid has become a mantra in the black American community, chanted by rote as a badge of informed "black identity." And it is true.

An increasing number of black thinkers are dedicated to working against the sense that victimhood is the keystone of being an African-American in the twenty-first century. But this mantra stands as the main obstacle to making our fellow blacks realize that the race seeking progress must celebrate its victories rather than downplay them, stress self-improvement rather than handouts, and treat problems as inconveniences rather than roadblocks.

So many of us want to "get past race." Many suppose that eliminating racial preferences, eliminating the "silly little boxes" on forms requiring people to indicate their race, or fostering seminars on "diversity" in the workplace are the crucial tasks here. Too few understand that the main obstacle to getting us out of our current sullen holding pattern is the conflict between young black men and police forces in our cities. This is not just "one more thing." It is the thing, and until it is addressed nationwide and solved, there will be no meaningful progress. ▪

When I was growing up in the 1970s, my elders defended the victim-centered perspective on the basis of representation in higher positions in society. "How many black men have you seen running a corporation?" "How many black people does President X have in real positions in his cabinet?" "How many black shows do you see on TV?" "How many black people do you see playing dignified parts in a white movie?"

Obviously, those questions are no longer possible. But today, with a black secretary of state and national security adviser, black television shows and movies produced by the dozens each year, and Atlanta of all places with a black female mayor, the victimologist position has a new crutch. Recite the ever more encouraging statistics on black economic advancement till you're blue in the face—the images at the front of all too many black minds are Rodney King, Amadou Diallo, and a tableau of cell blocks dominated by angry black male faces.

And this reflex stems from the outcome of the War on Drugs, which led to a focus on black men in searching for contraband narcotics, and played a large part in black men now constituting almost half of the prison population. Affirmative Action, reparations, Nissan car loans, Al Sharpton, the black-white test score gap, etc., etc.—in our moment it often appears as if profiling is just one of many issues on the race relations landscape. The "race question" can seem a roiling mess of endlessly interdependent ills. This leaves many whites privately inclined to just give up on blacks. Meanwhile, it shores up the defeatist strain even in more reflective blacks, often convinced that our race problem is so very "complex"—often a coded way of excoriating whites for how utterly insoluble a mess they have presumably left us with.

Imagine an America where blacks do not bop their heads in warm assent when they hear Tupac Shakur shouting, "Fuck the police! *Fuck* the police!" Imagine an America where black undergraduates do not flock to courses on Race and the Law to be taught that blacks are victims of the criminal justice system, because there are no longer any grounds for interpreting the legal system as racist. Imagine an America where for black children, developing a "black identity" in their teens does not mean internalizing a sense that whites are the enemy, and that to embrace school is to become one of them. Imagine an America where blacks chanting about "white hegemony" are a fringe element, hovering at the margins of elections, rarely sought on the lecture circuit, and publishing their books with vanity publishers.

Tantalizing vision. But it will never come to pass as long as the conviction reigns that white America is engaged in a war against black men. Today, racial profiling is not just one problem on the landscape of race relations—it is the main thing distracting African-Americans from sensing themselves as true Americans rather than a "people apart." Pull away this card and the whole house would fall down.

In *Losing the Race*, I argued that black America has been hobbled by three nested ideologies since the late 1960s. The adoption of victimhood as a racial identity (the cult of Victimology) spawns a sense that black people are subject to looser standards of judgment (the cult of Separatism), which in turns leads to a sense of intellectual excellence (beyond that applying directly to blacks) as something exterior to "blackness" (the cult of Anti-Intellectualism). Profiling encourages all three of these strains of thought.

■ ■ ■

The very physicality and invasiveness of being regularly stopped by the police, sharply interrogated, often frisked and sometimes even physically abused is uniquely suited to creating a sense of embattlement. We need only consider how many of us felt at airports after September 11, 2001, when the scanner seized on a belt buckle or packed-away knitting needle and we had to raise our arms and be subjected to a body scan by a stranger in front of dozens of onlookers. Imagine enduring this out on a city street with police cars stopped alongside, lights glaring and radios squawking. The black man who has undergone this kind of treatment—or even seen it happen to family members and friends—is one less receptive to recitations of declining black poverty statistics, and likely to see Condoleezza Rice as a fluke rather than as a personal inspiration. Imprinted with the statistic that fifteen black men had been shot dead by the police in Cincinnati over six years, only the most independently minded black Cincinnatian would see much wisdom in anyone's asserting that blacks need to stop framing themselves as victims.

Many whites are alternately perplexed and impatient seeing so many blacks grousing about the horrors of "racism" as if it were 1920. But profiling plays a major role in convincing blacks that racism is as prevalent today as it was in the past. Of course from a bird's-eye view, all indications are that it is not—economic indicators, the numbers of blacks in high positions, results from polling data, the rise in interracial marriages, and other facts relegate claims that "America remains hostile to blacks" to the realm of rhetoric. The friction between blacks and law enforcement is like the chimney standing after a house burns down, left alone as the most resistant feature of something otherwise reduced to shards and remnants.

Black Harvard sociologist Orlando Patterson notes that vestiges of racism are today concentrated among less-educated, working-class whites, and that police forces represent this layer of society. Patterson notes that the problem is that for many young black men, tense and often incendiary encounters with just these people are one of the most immediate interactions with whites they ever have. The statistics on general societal indicators, buried in dense nonfiction books reviewed in the *New York Times Book Review*, do not reach most of them and never will. They are first infused with the reflexive anti-white ideology of the elders in their immediate experience, and then directly impacted by the sting of sudden, edgy clashes with white public servants. As Wesley Skogan (political scientist and criminology specialist at Northwestern University) notes, people most fear threats that they have the least control over. Can we blame a seventeen-year-old black teen for feeling helpless if he is shoved against the wall by surly white policemen while hanging out in a park with friends? Can we blame him for feeling helpless even if the neighborhood is a hotbed of drug dealing and the policemen are acting on a concrete tip that makes checking him and his friends sensible on its face?

Instead, profiling lends itself to being interpreted as a replay of the racist animus that led to lynching in the past. To the outside observer, lynching is a historical curiosity that blacks would be best off "letting go." But for many blacks, the number of black men in jail suggests a covert way of expressing a deep-seated "fear" of "black masculinity."

And this sad reality stokes the most damaging misconception in black America today: that the existence of even vestigial racism stands between blacks and achievement. Misconception this is: many ethnic groups were subjected to virulent abuse in this country and rose to the top nevertheless, and this even included regular doses of what would later be called police brutality. Chinese and Irish people regularly had the daylights beaten out of them on city streets in the nineteenth and early twentieth centuries.

But these facts are distant history to most today, and often dismissed by blacks on the basis of an idea that antipathy to blacks is somehow more decisive than it was for these people. ("If you're white, you're all right; if you're brown, stick around; if you're black, get back.") It is the immediate that truly moves most, and this is all the more problematic in an age when events can be recorded and endlessly repeated before our eyes on tape. "Come early and stay late" if there is bias against you, says the black "conservative." The white conservative pundit rails against the "defeatist rhetoric of black leaders." And the black mother watching

TV making dinner sees the tape of Rodney King being beaten to the ground, while her son comes home listening on his Discman to his hero Tupac Shakur rapping about how much the po-lice hate the nigga. Racism doesn't hold black people down? The innocent Amadou Diallo being gunned down to the floor with forty-one shots does not exactly help make this case.

Few black men would assert upon questioning that they are "victims." On the conscious level black discourse encourages "black pride" and the fact that we are "a strong people." The victim-focused self-image, like so many that are most damaging, reigns tacitly. I recall a twenty-something black man—educated and, by outward indicators, unlikely to have grown up poor—at an African-American Studies conference charismatically crowing that he deserved Affirmative Action because of "what I have to go through as a black man in this country." A scattering of audience members chimed in with "mm-hmm"s. This was 1998, and thus the man was unlikely to be denied employment, education, patronage of a business establishment, or (in the Bay Area, at least) even the love of many white women if he desired it. He also gave all indication of being overall a confident, type-A sort of guy. The indignity he was referring to, essentially, was mistreatment by the police—say, the night when he was driving to meet some friends at a nightclub and was stopped and forced to endure a frisking because there was a report of a drug dealer lurking in the neighborhood. Experiences like this are the last bastion supporting a self-conception like his.

———

As such, profiling plays directly into a tragic situation where a race's self-image is based less on its positive traits than on its negative image in the eyes of whites. In the black community, it is un-fashionable to claim too loudly that the "black" person must be able to dance, speak Black English, listen to hip-hop, eat soul food, dress in certain ways, etc. Because these features perhaps have certain "ghetto" associations, they are certainly cherished, but with a layered ambivalence, and dwelt upon more readily in private. But there is one qualification considered too *sine qua non* to tiptoe around: the black person must be aware that whites see him or her through the same racist eyes through which they see other blacks. To give any indication otherwise is to elicit the sharpest of contempt.

Racial profiling is almost uncannily well suited to bolster this ideology, and unsurprisingly, today it is the Soul Patrol's battering ram of choice. Example: a black comedian on the Black Entertainment Network crowed in 2000, "If Tiger Woods thinks he ain't black, then wait till he gets pulled over by a cop!" The black audience howled in joyous assent. That is, Tiger Woods is laughable for trying to opt out of blackness because whites will always see him as "one of us." And how will it be made most bracingly clear that he is "one of us"? When he gets racially profiled.

––––––

Black entertainment culture also displays the crucial place that profiling occupies in the black American self-conception today. Black film director John Singleton has a poster of Tupac Shakur hanging over his lead character's bed in *Baby Boy* (2001). A black man two generations back would more likely have had Martin Luther King, Jr.'s image, and in any case there existed no young singer preaching alienation available for such a black man to celebrate. But this is today, and Shakur's work is endlessly eulogized in the black hip-hop press, celebrated in college electives, and recited by many young blacks—including college students—as readily as many young white collegians recited Elizabeth Barrett Browning and Edna St. Vincent Millay in the old days.

And Shakur is not even generally considered to be the most lyrically deft of rappers. A large part of his mystique lies in his encounters with the police and his spell in jail. The latter was possibly a frame-up, and many of his lyrics almost obsessively run down the police. If profiling and its aftermath in prison statistics had not come to the fore in the late 1980s, Shakur and his fellow "gangsta rappers" would not have struck such a chord among black listeners. If we could go back in time and play gangsta rap for young black college students in 1958, they would be baffled and repulsed, even after having seen black teens escorted into Central High in Little Rock under armed guard just the year before (blacks of this age are almost universally appalled by the likes of Tupac Shakur). Notice that there was no black music dwelling in this vein until the War on Drugs.

Another example was an episode of the early 1990s sitcom *Roc*, a kind of sepia version of *The Honeymooners* popular with blacks. Black actors on sitcoms have often felt it necessary to avoid "the *Julia* syndrome" by occasionally having an episode show that all is not sunny for blacks in America. On *The Jeffersons* in the 1970s, the result was an episode where George Jefferson saved the life of a Ku Klux Klan member by artificial respiration. Informed upon reviving of the physically intimate way Jefferson had saved him, he said that he would rather Jefferson had let him die. Chilling, but the implication was that these people were remnants, not a serious present-day threat—that is, remember where we *came from*. Series principal Charles S. Dutton's gesture in this direction two decades later during the War on Drugs? A show where Roc was thrown to the ground and hauled off to jail just for being in the wrong place at the wrong time. This time, the plot was torn from the headlines—remember where we *are*.

———

Nor can we be under any impression that profiling lends a sense of victimhood only to young men. The number of black men In Jail Or Involved With The Criminal Justice System feeds into the common wisdom in the black community that eligible black men are a rare find for available black women. The "Scarce Black Man Syndrome" becomes a form of victimhood for black women even if they are not the usual target of police profiling. To wit: whites' hatred of black men is seen as leaving black women lonely or mired in troubled relationships with partners unequal to them in aspirations and earning potential.

And this in turn creates more interracial suspicion, in conditioning an acute resentment among many black women of white women who "take our men." In a society where, in fact, racism is ever on the decline, it is inevitable—and, one would think, welcome—that romances and marriages between blacks and whites are on the rise. But in an America where young black men are disproportionately entangled with the criminal justice system, black women often see these interracial relationships as eating into the already atrophied pool of men they have to choose from. Once again, profiling is a linchpin in what keeps us from getting past race as so many would like us to.

■ ■ ■

The sense that blacks are a people under siege leads, with natural but destructive logic, to a notion that the black criminal is at heart an innocent, condemned at birth by a society that denies his humanity. How much can one expect, after all, from someone destined to be treated by the police the way we see they treated Rodney King in Los Angeles? Or even a black man who grew up hearing of the King and Diallo episodes—plus whatever similar cases erupted in their municipality that did not happen to get national coverage—discussed by his elders as evidence that whites remain implacably hostile to blacks' walking the earth? Remember—Rodney King and the resentment it sowed across America was more than ten years ago. Someone who was eight in 1991 is twenty as you read this.

Among many blacks the upshot of observations like these is a sense that while the white criminal is reprehensible, the black criminal must be "understood." This underlying conviction that black people are exempt from serious judgment is what I refer to in *Losing the Race* as the cult of Separatism. Profiling feeds directly into it.

For example, most whites were appalled to see blacks cheering O.J. Simpson's acquittal. But what led many blacks to entertain that Simpson was innocent was the revelation that officer Mark Fuhrman was on record as dwelling liberally on "the N word" in private discussions. This element instantly cast the case in a larger light, as a referendum on police brutality against blacks. Many objected that nevertheless, Simpson had been coddled for years by the LAPD, who had turned a blind eye to his wife-beating because of his celebrity. But much of the black jubilation over his acquittal came from a delight in seeing the police suffer "payback" for their oppression of black men in general.

The mostly black jury gave all indication of having operated under this ideological influence, almost willfully disregarding the actual evidence in favor of "vigilante justice." One jury member openly said that they had had no interest in considering the import of the DNA evidence, for example. Any claim that the LAPD's corruption was merely "anecdotal" is belied by the recent revelations that a cabal of its officers regularly framed young men during the 1990s. Simpson's savior, Johnnie Cochran, chronicles similar happenings in earlier times in his autobiography, a huge hit in the black community, helping to imprint on "the vine" a sense that the LAPD "had it coming."

Crucially, this imperative to stick it to the LAPD, and by extension the police in general, was felt so deeply as to outrank the issue of Simpson's guilt, which any idiot could not help but glean. This was another indication that the police profiling issue has become the keystone of black alienation.

And this kind of alienation is what has transformed the Civil Rights movement's focus on integration into the modern sense that our task is to define ourselves *against* the mainstream, in the hopes of preserving a sovereign black realm into which whites are forbidden to enter. In the late 1990s, black comedian DL Hughley built his sitcom *The Hughleys* around a black man who moves his family into a white suburb and is uncomfortable with the prospect that his children may lose their "black identity." This sounds so "normal" to us after three decades of "multiculturalism" and "the salad bowl." But note that in her classic play of 1959, *A Raisin in the Sun*, Lorraine Hansberry—whose bona fides as "authentically black" are as yet unquestioned—gives matriarch Lena Younger not one line expressing a fear that her little grandson Travis might "become white" when her family achieves her fiercely desired goal of moving to a white neighborhood. The idea back then was that we would all come together, a goal previewed by Hansberry, whose husband was white.

What, then, planted this antipathy to "the white man" thirty years later in Hughley, who is too young to have known the segregated America that Hansberry depicted, in which no network would have provided him with the series that has made him a millionaire? We get a clue in his segment of the stand-up comedy anthology film *The Kings of Comedy*. In the midst of a rollicking routine, at one point he does an abrupt detour into a reference to Amadou Diallo's having been shot forty-one times after policemen mistook the wallet he took out of his pocket as a gun. This glum observation contrasts so sharply with the jocular tone of the surrounding routine that it even throws the mostly black audience a bit. But Hughley risks it nevertheless, his sudden tart glare signaling that he felt that acknowledging the Diallo episode was an urgent gesture even in a party atmosphere. Tell DL Hughley to "get over slavery" and he, regardless of his exploding mutual funds, thinks about—profiling.

▪ ▪ ▪

Finally, the self-conception as strangers in their own land that profiling nurtures in blacks leads to a sense of school and learning as the lore of the oppressor. Writers like Diane Ravitch, Heather

Mac Donald, and Sandra Stotsky have chronicled the hijacking of education since the 1960s by a leftist distrust of traditional learning. Since then, a powerful current in education seeks to bolster students' "self-esteem" against a demonized "Establishment" by encouraging them to "express themselves" rather than learn facts and be trained in careful reasoning and concrete skills.

Because blacks are so well represented as educational administrators and teachers, black students end up in the line of the fire of people imprinted doubly by this ambivalence to mainstream teaching techniques: first by the convictions of their field, and second by their membership in a race taught that authenticity means nurturing a leeriness of white hegemony. And this is where profiling plays an indirect but powerful hand, because it is today the main support for that professional underdog ideology. As such, profiling, seemingly "just one more issue" regarding race, actually helps leave black children educationally handicapped.

The failure of black-dominated school boards to provide black students with a decent education becomes predictable. These people and the teachers they supervise are *overtly* committed to helping black kids learn. But their actions counteract this so often because they are guided by a *covert* sense of mainstream lore as the property of the "other"—i.e., the white people who are waging a War Against Black Men. The result is less that such people actively abandon their students than that their students' welfare becomes less of a priority than it should be. Naturally, salaries, promotions, and sinecures end up more heavily weighted than whether or not Dwayne and Tomika can read.

Nothing demonstrates this more tragically than watching black school boards take to the streets when state governments try to have outside agencies take over their districts, as in Detroit and Philadelphia. Amid the teachers' and board members' usual ful-minations at rallies, one misses a basic sense of the tragedy in black students getting high school diplomas barely able to read a newspaper article. They stand before the cameras insisting on "lo-cal control," Democrats-to-the-grave suddenly cherishing a Re-publican tenet. And most of us wonder about the elephant sitting in the middle of the room—that thirty years of these people's lo-cal control has churned out tens of thousands of semiliterate and largely innumerate graduates. Why don't these people see this issue as front-and-center? Ironically, the white public officials in suits are more alarmed at this tragedy than they are. Or not so ironi-cally—context explains the paradox. The black nationalist Oak-land school board member reads about the local "Riders," police officers who have been proven to have regularly persecuted and planted weapons on blacks, and as far as she is concerned, Shake-speare and how a bill becomes law in Washington can go to hell.

Or less hyperbolically, they are only so important, because "real" black people, aware that America is set against them, will only care so much about such things. And in their place, this per-son will embrace the idea that black students will be better off be-ing immersed in their "separate language," "Ebonics." While this notion only hit the national media in a major way in 1996, it has exerted an electric sway over many black educators for thirty years. And the sentiment lurks in less overt form among the general black population. Bernie Mac was another black comedian featured in *The Kings of Comedy*, and began starring in his own sitcom in the fall of 2001. In the premiere, he quipped about his fear that the children newly placed in his permanent charge might grow up speaking the Queen's English—i.e., end up not being "black."

Like most black people, upon questioning, Mac would probably assert that black kids must be able to speak standard English when necessary. But the sense of standard English as a stiff, itchy costume rather than skin plays into a general sense of books and learning as something "else"—that is, "white." This is the prime culprit in black students' lagging grades and test scores, which persist regardless of class. In a black America that assumes that black boys are on their way to encountering policemen like Justin Volpe, who sodomized Abner Louima with a broomstick, Mac's sense of standard English as the code of the oppressor will reign, like it or not.

Overall, the black educational establishment is focused more on decrying why black children *cannot* learn than how they *will* learn. Societal barriers to learning are one of the most urgently imparted facets in the training of graduate students in education, as powerfully imprinted "in the air" as in the formal curriculum. In this realm, a particular focus is white teachers' purported "bias against black boys." This genderization of the black educational crisis is, in fact, a distraction from the larger issue. The roots of the problem are a general racial self-conception as separate from "whiteness." Black women do attend college in larger numbers than black men. But racial preferences, paving many of these women's way into these colleges, mask serious deficits in these women's grades and test scores compared to whites and Asians. And besides, girls are as significant a presence as boys in the innumerable academic and journalistic reports of black teens allowing their grades to slip as a result of being teased as "acting white" for trying to do well in school.

But the attractiveness of crying for "the black boy" to legions of black psychologists, sociologists, and teachers is based on a sense that dwelling on the point is Doing the Right Thing, in calling attention to a general antipathy to black males in America. And what feeds that position most directly is the idea that the police prey upon black men—that the "black boy" of today is the innocent black teenager frisked against the wall tomorrow. Without this subtext, blacks in education would find the "bias against black boys" thesis less mesmerizing, and might devote more of their attention to solutions rather than indignant proclamations of impotence.

At the typical academic conference on race and education, the tone is set by black women earnestly indignant that America gives black children a raw deal. One need only attend a conference like this to see the following: As long as it remains true that "one out of three young black men is in jail or involved with the criminal justice system," black children will remain at the mercy of people more interested in shielding them from indoctrination by the enemy than in giving them the tools to succeed in their society.

■ ■ ■

Conservatives have leveled many arguments against the idea that profiling indicates that America remains a deeply racist country. These arguments are usually, in the strict sense, correct. But when it comes to profiling, we are not engaged in scoring points in a varsity debate. We are faced with an ideological tic bedeviling the black community since the late 1960s: that blacks will not advance in any meaningful way until there is no racism in the United States, and that black "authenticity" resists letting superficial improvements distract from this. This New Double Consciousness is due neither to stupidity nor self-righteousness, despite frequent appearances to the contrary. As I argued in the previous chapter, this ideology is a symptom of inner pain. It is wielded as a balm for a debased racial self-image, a legacy of the past whose echoes are still deeply felt just thirty-five years after the end of legalized segregation.

Many of us (including more blacks than we usually hear from) may wish black people would just "get over" this, but that is going to take a while. Sure, in an ideal world black "leaders" would take the numbers of black men in jail more as a call to address how open so many young black men are to stepping outside of the law, than as fodder for indicting whites as racists. But we are stuck with the here and now, where we are faced with a studied vigilance based on reflex and emotion rather than fact-checking. The sad fact is that under those conditions, statistics and hard logic will be of no effect in teaching black America that the police are not an occupying army.

If most of the rioters in Cincinnati in 2001 in the aftermath of the shooting death of a black man had criminal records, then they were "acting out" against a racist society that penned them into festering neighborhoods. If the police stop more black men because black men dominate the street drug trade, then the drug peddlers are "revolutionaries" playing "the cards they were dealt." If black-on-black homicides increase after a profiling controversy when officers refrain from stop-and-frisks—as happened in New York after the Diallo killing and in Cincinnati—then whites are now just letting blacks kill each other because they don't see them as human. (Reverend Damon Lynch, prominent black leader in Cincinnati, promptly leveled this type of charge in the summer of 2001.)

If black police officers "profile" as much as white ones, then they have been "turned against their own people." If Latino officers were the prime culprits in excessive profiling in Miami in the 1990s, then "they learned to hate the black man from whites." If Caribbean and African blacks thrive in America despite being equally subject to profiling (Abner Louima is Haitian; Diallo was from Guinea), then immigrants are an unfair comparison because they have a unique drive to succeed. And so on.

Diallo's case is especially illustrative. The mythology of his death is that four policemen surrounded him in a lobby and gunned him down like an animal. In fact, Diallo was at the back of the lobby, with one officer having entered. He mistook Diallo as drawing a gun and yelled, "He's got a gun!" at the same time scuttling backward out of fear. Only then did the other officers, frightened, undertrained, and mistaking the first officer's slip as evidence that he was being aimed at, run in with guns ablaze. That remains a hideous event, but it was due more to semicompetence, impulse, and terror than naked hostility toward Diallo. But the myth will persist, just as the dramatization *Inherit the Wind* has left forever the impression that William Jennings Bryan made a poor showing at the Scopes trial and dropped dead at the end, when in fact he acquitted himself fairly well and died peacefully a few days later of diabetes.

To return to DL Hughley as a demonstration case, he will probably not have occasion to learn the real facts about Diallo's death.
The case is now already years in the past, and the mainstream media are more interested in supporting victimology than giving evidence working against it. And if Hughley does happen to come
across the real story, he may well assume that the truth is being
covered up. Is he paranoid? Not necessarily, given regular revelations that just such cover-ups have been routine among police officers. A recent example is the Ramparts scandal in the LAPD,
where a coterie of officers operated beyond the bounds of the law
in a quest to corral drug traffickers, medicating themselves on
openly racist pep talks. Their ringleader (a Latino) revealed this
under duress in 2000 in Hughley's state of residence, where it was
widely covered in the local newspapers he is likely to read and on
the local news programs he is likely to listen to. And Hughley is
typical: local revelations of this kind, which are not rare, inform
the views on race of millions of black Americans.

The Fox network and *The National Review* can object till the
cows come home that profiling is necessary to stop the flow of
drugs into black neighborhoods. And they will be correct. But
what black Americans will retain, from the street corner up to the
boardroom and faculty lounge, is that young black men are routinely singled out and often abused in drug searches despite usually being innocent. And they, too, will be correct. And as long as
they are, racial profiling will stand as today's main enabler of the
dismaying, counterproductive sentiment that to be "authentically
black" is to maintain a quiet distrust of the white man, to never
feel quite at home if black people are not present, to sense integration as capitulation rather than the path forward.

■ ■ ■

My experiences since I wrote *Losing the Race* have made this ever more apparent. One black woman agreed with my statements about black students and schoolwork based on a television appearance I had made, and began corresponding with me as she read the book. As she got to the section on profiling, objection began to supplant agreement in her messages. She had worked in the criminal justice system, and when she saw that I could not be moved to concur with her that profiling shows that racism still determines black lives, she stopped writing. She was heartened to see a black writer arguing against the other planks in the "racism forever" rhetoric. But the crime issue was, for her as for so many, non-negotiable.

In one passage in the book, I describe how in one encounter I had with a surly police officer, I sensed that the only thing that kept it from developing into an unpleasant incident was that I have an educated-sounding voice, discouraging the officer from processing me as the criminal "type." One black reviewer on Amazon.com misread me as boasting about this, implying that other black men would not be "profiled" if they would just learn to speak more elegantly, and that I am in the meantime immune to abuse by the police. His disgust at this formed the basis of an indignant slam of a review. I mention this only to show how very sensitive this man was to the profiling issue, such that this one passage in a 280-page book elicited such an extreme response.

My dissertation adviser was John Rickford, who in addition to being on Stanford University's linguistics faculty is also the head of the school's African-American Studies program. His politics are unabashedly leftist. He was, for example, the most prominent black linguist supporting the Oakland School Board during the Ebonics controversy in 1997, and had no love for Shelby Steele's *The Content of Our Character* in 1991. Though he predictably does not agree with my sociopolitical perspectives, he has wished me well since *Losing the Race* was published, and we have maintained a warm relationship.

However, in the spring of 2001 he, someone who largely restricts his e-mail use to the brief and utilitarian, sent me a link to an article in a local newspaper describing two innocent black boys' violent encounter with the police. Appended to it was a calm yet urgent message to me to realize that when I write that black America's condition is much better than the Jesse Jacksons insist, that I am distracting white readers from tragic realities such as the boys' story. And in the past, John has objected to my views on race by recounting an edgy experience with the police that his son had as a teenager in the 1990s.

For Rickford as well as the Amazon reviewer and the criminal justice system administrator, any calls for blacks to "look on the bright side" and "stress initiative" are premature and irrelevant until stories like this are no longer commonplace in America. "Get over the past," many whites think. But even for a reasonable and sterling black scholar such as John, the past is still here. And he is not alone—he is representative of a burning resentment in black America over racial profiling and the massive number of black men languishing in prison.

▪ ▪ ▪

Surely our solution is not to refrain from focusing on young black men who exhibit clusters of traits and behaviors that reasonably suggest involvement in the drug trade. To do this would be inhumane, in leaving innocent residents of poor neighborhoods at the mercy of hardened criminals. The question is whether we can "profile" intelligently, in a way that does not leave black America feeling persecuted by marauding gangs of white men with guns.

Relevant here is the fact, downplayed by the bleeding-heart mainstream media, that many residents of these very neighborhoods often wish there were *more* of a police presence to protect them from the hoodlums over which they have no control. The key to clearing these neighborhoods of the young criminal element is to do so in conjunction with these residents, involving them closely in the police force's efforts to identify those most likely to be trafficking in drugs and the locations where they ply their trade. Police officers must develop an on-foot presence in these districts rather than just trawling through them in cars. They must become familiar and trusted by innocent residents who are as committed as they are to making the neighborhood safer.

Just this has worked well in Boston. This city has figured little in recent coverage of profiling despite its large disadvantaged black population. This is because cooperation between police officers and local residents has led to a decrease in drug traffic and other street crimes—without an attendant rise in black opposition to law enforcers. Black people are not insane, and regardless of lingering distrust of "whitey," no one on the block cries "racism" when the drug peddler who has corraled dozens of black boys into the trade and gotten many of them killed is taken off the street—as long as his fate is due to the combined action of the concerned people on the block and the police. In such cases, residents may even be more open to the sad reality that in police work, accidents will sometimes occur in the heat of the moment, such as in the Diallo case.

Obviously this advice is not original to me. I derive it from the counsel of many people whose opinions on the matter are based on career credentials in the law and criminology. However, too often we receive these people's messages as mere voices in the crowd—today's op-ed, what what's-his-name said at that colloquium; yeah, involve the community, of course. Rarely is it realized that short of making the Boston story a national one, we will remain mired in the stalemate most of us are so tired of. A vocal fringe of blacks will continue their quest to keep whites eternally guilty for the sins of the past. Most blacks sitting on the sidelines will be torn between privately wishing black teens and their parents would get their acts together and a "group" sense that black "authenticity" means placing the blame on whites so that they don't forget they are "on the hook." Most whites will shake their heads wearily, torn between a liberal pity and a conservative inkling that they are being had.

▪ ▪ ▪

This message is especially relevant to today's Republican Party, who would like to attract the black vote. They believe that they have something to offer in return for that vote: a platform better suited to the advancement of a people on the rise than the Democrats'. Many other ethnic groups are seeing this truth, and as more Latinos and Asians pledge their allegiance to the Republicans with each election cycle, black Americans are falling behind the curve.

Democrats, hostage to the theatrics of identity politics, see

African-Americans as piteous souls incapable of achieving without handouts. To condition a people to handouts is to disempower them. As such, a black America that continues to vote virtually to a man for Democratic presidential candidates is a black America without political representation. Moreover, the predictability of the black vote has long left the Democratic Party with no incentive to actually do anything to attract or deserve it. In our moment, the Democrats maintain their hold on the black electorate less through sustained efforts to improve black lives than through symbolic allegiance to the cult of the victim. As such, black Americans cannot look to them for genuine commitment to addressing the profiling issue.

Many Republicans suppose that they have already made proposals that one would think black voters would embrace. For instance, the Bush administration's Faith-Based and Community Initiatives were a more proactive approach to inner-city stasis than anything the Democrats have suggested since the Johnson administration. But the change they promised would be slow and indirect. And its emphasis on self-help can be suspicious and counterintuitive to a race trained since the 1960s—for better or for worse—to suppose that all that is holding the inner cities down is whites' refusal to write bigger checks or "bring businesses in." Similarly, the wisdom of workfare over welfare will only become apparent as years pass, as the children who grew up with mothers who worked every day prove less susceptible to falling into cycles of dependence.

Singing of these things on the *Wall Street Journal*'s editorial page preaches only to the converted. If Republicans seek the black vote, then because the profiling issue is today at the heart of reflexive black alienation, there is no more direct route to their goal than in making sustained efforts to heal the relationship between black people and police forces. This is all the more urgent given how much better a country this would create.

▪ ▪ ▪

Our task is to make it so that a generation—just one—of African-American people grow up without experiences leading them to process the police as blacks' enemy. This is for a very specific reason: *profiling and black incarceration rates are the last support for the victimologist position as a prevalent current in black thought.*

Victimology is already showing signs of decline otherwise. Millions of blacks in their mid-thirties like me, often married with children and in the prime of their lives, barely remember the heyday of the black radical (I was three when Dr. King was assassinated). Polls demonstrate that younger blacks are less likely than older ones to trace black ills to racism. Black politics is minting no new Al Sharptons. And "black conservatives" are nowhere near as lonely and beleaguered as they once were. I have taken much less heat than Shelby Steele did ten years before *Losing the Race* was published. There are times when I personally suspect that my positions—more centrist than right anyway—are the majority opinion in black America once we strip away certain cognitive dissonances.

Without the profiling problem, certainly some vestigial race-based discrepancies would remain. None of these, however, would be visceral enough in impact to shore up the melodrama and willful alienation that our Mary Frances Berrys are stuck in. Issues like small discrepancies in car loan deals, inconclusive suggestions that doctors are less solicitous toward black patients, and niggling head counts of the black "presence" on network television shows are not the kind of thing that sends people out to the streets. Unlike the naked realities of racial profiling, these issues are slight statistical discrepancies, where race is often but one of several factors, and they operate largely beyond the awareness of the individual.

If we could see *just one* generation of black people—that's all it would take—grow up in an America where systemic racism was limited to ever fewer phenomena of this kind, then as they became young adults, black Americans' perspective on racism would be similar to black Caribbeans' and Africans' response to even the nastier kinds of racism. Namely, that it isn't fair and must be addressed, but that black American lives remain among the most comfortable on the planet, that we had a lot to do with getting ourselves to that point, and that occasional inconvenience means that you get up and move on. And this generation would pass this on to the next one, parent to child, teen to toddler, teacher to student, in actions as well as words, in public as well as in private, in attitude as well as posture. This is how a culture changes. This is where, I think, most people white and black would like black America to go, and all of us are wondering just why it is taking so long.

We would have gotten there fifteen years ago if the War on Drugs had not intervened, a new log on a fire which was well on its way to running out of fodder. And so here we are, with the words *black people* still referring to a problem rather than to a proud, self-empowered ethnic group. The solution here is much less "complex" than often thought. When young black people see Tupac Shakur's song "The Streetz R Deathrow" as a quizzical period piece rather than "the way it is," we will finally be in the America that the Civil Rights heroes fought for.

3

"What Have You Done for Me Lately?"

The Reparations Movement

■ ■ ■

In 2001, America's leading race issue—in the media, at least—was the call from a vocal contingent for black Americans to be compensated for wages denied to our slave ancestors. "America must finally acknowledge slavery," we were often told. Randall Robinson's The Debt: What America Owes to Blacks *had hit the stores the year before, and played a large part in taking the reparations movement to a new level in terms of energy and media attention. The book was quickly taken up by black reading groups nationwide and was fiercely praised by black reviewers.*

The Debt *summoned the essence of the reparations movement so perfectly that I took it as a springboard for an address of the movement as a whole.* ■

I can buy a fancy car or two.
I can buy a big house in an exclusive neighborhood.
I can send my kids to private school.
I can work hard and empower myself.

Oprah Winfrey pulled herself up by the bootstraps. So if I work
    hard, someday, I too, can achieve the American Dream.
The fundamental problem with this rugged individualist
    dogma is that I would still be black.

This is from a piece by a young black woman in an undergraduate newspaper at UC Berkeley. It was written in
response to David Horowitz's notorious anti-reparations adver-
tisement, printed in several campus newspapers in the spring of
2001. We could find no more eloquent distillation of what renders America's race debate an eternal stalemate: the sense that for
black people, leading happy and productive lives is "beside the
point" in evaluating whether we are "oppressed."

The latest development in this holding pattern masquerading as
a "dialogue" has been the reparations movement. In this vein, Randall Robinson's *The Debt: What America Owes to Blacks* is useful
to us on two levels. In the local sense, only through a close exami-
nation of this book can we understand why so many African-
Americans, most neither poor nor even close to it, feel that they are
owed money denied to ancestors they never knew. In a broader
sense, *The Debt*, founded on the paradoxical sentiment of the black
woman's newspaper stanza, exposes why so many blacks feel that
a true "dialogue" on race has yet to happen. Robinson's cri de
coeur gives crucial insight into the path back to the mountaintop
Dr. King pointed us toward—but only as a negative example.

———

The reparations idea has been kicking around black discussions
since the beginning of the twentieth century, but has been bruited

about especially consistently since the Black Power era. The first book-length treatment was actually written by a white man, law professor Boris I. Bittker, in 1973 (*The Case for Black Reparations*). Perhaps not being a "family" product kept it from having significant impact. Since then, there have been some other books on the subject by blacks, either not widely distributed or, in the case of Sam E. Anderson's documentary comic-book-format *The Black Holocaust for Beginners* (1995), lacking the gravitas necessary to galvanize a movement. Robinson's is the first contribution to transcend these obstacles, a prominent manifesto for a movement revivified by Congressman John Conyers.

The title alone indicates the ideological underpinning of the new reparations movement. Bittker ended his book saying, "I have sought to open the question, not to close it." Robinson, although initially claiming "to pose the question, to invite the debate," clearly considers the moral urgency of reparations a closed issue. Bittker makes "a case" for reparations; in contrast, Robinson's subject is "*The* Debt," the definite article presupposing an unpaid bill. In "discussions" of this issue across the land, those who would question whether any reparations are appropriate are unwelcome. What is being termed an exploration is, in practice, a call to arms.

Predictably, Robinson presents this position as representing the whole race, the subtext being that whites' eternal hostility to blacks is the only reason the call could not be heeded. Yet to say that the foundations of his argument are questionable is putting it lightly. In fact, to embrace them would only perpetuate the un-focused, self-generating anomie that motivates his book. *The Na-*

tion, White Guilt Central as always, swooned over *The Debt* and designated Robinson "a worthy heir to W. E. B. Du Bois." But in fact the book only points up the misguided, disempowering ideology that the left foisted upon black America in the 1960s.

————

The first of Robinson's assumptions is that there has been no real progress in the black condition in America. "America's socioeconomic gaps between the races remain, like the aged redwoods rooted in a forest floor, going nowhere, seen but not disturbed, simulating infinity, normalcy. Static." But he writes this when almost 50 percent of black families were middle class in 1995 (defined as twice the poverty line), in contrast to only one in one hundred in 1940 and 40 percent in 1970. Static?

Those last figures were from hard data chronicled especially usefully in Abigail and Stephan Thernstrom's *America in Black and White*. But Robinson is instead fond of couching his arguments as allegorical "stories," in the vein of his fellow bard of data-light pessimism Derrick Bell. A "story" Robinson uses as a leitmotif involves his taking a certain black boy, "Billy," around the Mall in Washington, DC. Of course, "Billy" is from the inner-city Southeast, since the middle class *half* of black America is apparently just statistical (shall we say) static, while the poverty-stricken *less than a quarter* of black families are, as it is often put, "What's really goin' down."

Nowhere is Robinson's vision of his race clearer than when he points out that because there are proportionately more poor blacks than whites, poverty defines black America's image. Most black writers decry the "racialization of poverty" as stereotyping.

But after reading Robinson's passage three times I realized that he actually considers the "black"-is-"poor" equation accurate!

One revelation is key. Into what we could call his *Un Dimanche Après-Midi au Mall de Washington, D.C.*, Robinson paints "a black woman wearing thick owlish glasses, strolling hand-in-hand with a bookish-looking white man, and two black men with white women." He explicitly has all of the blacks on the Mall but "Billy" "attached to white people." Okay, I get it, Mr. Robinson: all black people who did not grow up like "Billy"—except, we presume, Robinson—are sellouts who marry outside of their race and are probably homely besides. In other words, it's not precisely that all blacks are poor—but that those who are not are "disloyal," "inauthentic."

Robinson has his reasons for that sentiment, as we will see again later, but he is hardly alone in insisting that the growth of the black middle class is somehow "beside the point," leaving the poor minority as the "essence" of black America. In their ten-point response to Horowitz's ad, initially posted on the *Black World Today* website, black academics Robert Chrisman and Ernest Allen, Jr., trotted out the distorted statistic that black people earn only 60 percent of what whites do. But this figure is dragged down by welfare mothers and the preponderance of blacks in the South where wages are lower overall; control for these factors and the differential is negligible. They then noted that over 23 percent of black families are poor, without including that about 10 percent of white families are. The omission is important, because it means that as of 2001, the black-white discrepancy in poverty was only 13 percent. Not perfect, but clearly progress. Millions of blacks have helped to turn what once was a gap into what is today more of a crack, and to depict the differential as "static" is a stinging insult to all of them.

Thus *The Debt* is symptomatic of a general implication in most arguments for "reparations," that even past the year 2000, "black" is shorthand for "poor," when this has not been true for decades. Paradoxically, many of the people most fervently embracing reparations are quick to condemn whites for thinking all black people are poor. Thus we are brought to a savage irony—the reparations movement is founded in large part upon a racist stereotype.

––––––

The "Why do white people think we all live in the ghetto?" complaint is usually wielded as a demonstration of the "racism" supposedly standing in the way of real black advancement. Indeed, for Robinson, another justification for reparations is that racism remains "unbowed" in modern America.

Yet Robinson claims this of an America where in 1993 more than one in ten blacks were married to non-blacks. Surely that is an important fact even if the black women in question favor "owlish" glasses. Is racism "unbowed" when housing segregation among blacks is now documented to be largely voluntary, and when antidiscrimination cases are regularly and successfully filed on behalf of black plaintiffs by *white* officials? Surely we have some distance to go—racism certainly is not dead in America. But even here, signs contradict Robinson's epically bleak assessment. Definitely the boys who dragged James Byrd, Jr., to his death behind a truck were bigots. But when the whites of backcountry Jasper, Texas, turn out in droves for his funeral, we must question the notion that whites are poised to turn the hoses on us again at any moment.

Of course things like the Jasper mourners or assorted statistics and personnel lists can reasonably be suspected to be just symbolic. But there are just as many more "substratal" signs that racism is abating in America. To quote and redirect the title of Lena Williams's Black Victimology primer, "It's the Little Things" where one sees this—if one is looking. Take popular culture. In 2001, Starbucks was including Billie Holiday's lynching portrait "Strange Fruit" in one of its music mixes, assuming that its latte-drinking white customers would see the urgency of this song as worth breaking the usual upbeat tone of their musical selections.

Or: increasingly movies for teens depict a world where, with no particular attention called to it, blacks and whites coexist in easy harmony. Crucially, the black characters are not "deracial-ized" as token brown faces, but instead are depicted as quite "black" culturally. *She's All That* (1998) was a typical example, and became a minor cult hit among teens. Black-white romances are also becoming downright ordinary on television and in movies—and not used as sensational ploys, but unremarked on in publicity and reviews. *Save the Last Dance* (2001) featured a willowy blond teen (Julia Stiles) falling in love with a black boy as he teaches her how to dance hip-hop style—a refashioning of the Astaire-Rogers trope for a new America. The interracial angle did not interfere with it becoming Stiles's break-out movie, nor was her having kissed a black man on film given any attention amid the frenzied publicity given Stiles before and after its release.

Nor was this movie exactly a "fantasy" pushing the envelope—the romantic apartheid of Robinson's youth is long gone in many parts of the country. When I was a teen in the 1970s it was already dissolving quickly, although still perceptible. As for today, as a still relatively young American I can attest that interracial romances like the one depicted in *Save the Last Dance* are nothing less than ordinary in many places in America. To put a point on it, in the circles I travel in—college campuses, the performing arts world, and the punditocracy—the white woman under forty who has not been romantically involved with at least one black man is an exception. For people of my generation and cultural context, the expression "interracial couple" is obsolete—it's too common to arouse much attention.

Yes, this is less likely in David Brooks's Republican-voting, tractor-pulling "Red" America, or Ralph Kramdenesque urban neighborhoods like Northeast Philadelphia or South Boston. But interracial romance is increasingly common even in those places, and *Save the Last Dance* and its ilk, like most pop culture, was designed to make a profit by depicting a reality a significant number of young Americans are familiar and comfortable with. As many black filmmakers will attest, Hollywood doesn't play: it is about cold, hard profit and has no interest in throwing millions of dollars into goodly gestures that won't pull in the shopping mall crowd, especially beyond the indie realm. Imagine a *Gidget* film where Sally Field jumped behind the bushes with a "Negro." Or even an episode of *The Mary Tyler Moore Show* ten years later where Mary had a fling with a black man. America has changed.

To wit: we are making progress, fast. Robinson most likely does not catch teen flicks, watch much youth-aimed television, or pay much attention to what's playing over Starbucks's sound system. Nor would one expect this of most men near sixty. But the fact remains that this is the data set Robinson is pronouncing upon: the America that children of all races are growing up in. These children will be grown-ups with children in just ten years—they are every bit as much "America" as Robinson's graying cohort.

Unfamiliarity with what's *really* goin' down is what makes Robinson, like the writer of the opening byline, scoff at notions of initiative as "rugged individualist dogma." Black poverty, for instance, is due to present-day racism:

> Modern observers now look at the canvas as if its subjects were to be forever fixed in a foreordained inequality. Of the many reasons for this inequality, chief of course is the seemingly incurable virus of de facto discrimination that continues to poison relations between the races at all levels.

Note that "of course," assuming that no reasonable person could allow that racism is on the wane, or that much black poverty is due to racism of the past creating a culture of alienation in the present. For Robinson, societal inequity is a sentence of doom rather than an inconvenience. This idea will sound familiar after Chapter One and we will return to it. But the fact remains that his views are refracted through a particular ideological prism. They are not the patently obvious "of course" truisms he supposes.

———

Robinson's argument is further based on a claim best designated "creative." Apparently I, despite growing up comfortably middle class in Philadelphia speaking nothing but English, am at heart an "African" person, more intellectually and spiritually akin to Nigerian immigrants than to anyone born in the only country that has ever been home to me. As such, for Robinson, I am to consider it a denigration of "myself" when the *New York Times* downplays a story about a lethal pipeline explosion in Nigeria. In such cases "We don't know what happened to *us* and no one will tell us" (italics mine).

The first problem here is Robinson's conception of "Africa," which follows the well-known sad tradition of "Afrocentric History." One of the most worrisome aspects of this oeuvre is its essentialization of "Africa" as a single culture, when the continent is home to hundreds of ethnic groups. The sense that being brown-skinned and speaking languages unlike English somehow renders all of these peoples as one is alarmingly close to "All Coons Look Alike to Me," as the old song went that got its black composer Ernest Hogan into such trouble in the 1890s. If a newspaper headline reads "Asians found adrift on raft," most of us spontaneously recoil at the notion that Chinese, Japanese, Vietnamese, Korean, and Cambodian peoples have been grossly lumped together. Yet throughout *The Debt* we are taught—by a black man—that the residents of four dozen countries speaking over a thousand languages are all simply "Africans."

Yet there is a certain agenda behind this "lumping" tendency. If we treat "Africa" as one culture, then we can claim the literate and technologically advanced societies of Ancient Egypt and Mali as "our ancestors." Accordingly, Robinson devotes another one of his allegories to a hypothetical forebear of ours from the civilization that built libraries in Timbuktu.

But what about the societies that most black Americans' ancestors actually came from? It is safe to say that not a single black American is descended from an Ancient Egyptian, and only a very small proportion of slaves were brought to America from as far north as present-day Mali. The English and American slavers drew the vast majority of their slaves from a swatch of the western African coast that starts below Mali at Senegal, and stretches down through Sierra Leone, Liberia, Ghana, Benin, and Nigeria, stopping in present-day Angola. Egypt is perched up on the northern border of Africa, thousands of miles to the northeast of this coastal stretch.

These West African societies, while developed far beyond the hunter-gatherer level, were preliterate ones with little technology, in no sense comparable in material or intellectual advancement to Europe or even the Mayan cultures of Central America. There are no ruins bedecked with engraved writing in Ghana, no records of astrological calculations in Angola. As the founder and president of the lobbying organization Trans-Africa, Robinson is surely aware that there is a profound difference between the history of Ghana and that of Egypt.

Here, *The Nation's* anointment of Robinson as the next Du Bois takes on an ironic truth. One of the assumptions of Civil Rights leaders of Du Bois's day that requires a certain historical perspective of us is that most of them, as good Victorians, quite openly considered Africans "backward." Exactly a century before *The Debt* was published in mid-2000, Du Bois was casually intoning before the first Pan-African Congress in London, "To be sure, the darker races are today the least advanced in culture according to European standards. This has not, however, always been the case in the past, and certainly the world's history, both ancient and modern, has given many instances of no despicable ability and capacity among the blackest races of men."

"No despicable ability"—this sort of thing simply would not go for most of us today. Yet one cannot avoid a sense that Robinson considers the actual cultures most American slaves were taken from as insufficiently "advanced" to build a case of aggrieved deracination upon. Current work in anthropology, however, shows us that the reason most West Africans (or many other of the world's peoples) had not created the kind of "civilizations" that Europeans had was largely an accident of geography. The plants and animals thriving on a particular temperate latitude were uniquely amenable to cultivation, naturally yielding a volume of surplus that swelled populations, thus in turn facilitating densely hierarchical societies where certain classes had the leisure to create technology.

Findings such as these—most masterfully presented in Jared Diamond's *Guns, Germs and Steel*—leave me with no sense of "shame" that my West African ancestors lacked libraries, pyramids, and muskets. To marginalize our actual ancestors in favor of Alexandria and Timbuktu is to base a case for reparations on a false conception of our actual history, and to abase the people whose lives were ruined to create us. In comparison, one imagines a descendant of Austrian peasantry singing of his roots in ancient Greece and medieval Toulouse, since after all a European is a European.

But the most glaring omission in Robinson's utopian depiction of my African homeland is that Africans themselves were avid, uncomplaining agents in selling other Africans to whites. Robinson instead depicts the slave trade as based primarily on "catching" individual slaves unawares. In his Africa allegory, an aging African dismayed at the decay of his society at the hands of white predators bemoans that "Our young people cannot sit still and listen to tales of glory from a dying old man while they fear being caught."

Robinson is hardly alone in this misconception, reinforced by dramatic pragmatism in the miniseries *Roots* and the movie *Amistad*, that most slaves were acquired via lassoing people while they were out on walks. The sad reality is that this method would hardly have netted Europeans enough slaves to furnish dozens of colonies of plantations, with each plantation often requiring as many as several hundred workers. Wouldn't Africans have just stopped taking walks? As a specialist in the history of the Creole languages spoken by descendants of African slaves, my career has lent me extensive contact with primary sources on the slave trade. In them, it is painfully clear that not just some, but most slaves were obtained by African kings in intertribal wars, and were sold en masse to European merchants in exchange for material goods. This tragic fact is well known to any specialist in the slave trade.

Of course, Robinson is not an academic, nor is there any requirement that one be an academic to make a case for reparations. But the fact that Africans sold each other is not exactly obscure out "on the vine." It is hardly rare to hear ordinary blacks of any number of sociopolitical persuasions note that "the worst thing is that back in Africa we were selling *ourselves!*" In the volumes of Maya Angelou's series of autobiographies that cover her residence in Africa, she more than once refers to Africans selling one another, and wrestles with how to forgive the Ghanaians she is living among for their collusion with the slave trade. At no point does she present this as new information—she assumes her readers know it. My sense is that many do not realize that this was the norm rather than occasional—but it is impossible that Robinson is entirely unaware of the practice in itself. Yet not once does he so much as mention this in the entire book, instead painting a portrait of Africans as a preternaturally perfect people.

Importantly, the practice also undercuts Robinson's notion of "African" as a single cultural identity that we were wrested from. Traditionally, Africans were like other humans in processing as alien people speaking other languages and having different customs. Even today, African immigrants to South Africa are experiencing open ridicule and discrimination from indigenous black South Africans, themselves a few steps out of apartheid. Certainly, in our world of global politics and wide communications, among modern Africans there does exist a certain sense of "Africans" as an entity distinct from whites. But in many ways, the idea of Africa as "one culture" represents the stereotyping colonialist *Weltanschauung* that Robinson considers to have gutted black America's soul.

———

Stereotyping can be a form of dehumanization, as Robinson is well aware. And Robinson certainly does not let dehumanization go unnoticed. For him, few things indicate it more than that, apparently, blacks' being wrested from another continent is treated as classified information in America. An example:

> Since this nation's inception, taxpayers—white, black, brown—
> have spent billions on museums, monuments, memorials,

parks, centers for the performing arts, festivals, and commemorative occasions. Billions have been spent on the publication of history texts, arts texts, magazines, newspapers, and history journals. Formulaic television and large-screen historical fiction treatments virtually defy count.

Almost none of this spending, building, unveiling, and publishing has been addressed to the needs of Americans who are not white.

But the melodrama here is almost staggeringly blind to reality. The National Endowment for the Arts and the National Endowment for the Humanities have both long had an outright bias toward funding projects oriented toward plumbing the black Americans' African heritage. Moreover, his portrait is only possible by restricting his purview to projects funded by federal taxes. The America I have spent my life in is one where museums in large cities frequently have exhibits of African art, and where performances by African dance troupes are a regular treat. Robinson writes when just a few years before, the media had been abuzz with reviews of Hugh Thomas's *The Slave Trade*, the publication of which was feted as a national event. Furthermore, Basil Davidson's briefer and more readable *Black Mother: The Years of the African Slave Trade* went through several printings after its publication in 1961, has never been a tough find in paperback, and was even reissued in a revised version in 1988. And on top of all of this, Robinson even includes both of these books in his list of sources.

Again, it's "the little things" as well. *Scientific American* has a page where they print excerpts from issues of the past. Naturally most of these citations are about science, but in a recent issue they featured a quotation from March 1851, subheading it "Open Sore": "The population of the United States amounts to 20,067,720 free persons, and 2,077,034 slaves." This suggests the editors' spontaneous consciousness of our country's racial history in a journal neither dedicated to sociopolitical issues nor even aimed at a black audience—that citation was culled for *white* readers. Nor did I have to hunt that one down. No literate American can help regularly stumbling across small signs like this that mainstream America is quite aware that a portion of its population were brought here in chains.

Richer is the implication Robinson draws from this presumed concealment of our African roots. To wit: the poverty and spiritual despair that black Americans are mired in results from a sense of rootlessness, from having been plucked from our African homeland. Noting often that a people must have a sense of belonging to a particular "culture" to thrive—debatable, but okay— he claims that "the armaments of culture and history that have protected the tender interiors of peoples from the dawn of time have been premeditatively stripped from the black victims of American slavery." Shepherding "Billy" around the Mall, Robinson sees the monuments as a statement from whites: *"This is who we are. This is who we are."* On the other hand, because there are no statues of African kings at the Mall, "Billy" is bedeviled eternally by the question *"Who am I? Just who the hell am I?"*

This argument, central to Robinson's presentation, is the most dangerous one in the book. Never mind that it is not exactly obvious that most whites process the Washington Monument as "who they are." Americans are not known for being a terribly historically minded people (compared to, say, what the Kosovo Polje means to the typical Serb).

But more problematically, Robinson's position flirts with the sense of separation from learning for learning's sake that is the prime source of the black-white performance lag in school. More than once Robinson takes potshots at "Enlightenment" learning: "Punic this, Pyrrhic that," he sniffs. He also repeatedly dismisses Hegel on the basis of an isolated racist statement that was, after all, typical of a man of his day. This courts misleading young readers into supposing that such passages were the meat of Hegel's oeuvre, thus turning them away from Hegel, and by extension, other "dead white male" thinkers. But these men's ideas are central to the philosophical heritage of the only society black Americans will ever consider home. It is a short step from "Punic this, Pyrrhic that" to another observation the black undergraduate made in the article the opening of this chapter came from, where she growls that so much of what she is expected to learn on Berkeley's "racist" campus is "white."

Robinson predictably falls in with the "Jonathan Kozol" camp, insisting that black students' problems in school are all traceable to societal inequities. For instance, he pauses to note that black students are lagging severely in school performance in Prince George's County, Maryland, because of "grinding, disabling poverty." But he writes this of a notoriously well-funded district (which he resides in), where the low grades and scores even from thoroughly middle-class black students have been covered by the local media for twenty years. There are academic articles on black students' problems with school in Prince George's County dating back to the early 1980s.

It is widely documented that much of this problem nationwide traces to a sense many black students have that school is fundamentally separate from the essence of being "black." A study by Clifton Casteel notes, for example, that where white adolescents tended to say that they do their schoolwork to please their parents, black ones tend to say that they do it to please the teacher. This stance is a product of a race-wide pull away from the old integrationist ideal in the 1960s, and the drive to define ourselves against "whitey" made a certain sense at that time. But few then had any way of predicting the awkward results this ideology would have as time went by. One of them is an ingrained sense in black peer culture that school is something "the white man" does. Robinson tosses off his "Punic this, Pyrrhic that" lines as a passionate salute to the race pride that Carter G. Woodson displayed in *The Mis-Education of the Negro*. But he fails to realize that this same sentiment has a lot more to do with black students' problems in Prince George's County's schools than the "poverty" of their middle-class suburban existences.

But most important is the very fallacy that it would make a whit of difference in Billy's psychological well-being to be taught that his essence was that of an Igbo boatman in the seventeenth century. I have rarely read a book by a black writer that demonstrates so little pride in the heritage of black people right here on these shores.

"Far too many Americans of African descent believe that their history starts in America with bondage and struggles forward from there toward today's second-class citizenship." Hear, hear—but Robinson's assumption that redressing this means harkening back to African villages is mistaken. Fewer positions on black uplift could be less promising than that we will lack inner pride until we studiously equate ourselves with people who do not talk, eat, move, dress, or even see the world the way we do, who are neither our immediate relatives nor usually even our close friends. Too seldom do "Mother Africa" advocates notice that, in any case, many Africans look askance at professional victimhood in black America, and are rather amused when we deign to consider ourselves "home" on African soil.

But ultimately, the Swahili lessons and the rest are a kind of theater, self-affirming in some ways but largely in a gestural sense. Most black Americans see themselves as neither "African" nor "white." Although rarely required to put it in so many words, black Americans think of themselves as a new race altogether. To Robinson this is obliteration of the self, the working-class black man in Cincinnati denying his primal urge to get back to Lagos. But this only demonstrates that the old "one drop" rule is now more fiercely wielded by blacks than whites. Post–Civil Rights history renders this understandable, but this does not make it "progressive." "What about us?" Robinson has "Billy" moaning, as if he is a village boy from rural Ghana. But in fact, "Billy" and his chaperone, in their speech, diet, clothing, music, technology, and even religion are—sorry, Mr. Robinson—much more American than African. Might one answer to Billy that it was "us" who worked this system against great odds and survived, who appealed to its ideological foundations in sparking a Civil Rights revolution that few blacks could have imagined even a decade before?

But that is not what Robinson wants the "Billys" of America to hear. He would be even less enthusiastic to hear it said too close to "Billy" that our ultimate ideal is for Americans of all colors to see the monuments on the Mall as the history of "us." Obviously this is a fraught business in our moment. This sentiment will not be created through mere exhortations, and will take several more decades to truly set in. But it remains the only place that we can logically see ourselves as heading, if we seek true interracial harmony.

Quite simply: *any human society known to history where groups coexisted indefinitely while maintaining their distinctness has been one based on social subordination or caste distinctions.* In any society minus these, people of different groups fall in love and produce hybrid children, and the result is that none of the original groups continue to exist in their original form. Usually there is a transitional period during which people on both sides of the divide rue the impending "death of their culture," and that is the phase that Americans are in now. But mixture wins out in the end. In the history of the world's peoples, endless waves of miscegenation are the rule, not the exception. Studies of the genomes of people across the globe are making this ever clearer, and all of the world's languages betray signs of this kind of ethnic mixture, most of it long lost to the memories or psychologies of the people themselves. Life went on.

To many blacks today, it's an uncomfortable notion that we will be subject to this human universal. It smacks of us being "co-opted" by the white man, "losing out." I address that reasonable fear in Chapter Seven; as a teaser, we tend to forget how "black" whites have become since we have been here. But for now, not even the tragedies of black history render America somehow immune from these universals of how ethnic groups come to share space in peace. Robinson, like most "multicultural" advocates, misses that if our goal is truly an absence of interracial tensions, then in the strictly logical sense, *the salad bowl can only be a pit stop.*

————

What about recasting our vision of what came *after* we were brought here? What "far too many Americans of African descent believe," in no small part because of books like *The Debt,* is that blacks have never been able to accomplish much of anything here, except the occasional superstars like Frederick Douglass. Robinson allows no room for the thriving black business districts in several cities just two generations past Emancipation, for the revolution of American popular music that African descendants sparked, for the fact that in the late 1800s, black university students were well known for taking top prizes over white students not in athletics or music, but oratory! Classical oratory!

Robinson processes all of this as marginal just as the geocentric astronomers I mentioned in Chapter One saw the stars that did not follow their expected orbits. Like those astronomers, he is operating according to a defeatist *paradigm* that restricts his view to a limited body of data. This paradigm is a direct result of the sidelining of black ideology in the 1960s by the triumph of the New Left among thinking whites. Bruised, inevitably, into a racial inferiority complex after centuries of disenfranchisement, black America naturally took this leftist ball and ran with it, egged on by whites newly committed to redressing the past.

The idea of staged pessimism as "progressive thought" seems self-defeating to the outside observer. But its appeal is that it offers a balm for insecurity, providing an ever-present "racism" to point out as depraved—thus detracting attention from the inadequacies one perceives in oneself. Shelby Steele made this point beautifully in *The Content of Our Character*. Time passes, and the message of that almost fifteen-year-old book seems to have faded, but it is a keystone to what ails us today.

Blacks have embraced this line, then, out of private pain and doubt. We must be under no impression that the "I would still be black" of the UC Berkeley writer's manifesto is a cynical ploy designed to elicit handouts and exemptions. That lady means it. However, it remains poisonously self-destructive to treat residual racism as a check on self-realization. And to the extent that *The Debt* is founded upon this paradigm, it is rooted ultimately in shame.

This sense that imperfect conditions render black success meaningless is all the more pernicious in being usually wielded tacitly. As I have noted, we are faced with a New *Double* Consciousness. On the *overt* level, most blacks are given to expressing pride and resilience. Yet Robinson offers a rare example of the New Double Consciousness spelled out in black and white:

> There are always those special few who achieve (or fail) against all odds. There are those, like me, whose families successfully defy mainstream society's low expectation of us. The exceptions, however, would not be numerous enough to allow the closing of the income gap, even if the coarse and tangible old brand of discrimination were to go tomorrow into some period of long-term miracle remission. This is so because a static, unarticulated, insidious racial conditioning, to which all Amer-

icans are subject, lifts the high-expectation meritless . . . and, more often than not, locks down in a permanent class hell the natively talented but low-expectation black.

That passage alone is rich enough to inspire several Ph.D. dissertations. It is precisely why Robinson can see nothing but misery in a black America where more people are middle class than poor. It is why he can even note that segregated schools often lent solid educations, but not notice that this belies his argument that today's sadder situation is due simply to poverty and racism. And it is why he can only see black Republican Congressman J.C. Watts, Jr., as "pliable" rather than as a man with legitimate opinions. Since black success is just a fluke until there is no racism in society, any black Republican must be adopting ideologies he does not believe in order to make a buck.

This sense of racism as rendering all black success "accidental" is the primum mobile behind the reparations movement. We see this underlined, for instance, in Chrisman and Allen's rebuttal to Horowitz, where they proclaim as if utterly self-evident, "Racism continues as an ideology and a material force within the U.S., *providing blacks with no ladder that reaches the top*" (italics mine).

It follows that when Robinson is confronted with the only true progress we will ever make, he can only see black women in "owlish glasses" "losing themselves." As a linguist who cherishes reading Chekhov and Tolstoy in the original, I found one of the most memorable passages in *The Debt* to be where Robinson sits at a Howard University commencement ceremony appalled when a black undergraduate speaker says "thank you" in French, German, and Italian, rather than in Swahili, Chichewa, and Wolof. "She was not a European American of any variety: She was an American of African descent. Why on earth was she iffing herself European?"

No, Mr. Robinson: this woman is "iffing" herself a new race entirely, one with a heritage as richly Western as African. In fact, given that no slaves were brought to America who spoke Swahili or Chichewa, learning them would no more return her to her roots than learning European languages. An heir indeed to Du Bois, who was fluent in German and would have had choice words for anyone who told him this was not a proper "black" thing to be.

But Robinson can only see this bright young black woman as illegitimate, because the late 1960s taught him, as he came of age, that the American establishment is so putrescent with racism that it offers us no worthy source of a sense of cultural belonging. Sure, Robinson, like anyone, has a right to his "politics." But in this case we must be clear just what these politics mean. In his contribution to the "Who's got the bigger Holocaust?" competition, Robinson has it that slavery

> has hulled empty a whole race of people with inter-generational efficiency. Every artifact of the victim's past cultures, every custom, every ritual, every god, every language, every trace element of a people's whole hereditary identity, wrenched from them and ground into a sharp choking dust.

As often in *The Debt*, the music has a certain pull, but this is a grievous insult to four centuries of black Americans. Could Robinson truly look Denmark Vesey, Sojourner Truth, Frederick Douglass, James Weldon Johnson, Mary McLeod Bethune, Paul Robeson, Thurgood Marshall, Rosa Parks, and Adam Clayton Powell, Jr., in the eyes and tell them that they were "hulled empty"? Could he even say this to the middle-aged black woman of a certain age working at the post office, to the black middle manager at Pacific Bell with a house and family, to Condoleezza Rice, or even, looking in the mirror, to himself?

But under this analysis as "hulled empty," not to mention poverty-stricken and thwarted by racism at every turn, it follows that blackness remains a condition of misery four decades after the Civil Rights Act. We are hollow chocolate bunnies, beached in an alien culture. It is unclear in Robinson's analysis whether he thinks we could find some new sense of self *if* racism were not jumping out at us from behind every tree, and just what sources we would turn to in forging that new sense of self. These "what if?" exercises are not his concerns.

Rather, his conclusion is that the only solution to our problems is to be paid.

————

The idea that we are Africans "hulled empty" renders Robinson's argument more evolved than the "Reparations 101" position: simply that blacks must be paid the money that their slave ancestors were denied. "Where's the money?" has become the watchcry of that version of the reparations argument.

By now, ripostes to "Reparations 101" have been recycled so widely by so many that they barely need exposition here: that many whites in America today arrived after Emancipation, that many whites owned no slaves, that racial mixture would render the very question of who qualifies as "black" tricky at best and arbitrary at worst. In the spring of 2001, reparations was a hot topic for middle and high school term papers, and nation-wide, students—many of them black—were posing these objections spontaneously.

I have also always felt uncomfortable with the idea of taking money meant for someone I never knew. Many black people I have spoken to consider this a procedural quibble overridden by the principle of the thing. I suppose my problem is that although I certainly feel "black American," I feel neither African nor in any sense just a few steps past being a white person's property. Given this, my connection to ancestors of six generations back who I know nothing about feels more academic than spiritual—and I would feel the same way if my ancestors were wealthy white barons. As such, I for one could not take their money. Nor do I feel—although here I am aware that I depart from the views of many—that even the least fortunate blacks among us are glosses on "slave." On the contrary, I feel that these people were hijacked from making their way upward by misguided white condescension and the black ideology it produced in the sixties, which went on to spawn books like *The Debt*.

But Robinson does not dwell long on the "back pay" angle. He and the reparations crowd have their responses to the standard objections, but the issues are ultimately too contentious to be promising as a case for extracting huge sums of money from a national government. As such, by 2001 the reparations "debate" had moved toward appealing less to slavery itself than its effects, specifically segregation and disenfranchisement. In this, the movement returns to the position advocated in 1973 by Bittker, who emphasized the effects of *Plessy v. Ferguson* as grounds for reparations.

―――――

But here we run up against an argument that invariably sets reparations advocates' eyes rolling: that *America has been granting blacks "reparations" for almost forty years*. When Robinson grouses, "Once and for all, America must face its past," one wonders just what he thought the "War on Poverty" was that Lyndon Johnson instantiated, with Adam Clayton Powell, Jr., dedicatedly steering sixty bills through Congress in five years as chairman of the Education and Labor Committee.

One result of this new climate was the expansion of welfare. As begun in the 1930s, welfare policies were primarily intended for widows. Chrisman and Allen get this right, adding that at the time more whites than blacks received welfare (they could even have added that through the 1950s, institutional racism ensured that black widows often got lower payments than white ones). However, they sail over the fact that in the mid-1960s, welfare programs were deliberately expanded for the "benefit" of black people. Much of the impetus came from white leftists who claimed that the requirements of the new automation economy made it unfair to expect blacks to make their way up the economic ladder as former oppressed groups had.

Pointedly, black employment rates were on the rise at the time. But the die was cast, and federal and state governments have since poured billions of dollars into a welfare program carefully tooled toward supporting unwed black mothers. None of this was termed "reparations" in the nominal sense. But it certainly provided unearned cash for underclass blacks for decades—as well as sinecure jobs for a great many others manning the imposing bureaucracy the policy created.

Some might see calling the expansion of welfare "reparations" as a mere semantic trick. But even leading Civil Rights figures can reveal themselves to see welfare in the same way. Here, for example, is Roger Wilkins—son of the former NAACP head Roy Wilkins celebrated as "Mr. Civil Rights"—in his recent book *Jefferson's Pillow*, referring to conservatives: "These same people regularly exert enormous efforts to destroy the fragile programs put into place in the sixties and seventies to compensate for the deep injuries done to blacks over the three and a half centuries of their legally sanctioned subordination." Note that "to compensate for"—that is, welfare was reparations for slavery.

But how welfare was expanded for blacks in the late 1960s is today a largely forgotten story, and this gap in our historical memory is a major obstacle to seriously evaluating the "reparations" idea. Blacks born after about 1960 never saw welfare as it was in the old days, and tend naturally to assume that the generations-deep welfare culture has been due simply to an absence of jobs, or racism barring blacks from all but a few of them. Even older blacks could easily have missed the transformation, as it was not treated as a headline event. King's assassination, urban riots, and the Black Panthers' mau-mauing escapades were more likely to turn one's head at the time. But it is no accident that welfare lurks only at the margins of depictions and discussions of black life before the late 1960s. Until then, welfare was harder to get and less generous, offering a stopgap but not a lifestyle.

Obviously, the new version of the policy was not successful in pulling significant numbers of blacks out of poverty. But America has not given up on the effort: today, welfare programs are thankfully being recast as temporary safety nets, with welfare mothers being trained for work. Time will tell how successful this revision of welfare will be. But signs are all good as I write, flummoxing leftists who insisted that welfare reform would leave black families on the streets nationwide. Meanwhile, reparations advocates have yet to propose any better solution, and the funds and efforts devoted to welfare-to-work are, again, a concrete acknowledgment of the effects of structural poverty. A society with no commitment to addressing the injustices of the past would restrict welfare payments to the temporarily unfortunate, 1930s style, and certainly have no welfare-to-work programs aimed at poor blacks.

Meanwhile, Affirmative Action policies were similarly developed to address the injustices of the past. Chrisman and Allen snap that "So-called 'racial preferences' come not from benevolence but from lawsuits by blacks against white businesses, government agencies, and municipalities, which practice discrimination." Nonsense: the moral urgency motivating these trained scholars does not justify historiography this willfully sloppy. Wasn't it Lyndon Johnson, white the last time I checked, who entered into history the famous line that "You do not take a person who, for years, has been hobbled by chains and liberate him, bring him up to the starting line in a race and then say, 'you are free to compete with all the others', and still justly believe that you have been completely fair"? Neither Adam Clayton Powell, Jr., Martin Luther King, Jr., nor the SCLC agitated for racial quotas—there is no black hero that Affirmative Action fans can point to as a pioneer. It was whites, converted by the leftism "blowing in the wind," who embarked on recruiting and then hiring or admitting qualified blacks into realms that had been closed to them before. This good-faith effort quickly transmogrified into quota systems, with lesser qualified blacks all too often given positions and university slots over better qualified whites. But then we cannot help suspecting that many reparations advocates would laud this as just deserts.

"Once and for all, America must face its past"—but has Robinson noticed that whites are often as horrified as blacks at any prospect of welfare or Affirmative Action being contracted or altered? It was the decidedly non-black Peter Edelman who resigned from the Clinton administration's Department of Health and Human Services in protest over the welfare bill. No members of the Congressional Black Caucus are on record as having even considered taking down their shingles. Meanwhile, the *New York Times*, which Robinson considers so remiss in its lack of interest in our African comrades, has spent years after welfare reform bending over backward to cast welfare-to-work programs in the most negative light possible.

Concurrently many whites in power fiercely hold to Affirmative Action. It was white men, William Bowen and Derek Bok, who devoted years to a book-length defense of the policy in their *The Shape of the River*. There exists no study remotely as substantial by any black author. Meanwhile, white University of California president Richard Atkinson has suggested working around the outlawing of racial preferences in California by eliminating the SAT. The most strident student organization at Berkeley seeking to reverse the ban on racial preferences in California, By Any Means Necessary (BAMN), has barely a black person in it and at this writing is led by a white woman. All of this demonstrates that the existence of structural poverty and "root causes" is now a central component of thinking white Americans' ideology. A healthy and powerful contingent among them consider it a moral imperative to compensate blacks through set-asides.

Indeed, most blacks about fifty or younger tend to tacitly process Affirmative Action less as a proactive policy than as "acknowledgment" or "payback." One can often catch short a black person who favors Affirmative Action by asking precisely what purpose it serves for middle-class blacks who do not need it. Such people's answers are often distinctly vague, the question having obviously never even occurred to them. This is no accident. For the black person who never knew an America without racial set-asides, Affirmative Action inevitably looks "natural." Having also grown up with most "black thought" treating racism as central to black identity regardless of life circumstances, most blacks can barely help but process Affirmative Action as "just." To wit: most blacks already process Affirmative Action as a "reparation," although they would not put it in just that way.

In other words: if I were assigned to develop a plan for black reparations, I would institute a program supporting poor black people for a few years while stewarding them into jobs—which is currently in operation. I would have the government and private organizations channel funds into inner-city communities to help their residents buy their homes—which is exactly what Community Development Corporations have been doing for years. I would give banks incentives to make loans to inner-city residents to start small businesses—something the undersung Community Reinvestment Act has been doing since 1977. (*No* ladder to the top, Messrs. Chrisman and Allen?) I would make sure there were scholarships to help black people go to school—hardly unknown in this country. I would propose that Affirmative Action policies—of the thumb-on-the-scale variety designed to choose between equally qualified candidates—be imposed in businesses where subtle racism can still slow promotions. If it were 1966, I would have universities practice racial preferences as well, even if this involved temporarily lowering standards somewhat for the sake of a greater good (although I consider the policy outdated today).

Finally, I would ensure that black children had access to as good an education as possible. Here, in real life, we have only just begun, with the Bush administration's commitment to increased testing and, more importantly, school choice. It's hard to miss that Bush is likely to weight paying off his backers more heavily than his commitment to "leaving no child behind." Within the first weeks of his administration his spokespeople were making it clear that their education platform was subject to negotiation. As time went by, Education Secretary Rod Paige was relegated to the sidelines, and in the end, the closest Congress came to vouchers was allowing children to transfer to other *public* schools. Not earth-shattering, but something. What would a Gore administration have done, bound to the teachers' unions for votes? Let's face it—nothing.

Meanwhile, reparations advocates have proposed no alternatives to date other than vague calls to give predominantly minority schools more money. But in many cases that's just what the government has been doing for thirty years to no effect. History clearly shows us that such funds would be misused, and I have a hard time seeing this as a substantially "progressive" position.

Thus, resigned though I am to being classified as a "black conservative," I do not believe that we blacks should be left to simply pull ourselves up by the proverbial bootstraps, and I never have. However, my quite spontaneous response to the reparations issue has always been that it seems to me that we already have them.

There are rich issues here, amenable to a number of conclusions. But the fact that Robinson and the reparations crowd cannot see the alternate views as even worthy of address indicates their true interest—assuaging the sense of inferiority to whites that gnaws at the black American soul. That may seem humane, but it means that they are not interested in actually improving blacks' condition in any concrete way.

Specifically, what renders all of the payments, grants, and set-asides ineligible as "reparations" for Robinson, Conyers, and company is that they did not come explicitly labeled as an apology for four hundred years of black suffering, and as an acknowledgment that whites are responsible for anything that ails anyone black in America. Robinson, for example, shows his hand in hoping that we can "wear the call as a breastplate, a coat of arms." In other words, what truly motivates Randall Robinson is the emotional kick, the therapy, of *calling* for reparations, not a sincere commitment to helping the race.

———

That may seem a tad cold. But nothing makes this analysis more clear than the most stunning aspect of Robinson's entire book. Namely, he devotes *less than three pages* to actually proposing the form that reparations might take, these pages only at the very end of the book. Even they are largely derived from a proposal made in a law review article by someone else. "A tangle of nameless, nebulous thoughts clamor for description," Robinson cries earlier in the text. And indeed the sum total of concrete directives he offers is a trust fund dedicated to education, recovering funds from companies that benefited from slave labor, supporting the current Civil Rights advocacy (onward and upward . . . !), and making financial amends to Africa and the Caribbean. Two-hundred-and-fifty-plus preceding pages are devoted to Robinson's fantastical portrait of an America not a millimeter past *Plessy v. Ferguson*, plus rather desultory recountings of Robinson's plush trips to Cuba and Africa (never mind that W. E. B. Du Bois often had to make his trips abroad in steerage). But to actual recommendations for progress, just two and a half pages, and then *fin*.

———

The most indicative contrast here is with Bittker's book, which dedicated several chapters to careful legalistic argument exploring how Section 1983 of Title 42 of the United States Code might be applied to obtaining reparations for blacks. Robinson, a graduate of Harvard Law School, would surely be capable of a similar effort. But mysteriously, he instead pronounces that "my intent is to stimulate, not to sate," having "by necessity, painted basic themes with a broad brush." But why on earth, if these issues are so urgent, is it "by necessity" that a 262-page book on reparations written by a *black lawyer* "stimulate" rather than "sate"? Throughout the book Robinson even regularly brandishes a studied pessimism that his call will be heeded—"I see no evidence of any will to do anything much." This seems almost incommensurate with devoting an entire book to his opinion. We can only understand this in realizing that *The Debt* and the movement it represents are dedicated less to actual change than to an emotional commitment to seeing whitey squirm. That is, "stimulation." Or better, making sure whites know they are "on the hook." We are, after all, "hulled empty." Powerless. Translated: children.

Once again the tragedy of what passes for "Civil Rights" in our moment stands out in sharp relief. Proactive protest has ossified into an empty gesture. Hooked unwittingly on the ironic high of being the underdog, too many black "leaders" today have forgotten that the protests of the late 1950s and early 1960s were driven by a commitment to forging a new paradigm, to building, to working toward interracial harmony. For almost forty years now, it has been considered "authentically black" in many circles to indulge in year after year of ceremonial agitprop while whites develop all of the policies—successful or not—that have attempted to improve the lot of the race. Enterprise or empowerment zones, the Community Reinvestment Act, the reform of welfare, and the Local Initiatives Support Corporation and Enterprise Foundation, shunting combinations of grants into inner-city communities, have all been white creations.

Thus it sadly follows that the most influential book-length treatment of the reparations case written by a black person devotes 99 percent of its text to theatrical channeling of Malcolm X's bared teeth and upraised fist. Meanwhile, the only book outlining nuts-and-bolts directives for an actual legal case for reparations was written by a white man, promptly went out of print, and is now forgotten.

In one sense, any black American cannot help but wish another one well when his or her book is successful. However, just as black radicals often fear that books by "black conservatives" may set the race debate back, the success of *The Debt* makes me extremely uncomfortable, especially when I envision young blacks reading it. Blacks of all political persuasions agree that there is a crisis of leadership in the black community. As such, we must ask: what kind of a leading thinker is it whose message for the black youth of America is that black success is marginal regardless of its prevalence; that we will only find peace by identifying with people of another continent who are largely alien to us; and that the measure of our strength as a group is how articulately we can call for charity rather than building for ourselves?

I'm sorry, Mr. Robinson, but this ideology does not represent me. *"You are owed. You were caused to endure terrible things,"* you tell me. But if by "you" you mean my African ancestors, I never knew them, and it is unclear to me that their experience was hovering over me as I frolicked in Montessori schools as a child. If by "you" you mean my elderly relatives who endured segregated America, again, I did not live through this era myself, and most of them derived a great deal more grace from their lives than your desperate allegories imply (and not one of them was "black bourgeois"). Furthermore, the abstract extent to which the legacy of segregation affects me is being dutifully addressed by "reparations" of long standing. This includes ensuring, through lowered standards for all blacks in academia, that to a quiet but pernicious extent anything I ever do in my chosen field will always be interpreted as something a burdened "Negro" does rather than something a human being does. Talk about "terrible things"—it is my burden to bear, but I can do quite nicely without any further "repair" in this vein.

Nor does *The Debt* represent my race as a whole, and this becomes clear in one more comparison with Bittker's monograph. One of its features that requires historical adjustment is that Bittker, even writing as the Black Power movement raged, matter-of-factly assumed that black Americans were a people holding a diversity of opinions. "Who is to decide whether a group that claims to be the vanguard is really only a body of stragglers because the army is moving in the opposite direction?" he asks.

As such, Bittker concludes that reparations ought only be paid to blacks who endured segregated schooling, this being in his view the only case that could be productively argued on a principled legal and moral basis. He rejects distributing payments on the basis of "blackness" alone, fearing that this would encourage a revival of the arbitrary conceptions of race that were used to justify slavery. He also distrusts distributing funds to any chosen set of black organizations, on the basis of the difficulty in deciding which groups could claim to represent all blacks. In another statement that—sadly—classifies his book as a period piece, he notes that "Among American blacks today, differences in economic status, geographical origin and current location, outlook, organizational ties, and educational background are powerful centrifugal forces that black nationalist groups have not succeeded in neutralizing."

This contrasts tellingly with another of Robinson's allegories, in which he imagines that all blacks are given a card outlining "black" political positions, allocating their votes strictly on the basis of how committed a given candidate is to the positions on the card. Thus even at a time when the academy and the media were ablaze with the black radical message, Bittker spontaneously saw blacks as an ideologically diverse people. But thirty years later, Robinson blithely assumes that the composition of the "black card"—presumably one espousing variations on the very hand-outs and set-asides that have so slowed the dissolution of "the color line" for decades—would be self-evident to all blacks. (What about the ones in the ugly glasses?)

It is here that Robinson reveals himself and those of his ideol-ogy as the "body of stragglers" Bittker refers to. Increasing legions of black people of all walks of life are realizing that pity has never gotten a race anywhere significant, and that countless ethnic groups in world history have risen despite residual racism.

The closest Robinson comes to acknowledging that there might be more than one morally legitimate way to think as a black American is in one of the oddest spots in the book, when he dis-misses—of all people—the black radicals of the Black Power era:

> For reasons that were never clear to me, they elected to set them-selves apart from those they presumed to lead by dressing and talking differently, using an unfamiliar idiom and cadence, leav-ing their voices up at the end of their sentences . . . They seemed deeply suspicious, often with good reason, of those blacks who had received from white institutions a liberal arts education, which I think they viewed as rather closer to indoctrination.

Thus for Robinson, this was a "body of stragglers" going against the tide. But does he not realize that these people were animated by exactly the ideology he dedicates a book to propounding? "Punic this, Pyrrhic that" and dissing the black girl who deigns to learn French, German, and Italian indicate the very distrust of "white" learning that became fashionable in the era of Stokely Carmichael. These people favored dashikis and exaggerated their black dialect out of the same spiritual disidentification with America that Robinson sees as the salvation of the race. (It was no accident that it was in the early seventies that some black scholars began creatively analyzing black English as an "African" language.) In other words, if Robinson considers these people the sort of "stragglers" Bittker was chary of granting stewardship of the race, then this would seem to be a clear case of the pot calling the kettle black.

———

In the end, *The Debt* is uniquely articulate not only in its title but in its cover, depicting Robinson himself. An affluent, poised black American man sits grimly indignant that his government does not acknowledge his essence as a Mandingo tribesman, considering the compensation given his race for decades invalid in not having been labeled as a groveling apology, and pretending to consider himself and all black Americans eternally "lost" as a result.

A hundred years from now, the marvelous inevitability of interracial mixture will have created a deliriously miscegenated America where hundreds of millions of *café-au-lait* Tiger Woodses and Mariah Careys will be quite secure in knowing that *American* is "who they are." For these new Americans, ancient essentialist tracts such as *The Debt* will stand as curiosities. Dissertations will be required to parse just why thinking people at the turn of the twenty-first century were inclined to treat this book and its ilk as urgent manifestos for uplifting a race. Confronted with archives of journalism and governmental records from our era displaying a virtual obsession with redressing the wrongs that had been perpetrated upon blacks, graduate students will cut their teeth on producing competing analyses as to why so many blacks in our moment saw "reparations" as an idea never given its due.

For now, however, the response *The Debt* must elicit in us is pathos: that is, to quote Mr. Webster, pity, sympathy, tenderness, and sorrow. For this book is not, as some might suppose, a cynical attempt to shore up the "handout industry" via "the blame game." Rather, this book and the entire movement to gain ourselves "reparations" that we already have is evidence of the spiritual stain that black Americans' history has left in our hearts.

However, we must beware a tendency for pity to transmogrify into condescension. The fine line between concern and disempowerment has been a prime source of black American misery the past thirty-five years. Thus to treat *The Debt* and the movement it represents as "progressive" is to give in to one of the more treacherous sides of our human natures. This would be especially tragic at a time when so many of us, despite the "stragglers" mired in a rhetoric that has outlived its usefulness, are making the best of ourselves as members of the newest race in the modern world.

4

The "Can You Find the Stereotype?" Game

Blacks on Television

...

I once appeared on a television talk show with a black professor, where as usual I was cast as the "conservative" voice in opposition to his "liberal" one. As we chatted during a commercial break, I asked him, "What kind of thing leads you to think that racism is really something you and I deal with on a daily basis? Really—I want to know." He said, "Well, for one thing, the depiction of black people in films." I asked him, as politely as I could, "If I may, since I know you have children and all, are you able to get out to the movies much these days?" "Yes." He nodded—but then we were back on the air.

At that time, over the past year there had been so many black movies depicting successful, thriving black people that even I, something of a film fan, had been unable to catch them all. Bamboozled, The Brothers, and Kingdom Come had just left the theaters. Meanwhile, vibrant black characters were a fixture in mainstream movies as often as not—not long after the taping I caught Sword-

fish, *where Halle Berry romanced two white male leads (one of them John Travolta) with not a peep in the script or from the media about these being "interracial romances." And for years by this point, a veritable flood of black sitcoms had been playing night after night on television, with African-Americans gliding across middle-class suburban sets indistinguishable from the ones decorating* Everybody Loves Raymond *and* Friends.

The professor's comment was typical of a reflexive observation often heard, based on a going wisdom among thinking blacks that the media paint a "misleading" picture of black life. That observation was valid twenty-five years ago. But things have changed vastly since then. Unfortunately the New Double Consciousness drives too many blacks to pretend that they haven't.

Few books demonstrated this better than Donald Bogle's Primetime Blues. *This exploration of that book addresses the dangers in insisting that anything a black person does in front of a camera is a "stereotype." The role that blacks play on television today is cause for celebration and hope. As a strong people, we must learn to admit when battles have been won.* ▪

Donald Bogle and I share having grown up in Philadelphia watching the growing presence of black Americans on television. Bogle has some years on me, having been in attendance since the 1960s. My memories of television begin in the early 1970s, when my mother required that I sit by her side to watch the new flood of black shows like *Good Times, Sanford and Son,* and *The Jeffersons,* as well as shows attending to race such as *All in the Family* and *Maude.* And of course, watching the entire run of *Roots* was de rigueur, even though it meant staying up past my bedtime for several nights in a row.

Part of this was surely due to black Americans' cultural affection for television. As Bogle notes in his *Primetime Blues,* a 1990 Nielsen survey showed that blacks watched an average of seventy hours of television a week as opposed to whites' forty-seven, and television was definitely a more central ritual in my household than in my white friends'. Yet my mother, a professor of social work, also considered black television a part of my early education in racial consciousness. She saw the shows as one way to help inculcate me with the basics of black history, the message that the whole world was not white, and that black America included many people not as fortunate as we were.

As we passed into the 1980s and 1990s, the black presence on television increased so incrementally that had I been born later, it would have been impractical to try to catch everything blacks did on the tube. In the 1950s, a white racist could be content that he or she would only catch blacks on television in the very occasional series, a few supporting roles, scattered variety show appearances, and one-shot dramatic productions a racist could easily refrain from watching. Today, blacks are so numerous on television in all of its genres, and represented in such a wide sociological and psychological range, that the same racist would feel inundated by blacks every time he or she turned on the set, incensed at how sympathetically blacks are portrayed and how intimately they interact with whites.

I have always seen this as a clear sign that the color line is ever dissolving in America. Bogle's *Primetime Blues,* however, is devoted to an argument that while progress has been made in the sheer numerical sense, overall the black presence on television has been an endless recycling of a certain passel of injuriously stereotypical images. The book will surely be interpreted by many as Doing the Right Thing, revealing the eternal racism always lurking behind developments that give the appearance of black progress. However, in the end the very founding of this volume upon that premise is more a matter of ideology local to our moment. Its very title marks *Primetime Blues* as a product of the sadly distortional, if well-meant, frames of reference that have dominated black thinkers' work since the late 1960s.

––––––

The early chapters on the 1950s and 1960s, however, are masterful, displaying Bogle at his best. Bogle did the chronicling of black popular entertainment a service with his *Brown Sugar* (1980), a survey of black "divas" from Ma Rainey to Donna Summer, bringing to the light of day the work of many figures who had faded from consciousness (especially before video made vintage performances more available). His 1997 biography of Dorothy Dandridge was a long-overdue chronicle of the life and work of this world-class beauty and gifted actress, who was denied the career she should have had by the naked racism of her era and died in despair at forty-two.

With the crisp prose and masterful eye for the telling detail evident in those books, in *Primetime Blues* Bogle takes us through black television of the 1940s, 1950s, and 1960s, bringing to light performances hitherto barely recorded in accessible sources. We learn that the very first experimental television broadcast, by NBC in 1939, was not, say, a half hour with Jack Benny, but a variety show starring none other than Ethel Waters. Bogle later traces Waters's little-known but fascinating television career, which included a stint playing the maid Beulah. This show was more representative of the black presence on stone-age television than its more frequently discussed contemporary *Amos 'n' Andy*, which even by the early 1950s was a rather tatty, recidivist affair rooted in minstrel humor by then passé, living more on the familiarity of the radio show than on freshness.

Beulah is remembered for depicting a black woman who has nothing better to do than center her life around the white family she works for, because she's waiting for her ne'er-do-well boyfriend Bill to propose. Of course, this is not an exclusively black trope: Shirley Booth's Hazel and Ann B. Davis's Alice on *The Brady Bunch* occupied similar spaces. But what makes *Beulah* so excruciating to watch today is that she is, in addition, none too bright. Only with the utmost fortification of historical perspective can one today endure the opening tags, where Beulah looks us dead in the eye and offers such aperçus as the fact that she is "the maid who's always in the kitchen—but never knows what's cookin' . . . ! HYEH HYEH HYEH HYEH . . ."

In its original radio incarnation, Beulah had been played by a white man, and for all of the discomfort this arouses in us today, Marlin Hurt's portrayal is a guilty pleasure. Few could resist laughing today hearing his uncannily accurate giggles, laughs, and intonations, picked up from his black childhood nursemaid, all the more evocative in the poised restraint of Hurt's delivery. (Hurt was truly amazing, also playing the man Beulah worked for, as well as boyfriend Bill.) Furthermore, on radio Beulah, while no

Einstein, was no dummy and got her licks in in Eddie "Rochester" Anderson style. Hurt died suddenly and his replacement, Bob Corley, was merely adequate in the role, but when Hattie McDaniel took over in 1947, she predictably reinfused the character with her trademark spark.

In contrast, the television version of *Beulah* was a glum, sodden affair, even for television of the era. Largely at the center of the action in the radio show, on television Beulah took second place to the anodyne comings and goings of the white family she worked for, all the more disturbing given that this family managed to out–Wonder Bread even the stock families of this type then prevalent in sitcoms. Today, Beulah's sidelining is especially hard to watch in its implication that these bland automatons are more interesting than her.

The show went through no fewer than three large black actresses in the lead role—Ethel Waters, Hattie McDaniel, and Louise Beavers. Beavers, picked up last and playing the role the longest, could barely conceal her lack of interest, walking through it as if she were in a children's play (which she essentially was). She eventually left the role because she was tired of it. And with that, having gone through all three of the leading black mammies in Hollywood, the producers simply closed shop.

Bogle is correct in noting, however, that the miraculous Waters managed to draw some kind of character out of the wan scripting. Waters's episodes are the only ones that approach watchability today, as she conveys a kind of warmth and sexual affection between her and Bill, and manages to give an appearance of intelligence and control despite what the lines nominally convey. Throughout her life Waters simply could not help filling empty space with sheer charisma in this way. Bogle movingly describes an episode of the usually frothy *Person to Person* in 1954 when Waters diverted the interview into sincere psychological self-revelation: Waters was intense.

Indeed, one of the strengths of *Primetime Blues* is Bogle's wise choice to cover television movies, specials, and guest appearances, as in the 1950s black performance history was made more here than in the all-too-rare black series. Waters appeared in a number of dramas and specials, and appeared in a savory episode of *Route 66* about the reunion of a group of jazz musicians that, in including not only Waters but jazz artists Jo Jones, Roy Eldridge, and Coleman Hawkins, stands at the top of my list of shows that ought be included in any future video anthology of early black television that *Primetime Blues* may inspire. Ex-boxer James Edwards had a brief eminence turning in nuanced and top-rate performances in numerous episodes of the drama anthology series popular in the decade. Sidney Poitier costarred in the early black-white "buddy" drama *A Man Is Ten Feet Tall*, eventually filmed as *Edge of the City* with him repeating his role. Dorothy Dandridge, Sammy Davis, Jr., the sadly forgotten Juano Hernandez, and Waters all got work in drama anthology episodes as well. It is easy to suppose that the only way to see blacks on television in the 1950s was through *Amos 'n' Andy, Beulah*, or Nat King Cole's short-lived variety show. However, Bogle shows that those watching at the time saw somewhat more black performance on their screens than this—although surely far from enough.

The sun began breaking through the clouds in the 1960s, as

the dawning of the Civil Rights Era brought race relations and "the Negro question" to the forefront of America's consciousness. Perhaps the most immediately memorable black icon of this era is Bill Cosby's erudite undercover operator Scotty on *I Spy*, portrayed as every bit the equal of his white partner, Robert Culp. (It was indicative to see Cosby decades later host Culp, by then a figure of the past, as a one-shot guest on *The Cosby Show*, rather than it being the other way around.) From our vantage point, we miss any indication of racial identity in Scotty, and this is largely true of other blacks in series of this decade, such as Greg Morris on *Mission: Impossible*, Lloyd Haynes on *Room 222*, and Nichelle Nichols's Uhura on *Star Trek*. To many analysts, including Bogle, this reflected white America's desire to "tame" the Negro beginning to be seen as a threat. This was part of it—but then only by the end of this decade would the salad bowl metaphor triumph over the melting pot one in most thinking Americans' consciousness. In an era when the main call from Civil Rights leaders was still for integration, many white producers and writers sincerely considered themselves to be doing good by portraying blacks without any particular "cultural" traits.

Today, however, the seams show in efforts like this, in ways that make the space blacks were assigned to fill require major historical adjustment. *The Dick Van Dyke Show*, for example, ventured an episode where the Petries are accidentally sent home with another couple's baby, the couple having been left with theirs. The snafu discovered, the other couple come to the Petries' to make the switch. They turn out to be black. The audience screams with laughter; the handsome couple sit down; there are a few more jaunty lines of dialogue capped by some jolly topper, and the episode fades out with the two couples sitting there in the living room all asmile. The producers' gesture was heartfelt. But I have always wondered: since the Petries surely did not just hustle the couple out the door right then, what did they all talk about after that? I assume we are supposed to think that they simply interacted as "people," talking about mowing the lawn and the crowds on the train into Manhattan. But we also know that this was an era a heartbeat past legalized segregation, and that interracial relations were hardly that simple, as they still are not. Only in the 1970s would sitcoms begin to explore what happened after that fade-out.

Drama shows, however, were somewhat more concerned with the tensions that would soon transform integrationism into separatism, although usually more interested in class and injustice than what we would call "diversity." Shows like The Defenders and The Nurses often addressed race issues. In East Side, West Side (which my parents always recalled fondly) Cicely Tyson as a social worker made a lasting impression sporting the first "natural" black hairdo on television. This show did not shy away from race-based episodes that were surprisingly rich for television of the era, including ones with Diana Sands, Ruby Dee, and James Earl Jones. (One of Bogle's nervier opinions is that Jones is a "fake old windbag"—I have always quietly thought so but would never have dared say it out loud!) And from our vantage point, Clarence Williams III's Linc on The Mod Squad, with his large Afro, thanks-but-no-thanks reserve, and "I don't fink on soul brothers," is most certainly anybody's conception of a Black Man.

A far cry from Beulah in the Hendersons' kitchen. Yet amid it all, throughout most of the 1960s there was not a single "black show" proper on national television. This changed in 1968 with *Julia*, starring Diahann Carroll. The response to this show from black commentators signaled that a new era in black American ideology had arrived.

Julia portrayed a middle-class widow raising a young son while working as a nurse. With "assimilated" Diahann Carroll's chiseled features and crisp standard English, *Julia* wore the race issue lightly. The occasional episode had Julia encountering and handily defeating manifestations of what was then called "prejudice," but this was depicted as an occasional excrescence rather than as a deep-seated societal malaise. Largely, however, *Julia* was a sepia version of the concurrently running *That Girl*.

Quickly black writers, actors, and thinkers fiercely condemned this little show for neglecting the tragedies of blacks in the inner cities. The Black Power movement was just then forging a new sense of a "black identity" opposed to the mainstream one. This naturally recast the suffering poor blacks—those most unlike middle-class whites—as the "real" blacks, and middle-class blacks as having some explaining to do in deserting their "roots." The black literati's response to *Julia* was predicated upon this then-new idea, now so deeply ensconced in much black thought as to no longer be processed as a "position" at all, that the very essence of blackness was suffering.

Obviously, then, a middle-class nurse living in a nice apartment and interacting easily with whites was "inauthentic." Objections to

Amos 'n' Andy in the early 1950s were based in part on the fact that even if the show was undeniably amusing in itself, this was one of the *only* depictions of blacks on television. Good point—but by the time *Julia* aired, black misery and the new "black identity" were not exactly absent on other shows. It was not that *Julia* was the only view of blacks on television: the problem now was with this side of black life being shown at all.

The profoundness of the shift in consciousness is revealed in the realization that black commentators just fifteen years before would have eaten up *Julia* with a spoon. *Amos 'n' Andy* is again a case in point: early in the book Bogle presents a list of objections to the show by the NAACP. Crucially, in a full page of complaints, the fact that the show did not address black poverty is not even mentioned. Most black thinkers of the period would have had no more investment in seeing the unfortunate dutifully "explored" on television than white viewers had in seeing Appalachia or the poor rural South depicted, and would have applauded a portrait of members of their race doing well as an advance from the "Mammy" days. And yet we can hardly say that the NAACP of the period, sponsoring efforts that would soon result in *Brown v. Board of Education*, was uninterested in black poverty. The difference hinged on the contrast between an ideology focused on achievement despite acknowledged obstacles, versus one focused upon the treacherous idea that achievement is just lucky until all obstacles are removed. This idea automatically casts those blessed with only ordinary capabilities and not blessed with luck—i.e., the poor—as "real" black people.

This ideology remains with us today. It includes Bogle, and as

such, it is at *Julia* that *Primetime Blues* takes a disappointing detour from intelligent survey into a narrow, almost numbingly cir-
cular litany. Namely, Bogle frames the thirty remaining years of
black work on television as an almost unbroken procession of
veiled injustice and exploitation. Bogle is hardly alone in this,
and his enviable gifts as a chronicler remain unassailable. But this
book remains important as an object lesson.

———

As of black television in the late 1960s, Bogle falls into the same
trap that mars the second edition of his *Toms, Coons, Mulattoes,
Mammies, and Bucks*. First appearing in 1973, this book, my first
primer on blacks in film, aptly identified the eponymous five
stereotypes as running throughout blacks' assignments in American movies. Bogle made the useful point that the "blaxploitation"
genre, whatever its visceral thrill and the work it gave black actors,
was recapitulating the very types on view as far back as *The Birth
of a Nation*. However, Bogle's update in 1989 revealed a man
with a hammer to whom everything is a nail. What was a valid
and penetrating thesis applied to blacks in film up to the early
1970s is reflexively applied to the next fifteen years, despite the
stunning maturation of the black role on the silver screen that occurred during the period.

Eddie Murphy is a dynamic phenomenon playing lead roles in
film after film, and often producing them as well? No—because
he is sexually appetitive, he is merely a recapitulation of the over-
sexed black "Buck" that chases the Camerons' young daughter off
a cliff in *The Birth of a Nation*. Was Lonette McKee's performance
in *Sparkle* a signature piece of acting? Not quite. Because she is

light-skinned, her sad fate in the plot renders her a "tragic mulatto," despite her character not being of mixed race. ("One wonders if McKee's Sister must, like Dandridge's important characters, be disposed of, as perhaps a kind of warning to other sexual, aggressive black women," Bogle proposes, with nary an attempt to demonstrate that this was on the mind of the Jewish scriptwriter.) And so on. Predictably, Richard Pryor, speaking for the ghetto, gets one of Bogle's rare stamps of approval—but with the qualification that he may exemplify a new stereotype aborning, the "Crazy Nigger."

Bogle transfers this same frame of reference to the rest of *Primetime Blues*, deftly pigeonholing almost every black contribution to series television from 1970 to 2000 into one of several stereotype categories. The result is a kind of game one might call "Can You Find the Stereotype?" which has increasingly slighter relationship to its data set as the years pass, and eventually becomes a kind of idle exercise that one regrets seeing Bogle waste his abilities upon.

All large, nurturing black women, for example, are "Mammies," recapitulations of Hattie McDaniel and Beulah. This includes Della Reese's Tess on *Touched by an Angel* as well as our beloved Oprah, whose inspiring success is thereby rendered suspect. Meanwhile, a feisty black woman who speaks her mind to men is a "Sapphire," the idea being that the Kingfish's shrewish wife on *Amos 'n' Andy* set a "stereotype" about the black female now best avoided. Thus our pleasure in watching LaWanda Page's immortal Aunt Esther on *Sanford and Son* or Nell Carter's lead character on *Gimme a Break!* and elsewhere must by all rights be a guilty one.

Furthermore, even nurturing middle-aged black men are evidence of racism eternal. I will never forget a black drama professor, quite oriented toward the "Can You Find the Stereotype?" game that Bogle's film book helped to legitimize, speculating in 1991 that the rotund stature of the black television fathers James Avery (*The Fresh Prince of Bel-Air*) and Reginald VelJohnson (*Family Matters*) signaled the emergence of a new stereotype to replace the Mammy, the "Pappy." However, the similarity of these two actors' body shapes turned out to be a coincidence—there has arisen no trend in casting fat black men as fathers. Yet Bogle, too, seems primed to find a "Pappy" stereotype in the air, dutifully griping that Lou Meyers's wonderful portrait of a grumpy but loving cook on *A Different World* was "something of a fussy mammylike character."

The prickly black guy, in the meantime, is the "Angry Black Man," stigmatized by the writers as "other" (Eriq La Salle's Benton on *E.R.*). Yet the black man, or woman, who does not stick up for the race is deracialized, "tokenism at its worst" (*Julia*, Brian Stokes Mitchell's "Jackpot" Jackson on *Trapper John, M.D.*). To be fair, one assumes that Bogle would prefer to see a happy balance be struck. But then he comes up with a way to dissect and condemn almost every attempt even in this vein. When Blair Underwood's Rollins on *L.A. Law* begins one subplot avoiding taking a race-based stand on a case, then rises into Politically Correct indignation, and finally withdraws into an ambiguous stance in the end—a pretty good depiction of how many successful blacks feel about race issues in our moment—Bogle chides the writers for taking the character "back to the mainstream shore." Avery Brooks's solemn, insular, culturally rooted Hawk character on

Spenser: For Hire is fascinating, but ultimately neutralized in lending his services to his white partner rather than working against the mainstream.

––––––

The problem with Bogle's framework is that as it is constructed, it is all but impossible for any black performance to pass as kosher. Instead, it becomes a "damned if they do, damned if they don't" exercise, designed more to feed the flames of indictment of the white man than to illuminate any actual truths. *Benson* was indeed a little dicey in depicting an intelligent, middle-aged black man as a butler in a governor's mansion as late as 1979. But within two years, the writers had him elected state budget director; eventually he became lieutenant governor, and finally ran against the governor himself. The series ended with Benson and the governor awaiting the election results together. One would think this series aggressively negated the Beulah stereotype, even at the expense of some plausibility. But for Bogle, what is significant is that the show ends with Benson "by his good white friend's side." Physically, yes—but watching the progress of an election in which he has attempted to unseat the man from his livelihood! One wonders how Bogle would have gotten around this ending if the writers had happened to end the series with Benson watching the returns by himself?

Along the same lines, to address racism in history (*Homefront, I'll Fly Away*) is to imply that racism is safely contained in the past. But then if producers refrained from depicting slavery and segregation on television, Bogle would decry this as "whites denying the wrongs of the past." Meanwhile, Bogle repeatedly dismisses as "self-congratulatory" shows where whites decry racism—but then if a black character wears racial indignation on his or her sleeve we are back to the Angry Black Man marginalized as "other."

This is not serious engagement with a cultural development. It is an exercise in promulgating professional underdogism, and as with most such work, it is often only possible at the expense of empiricism. In reference to Gary Coleman's savvy comments about racism in *Diff'rent Strokes*, Bogle sees an implication that such comments are acceptable "*only* out of the mouths of babes." One imagines black audiences at readings from the book nodding here—but the show came in the wake of a whole decade of Norman Lear sitcoms full of black characters far beyond toddlerhood sounding off confidently about racism in America. Children were the ones commenting on racism in *Diff'rent Strokes* because they were the black characters; the adults were white. Would Bogle have preferred the casting of a black maid to chime in? Or perhaps should the children's adoptive father Mr. Drummond have married a black woman—only for Bogle to peg her as "deracialized" in marrying white?

Bogle accuses *E.R.* of neglecting to fill in Peter Benton's personality. Granted, the show has given more attention to the white leads. Yet in the very episodes surrounding the death of Benton's mother that Bogle gives some space to, we were filled in on issues in his family background and the hills and valleys of his personality, rendering him much more than a mere Angry Black Man.

This bending of the facts extends to a tendency to read supposedly coded winks into performers' work that the actual evidence does not support. In his books, Bogle is fond of a notion that all black actors of the past were quietly seething at the roles they were forced to play. There is some truth here, but as with all historical inquiry, the idea that "they were really just like us" taken too far becomes ahistorical, implying that leading black ideologies have remained static over time. Bogle analyzes Hattie McDaniel's tendency to hold the viewer at a distance as evidence of possible "anger and frustration." But Bogle is looking at McDaniel through the post–Civil Rights era lens. McDaniel actually took a practical and unruffled view of her maid roles (famously saying, "I'd rather make seven thousand dollars a week playing a maid than make seven a week being one!"), made no statements suggesting the pent-up fury of later figures like Lena Horne, and was even a leader of a contingent of black actors who protested the NAACP's postwar condemnation of blacks' roles as servants in Hollywood. McDaniel needed the work, period, and would not live long enough to experience the change in the tide in the 1960s. She perhaps appears unenlightened by our standards, but the fact remains that the "militant" ideology so familiar to black people of Bogle's and my vintage was not yet mainstream in McDaniel's day.

Perhaps one of the last major black performers to fall on the other side of the ideological line was, pointedly, Diahann Carroll. During *Julia*, she told *TV Guide:* "Of course! *Of course, I'm a sellout*. What else would I be? I've sold my talents for a job I'm not particularly crazy about . . . *Isn't that what you do? Isn't that what most people do?*" And as late as the late 1960s, it indeed was. One had little choice, and for most blacks, the decisiveness of the obstacles would have made cultivating perpetual rage self-destructive.

No, the old-time Hollywood black actors did not love the limitations placed upon them—but few of them were inclined to actively parse their lives as sagas of victimhood either. That is a luxury more available to Bogle.

One of the saddest results of the ideological straitjacket Bogle filters black television through is that it leads him to dismiss more than a few very special and historically important performances. In *Gimme a Break!* of the early-to-mid 1980s, Nell Carter played a live-in housekeeper to a widowed white police officer (Dolph Sweet) and became essentially a surrogate mother to his children. Of course, according to Bogle, "For African-American viewers, *Gimme a Break!* was little more than a remake of *Beulah.*" But more properly this was what Bogle and assorted black commentators decided to make of it. I highly suspect that my even mentioning the show elicits warm nostalgia in many black readers. (In conversations with black people after the article version of this chapter appeared, not one but two of them spontaneously broke into singing the show's theme song, one of them even knowing the second version used in later seasons!) The show was quite popular in the black American community, in large part because the resemblance to *Beulah* was only superficial.

Beulah was meekly deferent to her employers; Nell brooked no nonsense from the Chief. Bogle may parse this as a revival of "Sapphire" (despite her decidedly unsexual rapport with Sweet), but most of us simply enjoyed seeing a black woman holding her own against a white man. Beulah never knew what was cookin'; Nell so much ran the house that the show barely skipped a beat when Sweet died during the run. Beulah's life outside the house was a cipher; Nell, on the other hand, was depicted as dreaming of a singing career, and Carter, fresh from winning a Tony on Broadway in *Ain't Misbehavin'!*, occasionally limned her character by singing (and always viciously well). "Do black people always have to sing and dance?" would be the party-faithful question—but then if Carter hadn't, this would be treated as suppressing her talent.

Nell was given a black female friend, and Bogle dutifully compares this to Beulah's empty friendship with simpleton Oriole. But if no such friend had been cast, then we'd be back to "deracialization," and Carter's chemistry with Telma Hopkins's Addy was so electric and genuine that my mother regularly commented on how racially "real" their friendship was. This extended to their pointed but affectionate spats, which Bogle sees as more hints of Sapphire, but which my mother accurately read as reflective of the black folk "fussing" tradition (the scenes would not have rung true with white actresses). My mother was exquisitely attuned to the depths of racism in American society, at the time teaching college courses on the subject. I do not believe that she was somehow misguided in not processing *Gimme a Break!* as a retread of the *Beulah* that she remembered seeing as a child.

But Bogle sees Mammies everywhere, in performances that deserve better, especially from a black writer. *What's Happening!* in the late 1970s was hardly Molière, but little Danielle Spencer contributed a bravura deadpan performance as the tattling little sister, fondly remembered by all blacks who watched the show. Yet for Bogle she was merely a "young mammy in waiting." *A Different World's* pitting Diahann Carroll as bourgie Whitley's mother against Patti LaBelle as down-to-earth Dwayne's was one of the most brilliant casting coups in television history, period. LaBelle, not a trained actress, walked away with her role so brilliantly that it led to her being given her own series a few years later. But to Bogle, LaBelle, because she is dark and not small (although hardly overweight), was "Mammy" again. Judgments like this ironically verge on "All blacks look alike," given that LaBelle's angular features and crisp, urban presence are not at all reminiscent of Hattie McDaniel. Thea Vidale's short-lived sitcom of the mid-1990s gamely tried to depict some genuine issues for a single black woman raising children on a tight budget. It wasn't a great show, but Vidale made the very most of it and I have always missed her since it went off. But because Vidale is a big, dark woman—well, you know.

Few vintage performances are immune. Sherman Hemsley's loudmouthed George Jefferson is apparently a retread of the "Coon." Yet Bogle at the same time captures the essence of Hemsley's brilliant characterization, in noting his "bouncy, brotherlike bop" entering the lobby of his and Louise's new "dee-luxe apartment in the sky" during the opening credits. That little clip, viewed week after week for over a decade, spoke to all black viewers, encapsulating the prospect of prideful black advancement while retaining ethnic identity in the bargain. The strutting bantam persona and savory line readings that Hemsley created gave vent to the frustrations that any black person of the time felt. He (plus Marla Gibbs's Florence) was why this essentially silly show lasted eleven seasons. Hemsley's genius is clear when compared to the actor originally cast with Isabel Sanford's Louise when the characters began as next-door neighbors on *All in the Family:* Mel Stewart's reading as George's brother was adequate, but the Jeffersons would never have spun off with him as the lead. Sherman Hemsley's George Jefferson was an acting triumph—in real life Hemsley is a low-key Buddhist—and dismissing the character as a mere "Coon" is unfair and, frankly, narrow.

———

A final trap Bogle's mission leads him into is apparently requiring that there be no black versions of tropes considered unexceptionable in mainstream entertainment venues. A group of urban, (mostly) upwardly mobile twenty-something friends congregating mainly in one improbably opulent Brooklyn apartment, some of them eventually hooking up—sound familiar? Indeed, *Living Single* was precisely a black *Friends* (although actually predating it by a season) and was a gorgeous, hilarious bonbon of a show at its height. Bogle criticizes the characters' obsession with sex and the transitoriness of their relationships. But most young sitcom characters are obsessed with sex, and television writers have traditionally refrained from having single characters get into permanent attachments because such new characters interfere with the chemistry of the show, and narrative plausibility would usually dictate that the show itself would have to end. How likely was it, for example, that an attractive young woman like Mary Richards on *The Mary Tyler Moore Show* would have no long-term involvements for seven years? Yet for Mary to remarry would have meant a different and probably doomed show. But to Bogle, business as usual in a white show is racism in its black equivalent.

One of Bogle's oddest analyses in this vein is his take on *Living*

Single's resident airhead Synclaire. Comparing her to Marie Wilson in the ancient *My Friend Irma* and Suzanne Somers in *Three's Company*, Bogle complains, "You had to ask why a Black woman on television should be stuck with a white woman's formulaic leftovers." But few people under seventy have even heard of *My Friend Irma*, a minor hit sitcom of radio and television in the 1940s and 1950s, forgotten as soon as it left the air in 1954. Not a single person involved with *Living Single*, including Coles, is likely to even be aware of the show. Certainly Suzanne Somers's Chrissy would have been a vivid memory. But Coles's warm, quirky Synclaire bore only a formal resemblance to Somers's jiggly, ephemeral cartoon. What Chrissy and Synclaire had in common was being stock sitcom dumbbells. But this is hardly a matter of Coles having had Somers's "leftovers" specifically foisted on her, much less of her having prepared for her role by holing herself up in archives to squint at grainy old episodes of *My Friend Irma*! Bogle, with his usual sharp eye, is correct in seeing a certain likeness between Synclaire and Wilson's Irma—a certain warm sexiness that both exuded within their "illogical logic." But the resemblance is accidental; the idiosyncratic sexuality Coles exuded was her personal contribution, convincing enough that her eventual marriage to Overton appeared much realer than any marriage Irma or Chrissy would have entered into.

Similarly, if white couples argue (*Roseanne, Married . . . With Children*) it is considered refreshing. But Fred Sanford and Aunt Esther's chitlin' circuit feuding (the characters' relationship being a kind of ersatz marriage) is a return to the Kingfish and Sapphire. But I for one adored Aunt Esther, seeing, as many black viewers did, an endearingly broad exaggeration of bits and pieces of any number of black women I had known. It is unclear to me that I should regret the many pleasures this character gave me because of an academic parallel to a character from a show created thirty years before I was born. Fred and Esther's relationship, along with the Kingfish/Sapphire one, traces back more plausibly to a general trope in American entertainment, the henpecked husband and the shrewish battleaxe wife. What I see in Fred and Esther is less a statement about black people than one of many *American* variations on the trope represented by, for example, Maggie and Jiggs in the old comic strip *Bringing Up Father*.

————

It is the post–Civil Rights separatist ideology that keeps Bogle from ever addressing the paradoxical nature of his expectations, such as his implication that there should be a moratorium on black participation in certain entertainment clichés long beloved by audiences of any extraction—including black ones. One senses that Bogle considers black television to have a special therapeutic mission that mainstream television is exempt from. In *Toms, Coons* (et al.), he proposes that "Black films can liberate audiences from illusions, black and white, and in so freeing can give all of us vision and truth. It is a tremendous responsibility, much greater than that placed on ordinary white moviemakers." At the end of *Primetime Blues* he considers television to have "a long way to go in honestly and sensitively recording African-American life."

And therefore, Bogle reserves his highest praise for, of course, *The Cosby Show;* the brooding, quirky, and still missed late 1980s "dramedy" *Frank's Place;* and the sensitive *succès d'estime* drama

I'll Fly Away, depicting a black maid working for an integrationist white lawyer in the segregated South of the 1950s. So vigilant against the Mammy stereotype, Bogle also appears to have a particular predilection for low-key, dreamy black women, heaping special praise on Louise Beavers, *E.R.*'s Gloria Reuben, *I'll Fly Away*'s Regina Taylor, and *Cosby*'s Lisa Bonet.

Working with this, we can construct a scenario that would presumably meet with Bogle's approval. All black television series will portray financially stable people, infused with a combination of intellectual curiosity and good old-fashioned mother wit. All characters will regularly display passionate commitment to uplifting the blacks left behind, while at the same time participating in mainstream society—but with a healthy dose of "authentic" anti-assimilationist resistance as well. All characters will be romantically fulfilled, but within the bounds of carefully considered serial monogamy. Humor will be low-key, avoiding any hint of "raucousness," and yet always with one foot in African-American folk traditions. Mothers and wives will be portrayed only by small, light-skinned women, who will never engage their husbands in anything but the most civil of manners. In general, casting of women will favor those of rather "dreamy" affect. Black characters cast in mainstream programs will at all times refrain from "nurturing" whites and display a primary rootedness in black culture, while at the same time refraining from going as far as being perceived as "angry" or "other."

To take a specific example, *Sanford and Son* should have been about Lamont working his way out of Watts by attending college, while Fred took continuing education classes alongside, but giving his white teachers hell along the way, resisting "assimilation." Instead of giving work to his old chitlin' circuit friend LaWanda Page, to avoid playing into the "Sapphire" "stereotype" Foxx should have let her languish in obscurity while a petite, reserved, light-skinned (and optimally "dreamy") woman was cast as Aunt Esther, with her and Sanford getting along warmly. The show should have been an hour-length drama, to more fully "explore" the "personas" and "issues." In later seasons, Lamont should have entered the corporate world.

But the first problem is that no one would have watched this show. For instance, in early episodes when *Sanford and Son* was finding its legs, Beah Richards played the "aunt" character ("Aunt Ethel"). Richards was a capital actress (one of her last roles was as Peter Benton's dying mother on *E.R.*), but the contained nobility that was her trademark generated no sparks with Redd Foxx, and *Sanford and Son* would have been a lesser brew if she had been retained.

More to the point, Bogle's requirements raise some troubling questions. If whenever a large dark-skinned woman plays a role where she is raising children she is a "Mammy," then what work would he prefer to see full-figured black women whose skin isn't light get? Presumably he would prefer all such women to be cast as, perhaps, maiden aunts or career women. But then they are "desexualized," aren't they? Bogle's framework unintentionally suggests a discrimination against heavy black women in television casting.

One also wonders whether there is any room for natural human exuberance in Bogle's ideal. I would feel that a vital aspect of the African-American essence was missing if *all* black shows were of the gentle tone of *The Cosby Show, Frank's Place,* and *I'll Fly Away.* Those dreamy women, for example. In this and other books Bogle gives the impression of having a special fondness for Louise Beavers, but having seen her in a good dozen of her film appearances, I have frankly never found her to be much of an actress. Even Bogle notes Gloria Reuben's "flat voice," and most viewers considered *A Different World* to have hit its stride only when the similarly flat-voiced Lisa Bonet left the show after the first season. Bogle claims that Gloria Reuben's *E.R.* character was someone "no viewer ever forgot"—but frankly, I did, and does it disqualify me as an enlightened African-American to admit that I prefer LaWanda Page over Lisa Bonet any day of the week? I doubt that I am alone.

What Bogle appears to miss is that this is, after all, commercial television. To the extent that the boob tube has never "honestly and sensitively recorded" white American life, to indignantly excoriate decades of powerful and increasingly influential black television artistry as a parade of "stereotypes" is to impose an unrealizable requirement upon the medium. In the eternal tug-of-war between art and commerce in popular entertainment, the latter has always come out on top. The art emerges here and there in the cracks, and as grateful as we are for it, we are just as aware that it is a sometime thing—e.g., the occasional *Cosby Show* or *I'll Fly Away,* paralleling the equally occasional *M*A*S*H* or *Hill Street Blues.*

Bogle is too deeply familiar with popular entertainment and its history not to know this. But this means that his proposition that an acceptable black television must shoulder a "tremendous responsibility" that mainstream television is exempt from is less a sincere directive than a cry of victimhood, designed to be sustainable despite any realistic developments no matter how positive. Bogle's natural impulse to parse fifty-plus years of black television in this way is more a reflection of the centrality of victimhood to modern black identity than of the facts, which would stun and elate a 1950s African-American brought to our era and put in front of a TV set for a few hours at any time of any day of the week.

———

This impulse to uncover purported rot behind all black success is so deeply ensconced among most black writers that many might find it difficult to imagine just what else a survey of black television could be about. Bogle is hardly alone in his approach to black television. There now exists a healthy literature of books and articles by black writers spinning out endless rounds of the "Can You Find the Stereotype?" game. Yet there are innumerable angles that Bogle and these other writers neglect, since they do not fit the arc of a victimologist argument.

For example, Bogle zips perfunctorily by the welter of black sitcoms on the new UPN and WB networks. True, the shows give a new name to lowest common denominator, operating on a ding-dong *Laverne and Shirley* level foreign to most white sitcoms since about 1980. And yet these shows are extremely popular with black viewers. The people who made a boisterous cartoon like *The Parkers* the top-rated show among blacks for a time do not share Bogle and his comrades' idea of an evening's entertainment. While Bogle waits for "honesty" and "sensitivity," millions of other African-Americans are happily sitting down to *Homeboys from Outer Space, The Wayans Brothers, Malcolm and Eddie,* and their ilk, these shows set to become as fondly remembered by many blacks coming of age in ten years or so as *Good Times, The Jeffersons,* and *What's Happening!* are by people my age.

It would be worthwhile to explore the fact that these sitcoms are so popular with black audiences while richer fare, such as the heavily black-cast and well-regarded *Homicide,* was not. Bogle is correct that there has always been a sad dearth of black dramas as opposed to comedies—but he never addresses the fact that this is partly because black audiences are less likely to take them to heart. His "Crazy Nigger" "stereotype" in film is also germane here. Chris Tucker's and Chris Rock's pop-eyed hijinks today bear out Bogle's prediction that Richard Pryor would spawn imitators. But black audiences love them to death, meanwhile staying away from *Beloved* and *Amistad* in droves. There are rich issues of culture, class, tradition, and psychology to be mined here that could engage writers from any number of political perspectives.

Contrary to common wisdom, studies suggest that blacks are *not* depicted as criminals on television today out of proportion to their representation in the population. In the early nineties, one study showed that black people constituted 10 to 12 percent of the characters in television dramas and committed only 10 percent of violent crimes; another showed that blacks committed only 3 percent of murders on television. And these results are not really counterintuitive. Many black readers will remember the sequence in the black movie *Hollywood Shuffle* (1987) depicting refined black actors as required to play hoodlums and criminals; a few years later a choice skit on the television show *In Living Color* made a similar observation ("The Black People's Awards"). But can we really say that this reflects reality today? Flipping through our sixty-odd cable stations, do we really find that as often as not, the black face we happen upon is jumping out of a window or cravenly begging for his life at gunpoint? Today, the answer is no. I would have liked to see Bogle explore this issue, charting the evolution of the black criminal on television (in the 1950s, the criminal was usually a working-class white) and possibly refuting the studies in some way.

Perhaps because they do not lend themselves to the "Can You Find the Stereotype?" game, Bogle largely neglects black variety shows after Flip Wilson, when, especially in the 1970s, these contributed some signature moments for black viewers. Who could forget little Janet Jackson's imitation of Mae West on *The Jacksons* in the mid-1970s? I also fondly remember Telma Hopkins and Joyce Vincent Wilson's savory skits as "Lou-Effie and Maureen" on *Tony Orlando and Dawn*.

———

Yet at the end of the day, let's be clear. The stereotype issue is hardly entirely invalid, and the black representation on television is not perfect. I can muster no positive take on Jimmie "J.J." Walker's sad takeover of *Good Times*, even though I was one of the kids in schoolyards shouting "Dy-no-MITE!!!" that Bogle describes. Furthermore, still too often black cast members are the ones with the least defined personas, a notable example as I write being Victoria Dillard's Janelle on *Spin City*, a character whose facelessness after six seasons would be unimaginable in any white character on any program. However, we are a long, long way from Andy and the Kingfish, or even Scotty.

Moreover, in broad view, a question the "Can You Find the

Stereotype?" tradition marginalizes is just why the issue is considered so urgent at all. The stereotype obsession presumes that anything short of "sensitive" and "honest" depiction constitutes an obstacle to black advancement. But this is a brittle claim. It was hardly a picnic when practically the only image of blacks on television was *Amos 'n' Andy*, granted. But given the profoundly richer scenario today, it is difficult to argue that Bogle's ideal, if implemented, would discourage a black youth from using drugs, lead a young black student to work even harder in school, or raise the rate of blacks opening small businesses.

On the contrary, a great many groups have worked their way up in American history despite naked stereotypes in entertainment, even ones naked enough to be perceivable without the mental gymnastics the "Can You Find the Stereotype?" crowd must exert. In other words, in the end it's just *television*—real life happens outside the little box. Okay, there is some evidence that television can affect behavior. But if from 1970 to 2000 blacks had been exclusively depicted "sensitively" and "honestly" on television, their history during the period would certainly have unfolded exactly as it did, with the same ratio of triumph to setbacks. The assumption that for blacks only, television must carefully reflect, often even airbrush, but never exaggerate or parody reality is a uselessly utopian one. The implication that black people in one particular country at one particular time are helpless without this fantasy renders us passive victims rather than masters of our own fates.

After all, *no form of entertainment has ever achieved, or even striven for, this vision in all of human history.* On the contrary, all popular entertainment throughout human history has been founded upon character "types," from Harlequin through Sapphire. Many of the very academics who would treat the "Can You Find the Stereotype?" game as "noble" in black Americans have devoted their careers to studying indigenous peoples' folklore, where they see the facile caricatures central to these tales as suddenly "charming," "symbolic," and "real." And this includes the stories central to the cultures of black Americans' direct ancestors. Why, exactly, is Anansi the wily spider, passed down the generations in folk tales native to West Africa and the Caribbean, any less a "stereotype" than George Jefferson? To assail all stock personages in black American popular culture as "stereotypes" is intellectually irresponsible unless one is prepared to answer that question.

Thus charting the persistence of stereotypes is no more an inevitable thrust of a survey of black television in 2001 than recounting discrimination would be in a history of Jews in America. Pointedly, Jewish authors would be less likely to find evidence of their triumphs discomfiting rather than inspiring—and even less likely to laboriously interpret every second female Jewish character on television since 1970 as a variation on Molly Goldberg.

But instead, this book, more aptly titled *Blacks on Television: A View from the Black Left*, will surely stand as the authoritative source on the subject, especially with its imprimatur and Bogle's established, and in many ways deserved, reputation. Like *Toms, Coons* (et al.), it will be endlessly borrowed from university libraries by black undergraduates in classes on Race and the Media, dutifully writing papers illuminating the "stereotypes" underlying almost anything anyone black has ever done on television. Black thinkers, many of whom, like most busy intellectuals and journalists, do not actually watch much television, will continue to decry "the scarcity of positive portrayals of blacks in the media." Sure, not watching much television in itself could be seen as a plus in an intelligent person (although I must admit a certain nonconformity on that score—I love TV, watch way too much of it, always have and always will). But then the chronicler of Thackeray is assumed to have trudged their way through the man's work regardless.

One result: the NAACP harangues the big networks—today watched by fewer people each year—as "racist" for not happening to have included black characters in a particular season's lineup. Kweisi Mfume's gambit here is almost a caricature of victimology—WB and UPN program whole blocks of black shows year after year, but Mfume gives "grades" to just NBC, ABC, and CBS as if it were 1975 and they are the only things going. And never mind that there are black people all over many of their long-running shows, regardless of how many blacks there happen to be in a given new season's lineup. Or that today, the viewer has dozens of channels to choose from, on many of which black faces are as often as not routine.

But white guilt and fear of boycotts drives the grand old networks to dutifully cast black actors in some roles written as race-neutral. The result is seasoned performers walking through glaringly token roles, rendering black-white "friendships" devoid of any natural chemistry. An example was Wendell Pierce in the one-season flop *The Weber Show* in the 2000–2001 season. Pierce is probably best known as the portly, inept swain that Lela Rochon's character wound up in bed with in the filmization of *Waiting to Exhale,* and as the "politically incorrect" black peddler thrown bodily off of the bus in Spike Lee's *Get on the Bus.* But he is also an accomplished stage actor; I caught him in 1994 as Doctor Astrov in a San Francisco production of Chekhov's *Uncle Vanya.* It was truly painful to see this artist in *The Weber Show* cavorting perfunctorily with white actors, looking like he had walked in from some other show or, worse, like a token "Negro" circa 1966. The white writers, hip to the "deracialization" gospel, made sure to shoehorn in the occasional exchange acknowledging the character's color, which in such a lightweight show only made the falsity of the whole business stand out even more.

But once again, damned if they do, damned if they don't. When Bogle revises *Primetime Blues* around 2015, he will certainly chalk up Pierce's place on this show and similar cases as evidence that even past the turn of the millennium, white America continued to refuse to see blacks as full human beings.

Hopefully another writer will tackle the rich subject of black Americans' journey through television history with a wider-lens view. There remains to be written a book about blacks on television that identifies the problems where they exist, but not to the point of treating evidence of progress as an embarrassment. This book will empirically address the complexities, victories, and pitfalls inherent in a post-oppressed minority's relationship to a commercial entertainment medium.

For now, though, we will have to make do with *Primetime Blues.* This is not altogether a bad thing, as the book is dead-on until 1968. But the remaining three hundred pages are devoted to a thesis unsupported by its data set, commercially unfeasible, and not even desired by most of the very community it purports to represent. Regardless of the reflexive pessimism of thinkers like Bogle, that community is well on its way to the truly integrated—dare I say "deracialized"?—future that is the only logical one possible. To people in that future, *Primetime Blues* will serve as a poignant document of an unwittingly self-defeating reflex in black American thought indigenous to the late twentieth century.

5

"Aren't You in Favor of Diversity?"

White Guilt and University Admissions

■ ■ ■

In my day-to-day life, I am a linguistics professor, not a "race pundit." Undergraduates are usually too busy with schoolwork and flexing their social muscles to be terribly interested in politics. They don't watch much television, they don't listen to NPR, they don't have time to read books beyond those assigned for their classes, and few have even heard of The New Republic, City Journal, or the other publications most of my race work appears in. Therefore, most of them only learn that I have "another life" well into a given semester—if ever.

I will never forget a conversation I had with one such student, the type who comes by the office a lot and evolves into a mentee of sorts. Because in my experience I find that many assume that all of my students are black (partly because it is the black ones I discuss in Losing the Race), I should specify that this student was Chinese-American. As we left the building, she said she had heard that I had been on the radio talking about Affirmative Action. "How do *you feel about it?" she asked. "Well, actually, I think in universities it's obsolete." Her immediate question, sincere and genuinely curious: "Aren't you in favor of diversity?"* ▪

That exchange has always stuck with me. She understood where I was coming from when I explained; it was by no means a spiky moment. But the question right at the tip of her tongue was highly indicative. For a student like this, exposed to the racial preferences issue largely by the college newspaper's editorial page and angry speeches by student activists out on Sproul Plaza, the racial preferences issue naturally boils down to "diversity."

In the same way, for many of us, the health of the economy boils down to "the deficit." Yet many economists argue that an economy can be healthy despite a deficit, and that we distract ourselves by making a false analogy between the national economy and our personal checking accounts. But unless one happens to cock one's ear to such arguments, we almost inevitably assume, from how newspapers and magazines frame the issue, that there could be no sound national budgetary policy in which "the deficit" was not a key issue.

Despite the insistence of Affirmative Action advocates, "diversity" is no more inherent to racial preference policies than eliminating the deficit is to a healthy economy. "Diversity" only made its way into the Affirmative Action debate a couple of decades ago, and through the back door at that.

It started with one man. In 1973 and then again in 1974, Allan Bakke was denied admission to UC Davis's medical school despite an A- grade point average and an MCAT score well within the tenth percentile. Given that black students were regularly admitted with GPAs in the C range and MCATs in the bottom third of the range of all applicants, Bakke charged the university with discrimination.

In the Supreme Court decision on the case in 1978, in contrast to the four justices in favor of UC Davis's quota system, Justice Lewis Powell concurred that quota systems like Davis's were unconstitutional. However, he submitted a widely covered hedge, asserting that it was appropriate for schools to base their decisions upon a quest for a "diverse student body."

That seems innocent enough on its face. But that argument provided a justification that universities quickly seized upon as a cover for admitting black students with significantly lower qualifications than white or Asian students. Ever since then, university administrators have regularly disguised their two-tier admissions policies by hiding behind the "diversity" idea.

Lately, courts are judging one university's policy of this kind after another as unconstitutional distortions of what the *Bakke* decision proposed. As I write, the most recent judgments have been against the University of Texas, the University of Georgia, and the University of Michigan Law School. As the dominoes fall one by one, a general reassessment by the Supreme Court of racial preferences in college admissions is imminent.

And I dearly hope that when given this opportunity, the Supreme Court will take the occasion to invalidate Powell's "diversity" opinion once and for all. I certainly am in favor of "diversity"—but only "diversity" among equals. The *Bakke* decision has taught a generation of young Americans that black students are more important for their presence in promotional brochure photographs than for their scholastic qualifications—an essentialization now as rife among black as among white students. This ultimately perpetuates the very underperformance that has made the fig-leaf "diversity" notion necessary.

White guilt is a dangerous and addictive drug, and for twenty-years-plus the *Bakke* decision has supported stricken higher education administrators in their habit. The "diversity" notion these people have been taught to espouse is a craven, disingenuous, and destructive canard, antithetical to interracial harmony and black excellence—and racist besides.

———

The very term "diversity" craftily overshoots the actual goal in question. Mormons, paraplegics, people from Alaska, lesbians, and poor whites exert little pull on the heartstrings of admissions committees so committed to making college campuses "look like America." Instead, the "diversity" of interest is tacitly considered to be brown-skinned minorities, especially African-Americans.

In the late 1960s, college administrations supposed that blacks' low representation on campuses was simply a matter of discrimination. The good-thinking white chancellor saw the task ahead as being to simply open the doors, providing some remedial assistance where necessary. But these efforts to bring qualified blacks into colleges and universities ran up against the uncomfortably small number of such people in an America just past legalized segregation. As for those who were admitted, university professors unsurprisingly proved unequal to the task of undoing the effects of fourteen years of underpreparation in the basic skills necessary for college coursework.

Meanwhile, the new hegemony of separatist ideology in black America had led to a sense that scholastic achievement was a "white" endeavor rather than an American one. In the massive feedback I have received since I discussed this phenomenon in *Losing the Race*, it is overwhelmingly clear that it was in the late 1960s that black kids started teasing other black kids who liked school as "acting white." This has become a central trope of black teen culture, that no African-American born after about 1955 can have missed, unless he or she happens not to have grown up around many black children. The "acting white" charge represents a general sense that school is, while perhaps necessary, ultimately something black people step outside of "themselves" to dwell in. The effects of this sense, subtle as often as overt, further decreased the numbers of black students qualified for top schools, as it continues to to this day.

Powell's decision was a typical trope of late-twentieth-century America: white guilt confronts the mundane fact that a group's rise from the bottom is gradual rather than instantaneous. His "diversity" construction was a benevolently intended back-door strategy, to goose along the utopian vision of a multihued college campus, even if this required rounding some corners here and there. But Powell did not know that his decision would become the linchpin of a reconception of the very purpose of higher education.

———

Powell did not intend, for instance, the brute quota systems that quickly came to reign on selective campuses. Many are under the impression that the "diversity" imperative plays out as a mere "thumb on the scale," choosing the brown-skinned candidate in cases where their qualifications are equal to a white one's. In fact, the reason many see opposition to racial preferences as "racist" is that they suppose this is all college administrations have been doing. It's an easy misimpression to fall into, as college administrators are trained to distort their admissions procedures as just this in public statements.

But it was almost impossible to maintain this illusion at, for example, Rutgers University in the mid-1980s, where I earned my bachelor's degree. After my first year there, it was painfully clear to me that, by and large, the black students were a rung below the general preparation and performance level of the white ones. Certainly there were plenty of white slackers, at what was at that time a "party" school. And certainly there were excellent black students. But they were exceptions rather than the rule, and the overall white-black discrepancy stood out in sharp relief. Even as a teenager with little interest in sociopolitics or admissions procedures, I easily and spontaneously perceived after a couple of semesters that black students were admitted under some kind of quota system.

The Rutgers top brass had long maintained that race was used as just "one of many factors," as the *Bakke* decision had counseled. But a few years after I graduated, a student working in the admissions office blew the whistle, revealing that black students were regularly gathered into a special pool and admitted according to significantly lower grade point averages and standardized test scores than other students. Nor was Rutgers unique. Similar findings have emerged since in system after system, including the state university systems of California, Texas, Michigan, and Georgia.

Even in their pro–Affirmative Action manifesto *The Shape of the River*, William Bowen and Derek Bok admit and painstakingly document that this practice has been par for the course in selective universities across the nation for thirty years.

Before racial preferences were banned at the University of California at Berkeley in the mid-1990s, the quota system had been as obvious "on the ground" as it had been at Rutgers in the 1980s. One older white professor of avowedly leftist politics confided in me that since the early 1970s, black students had bombed in his classes so often that he had found himself fearing that any black student he saw in his class on the first day might be a problem case. I have heard similar testimonials from many professors across the country. A white man who had worked as a remedial composition tutor at Berkeley observed that he had worked with so many minority students hopelessly underprepared for work at the Berkeley level that he had found himself questioning the wisdom of racial preference policies, despite his leftist persuasion.

Many would dismiss observations like these as the product of "bias" and "stereotyping." But given the dossiers that black Berkeley students were submitting, it would have been surprising if these discrepancies had not been apparent. Stephan and Abigail Thernstrom in *America in Black and White* note that black Berkeley students who enrolled in 1988 had an average SAT score below 1000, as contrasted with white students' average of over 1300. The highest quartile of black SAT scores in this class clustered at the bottom quarter of those of all students'. The average GPA among black students was B+, rather than the straight-A average required of white students. Nor was this a mere Berzerk-ley aberration: in 1992, the gap in average SAT scores between black and white entrants was 150 points at Princeton, 171 at Stanford, 218 at Dartmouth, and 271 at Rice.

Graduation rates also reflect these gulfs in preparation. The Thernstroms document that of the black students who entered Berkeley in 1988, 41 percent did not go on to graduate, while only 16 percent of whites ones in that class did not. Bowen and Bok show that at twenty-eight top universities, black students in the class of 1989 were about three times more likely to drop out than white students.

Many would argue that the latter problem was due to financial issues rather than the sharp deficits in high school grade point averages and SAT scores. But the burden of proof is upon such people to identify just why grades and scores would *not* contribute significantly to a student's chances of finishing college. Few of any persuasion have any problem seeing a causal link here when it comes to white students.

In general, the argument that grades and scores are irrelevant to assessing a candidate is not only illogical, but refuted by the evidence. For one, no one would argue that a student with perfect SAT scores is only a "possible" good match for Harvard. Nor would anyone venture that a student with an abysmal SAT score was prime Harvard material. This frames the glaring lapse in argumentation of those so chary of grades and SATs: precisely what leads to the conclusion that for some reason, SAT scores in the middle ranges have no predictive power?

Obviously this makes no sense at all, and hard facts bear out the clear reality. For one, the Thernstroms show that graduation rates of black students starting at Berkeley in 1988 fell in virtual lockstep with lower SAT scores—hardly the result we would expect if there were no connection between achievement level and graduation. Bowen and Bok even note that SAT scores *overpredict* black college students' performance in college—that is, black students do *less* well than their SAT scores would predict, not better.

Yet the sense of Diversity Über Alles forces racial preference fans into the mental acrobatics of supposing that "leadership skills," helping to write the yearbook, and "spunk" are as germane to evaluating a student's scholastic potential as, well, how well they did in school and how well they can do word analogies, eighth grade math, and some logic problems within a set amount of time. But leadership skills and "spunk" are distributed among white students as equally as among black ones—surely black people are not innately "perkier" than white ones. As such, the admissions committee that cheerily concentrates on these factors in evaluating black students, in all of their good intentions, is designating black people incapable of excelling in the decisive arena of classroom ability. In other words, in the name of "diversity" black students are exempted from serious competition. One always wonders how white professors and administrators sitting on these committees would feel to see their own children evaluated on their "spirit" rather than how well they did in school.

———

Could we make a case that this exemption is justified in view of a larger good? Many suppose that bending the rules for "diversity" fosters interracial fellowship on campus that students will carry with them after they graduate. In my less politicized days, infused with the sense that I could not be a "good" person without supporting racial preferences, I tried to hold to this idea for years. But in the end, it just doesn't wash. College campuses, in all of their "diversity," are among the most racially balkanized settings in America.

Separate black fraternities and sororities thrive. While they emerged early in the 1900s because whites did not welcome black applicants, today black Greek organizations are thoroughly un-enthusiastic toward whites. One of the most sadly ironic little news flaps in late 2001 was a quest by the University of Alabama to "desegregate" its Greek organizations. The tragedy is that the whole effort by now had an antiquarian cast, reminiscent of the era of "Negro" leaders in black-and-white photos calling for "integration" circa 1957, with crew cuts and cat's-eye glasses, holding filter-less cigarettes. The modern black fraternity has not the slightest interest in admitting white pledges, nor are any but the occasional black students seeking to join "whitey's" fraternities and sororities. Across America, the black student who pledges a white fraternity or sorority is generally dismissed by black students as a self-hating "sellout." At Stanford in the late 1980s and early 1990s, it was also understood among black fraternity members that one was only to date white women undercover—to do so openly compromised one's "black identity." Harmony this was not.

Universities also typically host black graduation ceremonies, the idea being that one's achievement is less a human or American one than a "black" one. I attended one such ceremony at Berkeley where the invited speaker was apostle of interracial harmony Derrick Bell.

Classes in African-American Studies are billed as lending black students pride in their heritage, but in practice, they often double as exercises in fostering hatred of The White Man. At Stanford, where I earned my doctorate, I was a teaching assistant in a predominantly black class on Black English. In itself, the subject encompasses much more than mere street slang, extending to grammatical structure, literature, and educational issues. But the class discussion devolved so often into visceral dismissals of whites that one white student complained to the professor that he felt that any opinions he ventured beyond genuflections to cries of victimhood were unwelcome—and he was right. In a class I taught at Berkeley on black musical theater history, when a white student suggested that the lyrics in rap music were misogynistic, several black students (led by a woman) dressed her down so vehemently that they left her in tears.

Nor are these incidents mere isolated events. They fit into a general atmosphere where black students are tacitly taught that black "authenticity" means hunkering down behind a barricade glaring hatefully at the white "hegemony" on campus. Black students typically cluster in their own section of dining halls, throw their own parties, often have their own theme houses, and are in general ushered into a separatist ideology that they often did not have when they came to campus. In John H. Bunzel's *Race Relations on Campus: Stanford Students Speak Out*, black Stanford students in the early 1990s report being expected to "talk black, dress black, think black, and certainly date black." This squares with what I saw in my graduate years on the campus at that time, where for the black student disinclined to toe this line, edgy conversations with other black students questioning their "blackness" were a regular part of their campus experience.

I suspect that many black people see this kind of thing as a healthy nurturing of "black identity." When conservatives claim that it works against "integration," it seems a rather athletic feint for many of us—I openly admit that on an off day, it still throws me sometimes. We post–Civil Rights babies, in particular, are taught that our main task as we come of age is to resist "becoming white" to the full extent that it is practical.

But the passing comforts of cultural fellowship come at a price: in a larger perspective, black balkanization on college campuses does as much harm as good. A black acquaintance once told me that any occasional racist experiences she had had during her college years were dwarfed by the overriding hostility from black students scornful of her white friendships and activities. Only the most ardent black nationalists—a mere fraction of black America—could see this as a healthy state of affairs. And meanwhile, as Bunzel notes, white Stanford students enduring constant charges of undefined "racism" from black students often become less interested in interracial outreach than they were as freshmen. I have seen that trend on several college campuses that my life has led me to—it's almost a cliché among white upperclassmen.

Scratch the surface and one finds that the notion of "diversity" many advocates propose is a matter of maintaining one's missiles at the ready. After black University of California Regent Ward Connerly spearheaded the outlawing of the use of racial preferences in University of California admissions, some black locals formed a committee called Citizens Against Ward Connerly. At one event, one representative opened her speech by declaiming that "Ward Connerly wants the University of California to be all vanilla—and I don't like vanilla." She intended this to elicit audience approval in a predictably rally-like atmosphere. But given that half or more of the audience was white, the laughter was nervous and hesitant. Thus she dutifully appended, "I like to have some mix-ins— chips, nuts . . ." But no—what she said the first time illustrated that the people so furiously committed to "diversity" are not interested in working toward a color-blind America. Their goal is to ensure that the privileges of a college education do not distract black students from the urgent task of keeping the fires of reflexive black alienation burning.

In her book *Why Are All the Blacks Sitting Together in the Cafeteria?* black psychologist Beverly Daniel Tatum cheers that this is due to black students' "anger and resentment" at the "systemic exclusion of Black people from full participation in U.S. society." But while fashioning a notion of "exclusion" that accommodates a black secretary of state and national security adviser will be tricky, it will be downright impossible to fashion a notion of interracial harmony illustrated by the separatist tableau that Tatum considers so righteous.

———

It is perhaps for this reason that "diversity" is typically defended less on the basis of bonding than on mere "exposure." The idea endlessly prattled is that this "exposure" to other groups is a crucial component of a college education in a multiethnic America. The notion was given its first official rendition in Powell's *Bakke* decision, where he argued that universities would benefit from selecting "those students who will contribute most to the robust exchange of ideas."

In light of the fact that the *Bakke* case concerned a medical school, just how being black qualifies one to especially "robust" observations about surgical incisions and metabolic pathways is hardly obvious. Nevertheless, in practice the tacit assumption has been that within these "robust exchanges," it is less important that black students learn about the ways of the white devil than that whites learn about the blacks they find so alien, threatening, and despicable.

But the person reciting this line generally looks off into the distance rather than into their interlocutor's eyes, as people tend to when mouthing a dogma rather than expressing an opinion they genuinely believe in.

For one, on a campus where black students are let in under the bar, white students often get their first "exposure" to wondering whether black people are not as sharp as they are. It is difficult for me to imagine how even the best intentioned of white students could have avoided this conclusion at, for example, Rutgers in the 1980s. There is a deathless lie reigning in most discussions of this issue: that most black students come from disadvantaged circumstances, their life histories rendering even a better-than-average performance a miracle.

Yet at selective schools, the black student from the inner city has been vanishingly rare since the late 1960s, when some schools briefly and unsuccessfully experimented with seeing if such students could excel in top universities without having had the necessary preparation. Among the black students in the last class admitted to Berkeley under the racial preference regime, over 65 percent came from households earning *at least* $40,000 a year, while the parents of about 40 percent earned *at least* $60,000 a year. Of the black students admitted in 1989 to the twenty-eight selective universities surveyed by Bowen and Bok, just 14 percent came from homes earning $22,000 a year or less.

But white guilt will find a way, leading many who ought to know better into some of the lowest moments of their careers as professional thinkers. In *The New York Review of Books*, Ronald Dworkin came up with the pièce de résistance in this vein in 1998 in one of the myriad smitten reviews of Bowen and Bok's book. For Professor Dworkin, even a middle-class black student who lacks stereotypically "black" traits ought be admitted under the bar—because such a student embodies a lesson for whites that the stereotypes are inappropriate. Yet we can be sure that Dworkin would not hear of his own children being admitted under a quota to serve as museum exhibits for gentiles. And meanwhile, precisely what traits do middle-class black students display that are so unique, unexpected, and challenging that the white student who fails to learn them risks being a washout in the management job they begin after graduation? I have found repeatedly that middle-class black students asked to list a few such traits regularly draw a blank.

And even if a significant number of black students at selective schools did come from the 'hood, just how is "learning about" their cultural traits so vital to white students' educational experience? In African-American Studies courses on the very same campuses, blacks are taught to decry the stereotype that all blacks are poor. Wouldn't a four-year tutorial in the vibrancy of ghetto life reinforce that very stereotype? Poverty is a tragedy, not a lifestyle.

―――

None of this is rocket science. Every college adminstrator knows that "diversity" is code for "at least five percent black faces with a goodly sprinkling of Latinos." They also know that this is only achievable through quota systems euphemized by artful terminology, chronic double-talk, and outright lies. Nor do any of them miss, as black students dutifully erupt in furious protest every second spring over manufactured or trivial instances of "racism," that in practice campus "diversity" means black students carefully taught that they are eternal victims in their own land.

Yet all of this cognitive dissonance is considered a tolerable downside of what many decision makers consider a *sine qua non* moral imperative. Under the view that societal inequity bars most black students from having a chance to truly qualify for admission to top schools, the idea is that the moral white person must compensate for this by letting black students in through the back door. Rutgers president Francis Lawrence popped out with a gaffe in 1994 that quota systems were necessary in admissions given that black students do not have "the genetic hereditary background" to do but so well in school. He was predictably reviled for the clumsy terminology, but what he meant was that the reasons so few black students qualified for admission to Rutgers was a legacy of centuries of disenfranchisement and segregation.

And he was quite right. But here we face perhaps the most tragic aspect of a previously reviled group's climb to the top: there comes a point where a people can only achieve at the same level as the ruling group if the safety net is withdrawn.

When word got around at Berkeley that racial preferences were likely to be outlawed, one often heard from concerned faculty and administrators that preferences should only be eliminated "when the student body looks like California." But this superficially reasonable conclusion assumes that equal opportunity guarantees equal outcomes, and that if outcomes are in fact unequal, then the only possible culprit is "racism." But that conclusion is false. The sad fact is that extended disenfranchisement often leaves a group ill-equipped to compete at the highest level even when the doors to success are wide open and ladders to the top are beckoning. This is partly because of the well-known obstacles to achievement that disadvantaged status lends, but in equal part because long-term oppression often creates a cultural identity oppositional to the ruling establishment. The black student who only pulls B's and C's because his or her friends think that making good grades is a "white" thing to do is not a victim of present-day discrimination.

These realities are not pretty. But what they mean is that a crucial component in a group's rise to the top is learning tricks to a new trade. Those growing up under conditions that do not offer a direct path to accomplishment have the burden, unfair but hardly limited to blacks, of learning how to turn lemons into lemonade, as oppressed groups in America have done for centuries. A group pervaded by a sense that to achieve in the mainstream is "inauthentic" has the similarly grim but ineluctable task of refashioning its self-concept to encompass moving ahead in the only society it will ever call home.

And here is the rub: lowered standards are directly antithetical to either of these endeavors. *A people can only hit the highest note when it has the incentive to do so:* this is a fundamental tenet of economics and psychology. Perhaps the most sobering reality that black Americans face today is that even our history cannot exempt us from this deathless fact of the human condition.

It must be clear that my opposition to racial preferences is not based on whether they are constitutional, or on whether they are commensurate with "democracy." I am not just tossing my hat into that rhetorical arena here. Make no mistake—those arguments are valid. But I see little hope of making black audiences see the poison in these policies by referring to the Founding Fathers and arcane points of legal argument. The leftist sense that the very rules of the game in America are illegitimate is too deeply ensconced among most blacks for arguments like this to carry much weight. After all, the Founding Fathers were often slaveholders; the American legal system is set against blacks anyway because "One out of three young black men is in jail or involved with the criminal justice system"; etc. Judges and avowed conservatives will be swayed by philosophical and moral arguments against racial preferences, but the message black people beyond these realms need to hear is closer to the ground.

Specifically, my argument against racial preferences is based on a purely logical conviction—that they prevent black students from showing what they are made of, that they dumb black people down, pure and simple. The rank injustice that blacks have suffered in America is obvious. But the fact remains: students growing up in a system whose message is "You only have to do pretty darned well to get into a top school" will, by and large, only do pretty darned well, with the exception of the occasional uniquely driven shooting star. As such, *to enshrine "diversity" over true excellence nothing less than condemns black students to mediocrity.* This is the inevitable result, regardless of good intentions, of denying them—and their parents, high school teachers, and guidance counselors—the one thing that elicits the best in anyone: the unavailability of any path but individual initiative and perseverance. That's not "politics"—that's common sense.

————

This is also where arguments that racial preferences are necessary as recompense for the horrors of the past come a-cropper. After one presentation I made, a furious black questioner asked me how, if I am against racial preferences, we "make up for the fact that whites benefited from societally ingrained preferences for centuries." In a similar vein, Harvard sociologist Nathan Glazer has reversed his longtime opposition to race-based admissions policies on the grounds that whites "owe" blacks due to the injustices of the past.

But in all of their sincerity and concern, what people like Glazer do not understand is that this "tit for tat" conception of racial preferences stands directly in the path beyond our racial dilemma. The emotional balm of intoning "We owe them" is obvious, but what makes whites feel goodly does not necessarily give black students the tools to truly excel. As I have written and said before, one can only learn to ride a bicycle by being let go to master the subtle muscular poise of the endeavor by oneself—as long as the training wheels are on, one is not truly riding a bike. Birds learn to fly by being dropped out of the nest. One gains fluent command of a foreign language by living for an extended period in a setting where it is impossible to use one's native tongue for any length of time.

Just as being black does not somehow exempt one from any of these obvious realities, black students will only gain the knack of achieving their highest potential in school by being required to do so. Short of this, top-rate black students will continue to constitute the tiny coterie of uniquely gifted seniors—as many of them children of Caribbean and African immigrants as black American—that emerge each spring for admissions committees to fight over in almost unseemly fashion. Asian students, for example, have never had the occasion to embrace the illusion that there was any way to the top but showing their stuff hell or high water, which is why they do so in such large numbers. A university administration culture where black students are denied the opportunity to do this is, quite simply, a racist one.

———

Pushing it? Maybe. But what are we to make of various university officials' apparent conviction that black people are the only ones in American history who cannot triumph over societal and historical obstacles? University of California president Richard Atkinson was so discomfitted by the fall in black and Latino admits to the top UC campuses Berkeley and UCLA that he proposed eliminating the SAT I from admissions requirements altogether. Never mind that after the elimination of racial preferences, black admissions fell only on these two flagship campuses but rose in several of the other UC schools, or that the University of California is deeply engaged in efforts to prepare minority students in middle and high school throughout the state to submit competitive dossiers to UC, or that, for example, at Berkeley black admissions rates have risen every year since the first one when admissions were race-blind.

Nevertheless, Atkinson is apparently so skeptical that any of this will bear substantial fruit that he does not even consider it worth waiting to see results that, after all, could not have been expected to emerge overnight. Instead, what he sees is the "resegregation" that black and Latino faculty, administrators, and white comrades-in-arms warned of back in 1998. The implication was that Berkeley and UCLA were the only colleges in California worth attending, such that students denied admission would have no choice but to resort to lives of crime and destitution.

But this is apocalyptic nonsense. Certainly, over the past few years many black students who would have been admitted to Berkeley before, most taking their place in the open secret of a two-tiered system, are now attending UC Santa Cruz, UC Davis, and other solid but second-rank schools. And at these schools, they are much more likely to thrive and succeed than they would have been in the legendarily demanding atmosphere of schools like Berkeley and UCLA. Their sense of achievement ought to delight those who consider the development of self-esteem one of education's primary goals. Moreover, on these campuses, black students learn that they are as qualified as their classmates on the basis of everyday, concrete successes, rather than having to assert it on the basis of empty, tribalist rhetoric. Armed with this true confidence, black students will be less likely to compensate for private feelings of inferiority by retreating to their own sides of the cafeteria.

Atkinson's conviction that this is a return to the era of Orville Faubus reveals a strangely dismissive stance toward these schools for someone entrusted with their stewardship. And contrary to the impression that to sort out black students meritocratically is somehow an injustice, the majority of the student bodies at these second-rank schools are, after all, white and Asian. The demise of racial preferences in the UC system has simply brought black students before the same combination of skill, initiative, and serendipity that have long been the lot of non-"diverse" college applicants worldwide.

And this brings us to the oft-heard claim that black students must be admitted to top schools beyond what their qualifications justify because these schools' prestige, and the connections one makes attending them, are crucial to success in later life. James Fallows noted in a piece in *The Atlantic* that "the four richest people in America, all of whom made rather than inherited their wealth, are a dropout from Harvard, a dropout from the University of Illinois, a dropout from Washington State University, and a graduate of the University of Nebraska," and added that top universities are sparse among the résumés of members of Congress, Nobel laureates, industrial leaders, and even U.S. Presidents. As to black Americans specifically, the Thernstroms have noted that of today's African-American congressmen, army officers, people earning Ph.D.'s from 1992 to 1996, MacArthur Foundation genius award winners of 1981 through 1988, and top fifty business officials, none but a sliver attended top-rated selective colleges. Thus "diversity" serves no better as a fig leaf for fostering black excellence beyond college than within it.

———

And a fig leaf it is, distracting us from the true nature of the task before us. For most, Powell's nuanced counsel that "diversity" be just one factor in evaluating an admissions file is lost to the ages. The typical person knows nothing of an obscure Supreme Court case decided under the Carter administration. Instead, one simply comes of age hearing "diversity" bandied about as a prime justification for racial preferences.

And meanwhile, our moment indoctrinates one, especially on college campuses, with the piety that racism is at the root of all racial discrepancies. The inevitable result: seeing furiously self-righteous people agitating for "diversity," one processes an implication that without racial preferences, "racists" would dismiss qualified black applicants' files.

But university administrators resoundingly refute this fear. In the university systems of California and Texas, in the wake of the elimination of their racial preference policies, administrators have responded with deft "end runs" designed to target minority applicants regardless. UC proposed elimination of SAT I, while Texas proposed a policy of admitting the top 20 percent of students from a deliberately selected array of predominantly minority schools. Meanwhile, University of Michigan president Lee Bollinger became a media darling for his opposition to the decision against the university's law school, and his support for the upholding of racial preferences in the undergraduate school in a concurrent case. Overall, a person could not be appointed a university president today without being committed to racial preferences in one guise or another—pointedly, in the fall following the decision against Michigan, Bollinger was picked as president of Columbia University. Thus we cannot defend the "diversity" argument as holding white administrators back from discriminating against black students. That argument may have made sense in the late 1960s, but today it utterly lacks foundation.

Many know this, but suppose that "systemic racism" prevents

black students from hitting the highest note, and that short of racism, blacks would constitute exactly 13 percent of every selective university in the United States. As such, black students submitting substandard applications to top schools are seen as diamonds in the rough, their grades and scores obscuring vaster ability, such that to refuse them admission is to turn away students equal in ability to the white and Asian ones with A+ averages and SATs above 1400. And thus, "Aren't you in favor of diversity?" is interpreted as "Don't you like black people?" And nothing chills most of today's thinking white Americans to their bones more than the notion that they might be racist. Naturally, then, admitting black people to top schools under the bar becomes imperative. Meanwhile blacks cheer, equally misguided by the misimpression that racism is the only possible cause of unequal performance.

But once again, "racism" is no longer the main thing keeping black students from doing as well in school on the average as others, and their unequal performance does not mysteriously vanish once they hit college. This means that racial preferences do not, as so often thought, "correct" a "raw deal" that black students have been saddled with. They merely sanction and perpetuate a culture-internal sense of separation from "school stuff." This, in turn, is an outgrowth of a post–Civil Rights sense of the mainstream as a malevolent alternate universe. And when black students bring this sense to the campus and sequester themselves in their own dorms, parties, and social circles, it makes a mockery of the "diversity" that so many see as the justification for what is, in fact, institutionalized condescension.

George Orwell deftly demonstrated the power of words to bolster social injustice. A university culture truly committed to erasing the sins of the past will champion "diversity" in its true sense, infusing its discourse on race with a range of views wider than variations on melodramatic capitulations to victimhood. Since 1978, the term has been recruited as a flimsy and evasive perversion of justice, appealing to the weakest aspects of our nature. This new definition of diversity helps no one, least of all black students. It is high time we relegated it to the dustbin of history.

6

The Unbearable Lightness
of "The 'N' Word"

...

*The very first media interview I ever did was on "The 'N' Word,"
for a piece on the leftist Bay Area radio station KPFA back in 1995.
It was no accident that the new black linguistics professor at Berkeley was sought out on this particular subject. Nigger is an eternal
"race topic," always good for a talk show episode, ever thrust in our
faces by rap music, and once every couple of years popping up as evidence that a white person in the media spotlight is a "racist."*

*Years later, writing a review of Randall Kennedy's nigger: The
Strange Career of a Troublesome Word brought me out on the
topic again. Ultimately, for me nigger is like hip-hop: we can't change
it and it's beside the point anyway. Casual speech will submit to
policing no more than people's musical taste, and no amount of
literary musing will impact the life cycle of this pungent and heartfelt little word—especially given that black people today cherish it
much more than whites. And at the end of the day, to expend energy telling the white man not to call us a name is a distraction.*

Once we have Done the Right Thing for ourselves—which is what interests me—the word will no longer seem so interesting.

However, this chapter presents my feelings on what this word tells us about where we are and where we are going. ▪

N o white person calls me "nigger"—at least not when I'm around. The white people I come into contact with seem aware that the word is today "the filthiest, dirtiest, nastiest word in the English language," as prosecutor Christopher Darden put it during the O.J. Simpson trial. I know *nigger* mainly as an affectionate in-group term favored especially by black men. Beyond this, for me, *nigger* exists largely as the media's euphemism "The 'N' Word," discussed more than used, the discussion usually exploring the popularity of the word among blacks. I suspect that this experience squares pretty well with most readers of this book.

Randall Kennedy's *nigger: The Strange Career of a Troublesome Word* starts out with a chronicle of various recorded uses of the word in days gone by. When Booker T. Washington dined with Theodore Roosevelt at the White House, South Carolina Senator Benjamin Tillman groused, "The action of President Roosevelt in entertaining that nigger will necessitate our killing a thousand niggers in the South before they will learn their place again." That one hits home in how it casually situates *nigger* in a sentence with such elegant syntax, like a clump of mud set in molded aspic at a dinner party. Harry Truman was polite to Congressman Adam Clayton Powell, Jr., until Truman's wife backed the D.A.R.'s refusal to allow Powell's wife, acclaimed pianist Hazel Scott, to perform at Constitution Hall. After Powell attacked Truman's wife in the press for this, Truman referred to him as "that damned nigger preacher." In 1947, members of the Philadelphia Phillies yelled the likes of "We don't want you here, nigger" at Jackie Robinson from the dugout as if "synchronized by some master conductor."

Often calls to ban *nigger* from American speech are defended on the basis of such chronicles of the word's use in the past. But in the second section, Kennedy presents an almost numbing parade of uses of *nigger* right here in our post–Civil Rights Act era, quite free of euphemism or irony. Illinois, 1977: a black man returns a defective product and the sales clerk writes on the sheet he asks him to sign, "Arrogant nigger refused exchange." Ohio, 1994: a white employer calls a black employee a "sleazy nigger." North Carolina, 1995: District Attorney Jerry Spivey sees the Denver Broncos' Ray Jacobs talking to his wife and, drunk, says, "Look at that nigger hitting on my wife." Florida, 2000: white graduating seniors conclude a violent screed against a black teacher in a newsletter with "Die nigger."

These observations are useful, even urgent in their way. As increasing numbers of blacks and whites are speaking up against the culture of professional victimhood hobbling black America, it is becoming almost a cliché to chant, "Of course, racism is not dead." But rarely is that phrase bolstered with sustained illustration. For many writers, one suspects the phrase is a kind of genuflection. It is easy to suppose in 2001 that there is barely any overt racism left in the United States beyond scattered hate-group yahoos most of us never meet. Kennedy's procession of mundane cases like this are ample illustration of what lurks beneath surface politeness among many whites. And the sheer number Kennedy adduces usefully implies the tip of an iceberg. The cases documented in court records are like the particular ancient creatures that happened to be fossilized—the preserved evidence captures only hints of a vaster reality. Much of the reason I don't get called *nigger* is that such language is especially stigmatized in the academic and artistic realms I circulate in, which are, after all, rarefied corners of a much larger America.

————

But Kennedy's book is not just one more book by a black academic dressing up the blame game in its Sunday best. Where many see blacks' use of *nigger* as evidence of self-hate, Kennedy is heartened by it. He even goes so far as to give his stamp of approval to what we might call "*nigger:* stage three," where whites use the term as an affectionate one with their black (and sometimes even white) friends. Even before the book's publication, leftist black academics were already screaming foul as if "synchronized by some master conductor," taking the line common in such circles that the word must be "stamped out." Notoriously screechy columnist Julianne Malveaux's judgment: "You are just giving a whole bunch of racists who love to use the word permission to use it even more." From Columbia's law school, Patricia Williams contributes "Seeing [nigger] floating abstractly on a bookshelf in a world that is still as polarized as ours makes me cringe." And of course, the inevitable accusation of mercenary motivation: Houston Baker from Duke's English department makes sure to get in "I see no reason whatsoever to do this, except to make money."

But views like these take their place in a long line of vain attempts throughout written history to ban the use of words that offend. There is not a single recorded instance to my knowledge of a word that was truly driven out of usage by fiat. The most one can do is drive a word underground—whereupon its taboo status lends it more power not less, rather like the cachet drinking alcohol took on under the Volstead Act.

Kennedy's game tolerance of the extensions of *nigger* among blacks and then back to whites is on the right track. Human speech—intimate, spontaneous, and largely subconsciously controlled—allows only commentary, not editing. As such, he usefully focuses on the black use of *nigger* and *"nigger:* stage three" as evidence of the word's dynamic transformation over time, even seeing blacks' adoption of the word as a kind of agentivity, a self-empowered response to the word's original use as a slur. Indeed, not only is it inherent in words to hang around despite attempts to submit them to pogrom, but it is also inherent in them to change in meaning over time.

And not just the sexy, controversial ones. *Silly* began as meaning, of all things, "blessed"—its evolution into its current meaning was a gradual, incremental process over several centuries. *Innumerable* began in its literal meaning: "unable to be counted." But since something hard to count is usually numerous, the meaning has slowly evolved into "many." It is things like this that make understanding Shakespeare's language challenging. For him, *wit* meant "knowledge" (preserved in the expression *mother wit*), not Noel Coward's sense of humor. When Polonius tells Laertes, "And these few precepts in thy memory look thou character," by *character* he meant "write." And in original Shakespeare folios, we can still see orthographical echoes of the fact that *good-bye* began as "God be with you." The ugly nature of *nigger*'s past and present does not exempt it from this universal process of eternal transformation. All words are like the clump in a Lava lamp, and *nigger* is currently squishing around in the little hourglass like all the other words.

Kennedy is especially good in situating the campaign against *nigger* within the context of the hate speech movement. He staunchly comes out in favor of treating *nigger* as an example of "mere words" rather than classifying its utterance as a legally prosecutable assault. For one, this encourages deceptive manipulations, such as Tawana Brawley's claim that white police officers raped her and scrawled *nigger* on her body in feces, now proven to be false but enshrined as a symbolic legend by scholars like Williams. Then there is the tripwire sensitivity to perceived insult, often leading to unjustifiable firings. Kennedy takes us back to widely covered cases such as the firing of municipal supervisor David Howard in Washington, DC, when he used the word *niggardly* discussing a budget, and the dust-up in 1997 over the Merriam-Webster Collegiate Dictionary's definition of *nigger* as "a black person—usu. taken to be offensive."

In the latter case, a black computer technician read the definition as implying that all black people are "niggers" and even elicited a boycott threat from Kweisi Mfume. But she was deaf to context: dictionary entries record what a word is used to refer to, and sadly, the original meaning of *nigger* is indeed often intended as a statement about all black people. Kennedy notes that this implies sanction no more than the same dictionary's listing for *honky: "usu. disparaging:* a white person." Cases like this are dismaying given how readily many black thinkers and leaders insist that whites view black misbehavior "in context." Critical Race Theory, calling on minorities to adopt the history of their race as personal stories, goes so far as to overextend context. Conversely, the dictionary case and the general call to classify *nigger* as "hate speech" instead overlook context, in the service of what Kennedy aptly terms "formulaic rage."

Kennedy also casts incisive light on frequent claims that the use of *nigger* is "on the rise." Malveaux, for instance, claimed in her comments on the book before its publication that the use of the word is "escalating." But how many of us could seriously say that *more* people are casually tossing the word around than they were in the past? We may see its use in the news more—but isn't that because it is processed as a shocking lapse, whereas in the past it was ordinary? Along those lines, Kennedy objects that "too often the dramatic retelling of an anecdote is permitted to substitute for a more systematic, quantitative analysis." As always, Kennedy is valuable in being committed to racial justice (such as in his underread book *Race, Crime and the Law*) while having no patience with subverting empiricism to the theatrics of playing the underdog. As such, he often throws the cold water of cool, common sense upon issues too often cloaked in glib histrionics: "After all, even when one is able to say that the number of reported incidents in a certain year was greater than the number of reported incidents in another year, there remains the problem of determining whether the reporting itself was a mirror of reality or a result of efforts to elicit from subjects their dissatisfaction with conduct they perceived to be offensive."

Kennedy's most useful point on the "mere words" issue is that the use of *nigger* is not only increasingly infrequent in public, but in the end less harmful than the subtler operations of racism that can genuinely impede self-realization. As he quotes Henry Louis Gates on the subject, in a sterling three sentences:

> The real power commanded by the racist is likely to vary inversely with the vulgarity with which it is expressed. Black professionals soon learn that it is the socially disenfranchised—the lower class, the homeless—who are more likely to hail them as "niggers." The circles of power have long since switched to a vocabulary of indirection.

Thus focusing discussion and legislation on *nigger* channels our attention to the least harmful reflex of racism.

Here is where once again, many black thinkers miss, or perhaps overextend, context in favor of the easy emotional score. In the vein of Kennedy's and Gates's point, I might note that I dissimulate a bit in saying that I have never been called a *nigger* to my face. A hard-drinking, working-class white man in the apartment complex I was living in once mumbled "just a nigger anyway" after we had had an altercation over his screaming at his wife outside my apartment until two in the morning. But for me, this elicited neither rage, chills, nor tears, but a sense of victory. After all, I was just out of graduate school and was on my way to a rewarding career and a comfortable lifestyle. He, on the other hand, may very well still live in that crummy complex, and had clearly gotten about as far as he ever would in life. His use of *nigger* was a defensive yelp of last resort.

This, for me, did not count as being "called *nigger*." The reason the word is such a hot potato is that its use supposedly cuts the addressee like a knife, reviving memories of how blacks were treated in decades past, disrupting our still-fragile egos. But I cannot say that getting this from that man under those circumstances made me feel that Redwood City, California, in 1994 was Birmingham 1963 all over again. Frankly I took it as a musical return to the tonic, a pleasantly unequivocal sign that I had won the fight.

Maybe I would feel differently if the head of my department called me a *nigger* in my office one afternoon. But the chances of that are, roughly, nil, and where racism touches me, it is in ways much subtler, and difficult to subject to legislation.

———

But in many ways Kennedy could have gone deeper on the underpinnings of how *nigger* is evolving. Yes, words' meanings always change, but it does not quite do to simply celebrate black comedians' rampant, jolly reveling in the word as a rejection of "boring conventions," as Kennedy has it. Words' changing meanings do not always indicate progress.

For example, the word *hussy* has its roots in the innocent "housewife" (Old English's *huswif* gradually transmogrified into *huzzif* and then *hussy*). Many want *nigger* to disappear, but sometimes a word disappears only because other terms have arisen to convey the same sentiment more surreptitiously. As I asked in an earlier chapter, whatever happened, for example, to the term *token black*? As late as the 1970s it was wielded to call attention to the dehumanization of blacks by placing them in prominent positions as a cynical, quick-fix way of deflecting charges of racism.

Today, however, the left sees this very brand of tokenism as permissible in the name of "diversity." Thus "Affirmative Action" has eased out *token black*, distracting many from the fact that too often, it is just this that the policy has fostered.

Along these lines, blacks' in-group use of *nigger* is certainly one part affection, as Kennedy notes. Worldwide, humans recruit disparaging epithets as terms of endearment—humility is a necessary prelude to intimacy. In an episode of *Seinfeld*, George Costanza falls in with a clique of businessmen who refer to one another affectionately as "bastard" and picks up the habit as he is accepted among them. One often can hear white friends referring to one another in jocular vein as "motherfucker." In Russian, the term *muzhik* technically means "peasant," but has evolved into a term of affection, indicating that a man is the "genuine article," a fine fellow. Young white women occasionally recruit *bitch* in this fashion: in the early 1990s at Stanford, a student-written feminist 'zine was called *Critical Bitch*. (The solicitation for submissions read, "Don't just be a bitch—be a critical bitch!")

It is thus no accident that, as Kennedy notes, even Asian teens in California are heard calling each other *nigger*, in line with their adoption of hip-hop fashions, musical tastes, speech, and attitudes. More than once in the Bay Area I have thought I was hearing black teens only to see when they passed that they were Chinese or Filipinos. In that vein, blacks' use of *nigger* is, to an extent, a warm leveler, equivalent to a sense among many people that getting intoxicated together is a kind of initiation of spiritual brotherhood. Among many black men, one has not really "arrived" as part of the group until one is being called *nigger*.

But only briefly does Kennedy acknowledge the equal role of

self-hate in this. It is significant that it is this term, among others possible, that has acquired such cachet. If affection and solidarity were really the only factor, then *motherfucker* alone or its ilk would do the trick. Blacks' use of *nigger* contains an echo of the internalization of whites' contempt. It conveys not only that you are "a reg'lar fella," but that you are "nothing but the lower organism that whitey thinks you are." All is not well when an obbligato like this bobs and weaves through casual conversations among black men across the United States.

There are times when this aspect of the meaning is painfully clear. For example, Truman calling Powell "that damned nigger preacher" was ironic when situated within a larger "context." Some years later as Martin Luther King, Jr., began to steal Powell's thunder, Powell dismissively asked, "Who's this nigger preacher?" That assessment responded in part to King being darker complected and from humbler circumstances than Powell, who was a physically near-white scion of bourgeois upbringing. Translation: King was, if we may, "blacker" than Powell. And thus, to Powell, a nigger.

Thus call blacks' use of *nigger* affectionate, creative, or a coping mechanism, but it's more than just a cheeky refusal to be "boring." And this extends to "*nigger:* stage three." Kennedy actually describes two uses in this vein. One is whites' careful use of it among their black friends. Kennedy notes a nimble depiction of this in Spike Lee's *Bamboozled*, where a "down-with-it" white producer cockily prides himself on knowing the taste of "niggers" better than the educated, buttoned-up black protagonist. My feelings about this usage are more ambivalent than Kennedy's, but only marginally so: overall, it recapitulates the challenging blend of affection and dismissal of "*nigger:* stage two."

But the other "*nigger:* stage three" trope is whites' occasional attempts to fashion *nigger* as referring to people of all races who display inappropriate behavior, weak character, and slovenly speech. The most memorable recent example was Senator Robert Byrd's controversial remark "I've seen a lot of white niggers in my time." Now, ideally, it would be lovely if *nigger* really did shed any association with a particular race, becoming synonymous with *wastrel* or *asshole.* But in our moment, this use of *nigger* makes me cringe a bit. What I hear in the "white nigger" term is "white person who is so disreputable as to compare with the worst among even *black* people." The subtle implication is that the lowly black person is the lowliest of all.

At the very least it reveals a certain obsession with "the Negro" and his character. After all, why are we not using *wop, spic,* or *kike* in this way? Some might object that these terms are all now a tad archaic, but this only begs the question as to why these terms were not recruited in this fashion when they were current.

———

But one reason Kennedy does not push this hard on these issues is that the book is really more a brief fascicle of three colloquium talks than a self-standing monograph—only about 175 pages, with largish print and airy spacing. Much of the text consists of taxonomic outlinings of legal cases in which *nigger* has played a part; the second section particularly shows its roots in the law review realm, although Kennedy is a graceful writer.

But at the end of the day, the brevity is one more of the book's strong points, in its way. In the year 2002, a plangent, three-hundred-page disquisition on the word *nigger* would be a melodramatic, backward endeavor. The obsession among many with *nigger* boils down to roughly "I am a strong and self-empowered person. Therefore the mere utterance of a racial slur referring to my race will reduce me to tears and helpless rage."

This is a curious manifesto for a race on the rise, and I suspect Kennedy would agree. One of his best passages:

> In stressing the "terror" of verbal abuse, proponents of hate-speech regulation have, ironically, empowered abusers while simultaneously weakening black students by counseling that they should feel grievously wounded by remarks that their predecessors would have ignored or shaken off.

When a white person throws *nigger* at a black one, what they are saying is "You are inferior to me because of your race." The sad and simple fact is that as long as a black person can be reduced to sputtering despair by this word, then deep down they believe the charge. To put it another way, recruiting Senator Byrd's take on the word, it won't hurt you to be called a nigger unless you think you are one.

Our problem is less a word than a racial self-image. If black Americans truly love themselves, then Kennedy's two cents—businesslike, bite-sized, and focused on moving ahead rather than wallowing in the past—is just about all we need on "The 'N' Word" in book format. And after we've read the reviews and heard the lively talk radio shows in the wake of the book's appearance, let's get back to rebuilding the inner cities and addressing racial profiling.

7

"We Don't Learn Our *History!*"

...

This essay began as a tiny seed, an op-ed for the Baltimore Sun. *I later developed it into an article in* City Journal, *and this is an expanded version of that piece.*

The Sun *op-ed elicited an angry response from Baltimore's black history museum, charging that I was merely shilling for the "neo-conservative" agenda. But we must get past the assumption that any black person who writes outside of the "racism is everything" agenda is merely trying to make a buck.*

I write this essay out of convictions just as deeply felt as those that drive black writers from the hard left. It pains me that every February as Black History Month rolls around, black talk radio is abuzz with callers claiming that "We don't know our history." The problem is a different one. ■

"Our problem is that we don't learn our *history!*" One often hears that said in the black community. It is another one of the key mantras, alongside "One out of three young black men is in jail or involved with the criminal justice system" and "We have to make sure white people know they are on the hook."

But is black history exactly an obscure topic these days? There are now thousands of books on the subject written for all ages. Henry Louis Gates, Jr.'s celebrity has ensured that his and Kwame Anthony Appiah's new *Africana* encyclopedia has been decidedly hard to miss. Mainstream history textbooks now acknowledge blacks' role in American history much more substantially than thirty years ago. As I write, an exhibit of artifacts from the wreck of the slave ship *Henrietta Marie* has sold out at one museum after another nationwide. Black history has been well sampled in films and on television; one can amass an imposing collection of videos on black history, as many libraries and African-American Studies departments have. Black History *Month* has now been prominently celebrated by schools and the media annually for almost thirty years. One could reasonably ask just what more one might expect in terms of keeping black history in the public eye.

The problem is not that black history is "hidden" or unavailable. People who insist that we "reclaim" and "uncover" our history are stuck in a conditioned reflex that arose in a situation now long in the past, just as we continue to refer to CDs as "albums," a term that arose before LP records when 78s ran only a few minutes and were often sold in eights, tens, or twelves in actual "album" packets.

The real problem reveals itself in a talk show appearance by James Baldwin in the late 1960s. "You brought me here in CHAINS! You brought me here in CHAINS!" Baldwin exclaimed to the interviewer. Baldwin here neatly summoned the sense of our history that most blacks have. There is a lip service paid to blacks having "survived" in this country. But the most immediate perception is that we were brought here packed in ships, treated like animals for 250 years, and then relegated to the margins of society for the next hundred. Then many black thinkers downplay even the progress made since, depicting modern black America as a variation on slavery, right down to condemning many successful blacks as "house niggers."

The result: for most of us "black history" summons grim images of endless degradation. This leaves black Americans feeling as if we are eternally just getting started, picking ourselves up after four hundred years "at the bottom of the well." But a people with no substantial source of inspiration from the past is one spiritually weakened, especially one in the process of reconstructing itself.

Our question, then, is not how we can make black Americans aware of their history. That battle has been won, and anyone who claims otherwise would sing a different tune if transported by a time machine into 1950 to see just how available black history was to people living in the era of *I Love Lucy*. Our question is whether we can make anything useful to us of a history that does begin, after all, with us being brought here in chains. The answer is yes—but not in the ways many suppose.

———

For many, what has happened to us in this country is too demoralizing to focus on except as a source for indicting whites. Whatever the value of this, it does not create a sense of personal uplift. The sense of emptiness here leads to the "Mother Africa" ideology.

Our treasuring of this bloodline is a moral advance over the condescension most black Americans had toward "the African" in the days of yore. But there are grave pitfalls in styling Africa as black America's "first act."

The "Afrocentric History" school, for example, is founded on the idea that Ancient Egyptians were "black," that the Ancient Greeks stole their philosophy from Egypt, and that the Western intellectual heritage was therefore a "black" creation. Over the past thirty years, this frame of reference has led millions of blacks to trace "themselves" to the technologically advanced civilization of Ancient Egypt.

Advocates cherish this idea as giving black students a sense of historical importance. The problem, however, is that this school of thought has no factual basis. There are now several book-length treatments that decisively refute all of the tenets at the heart of "Afrocentric History." Some are written on a level that only a career academic is likely to get much out of, but I recommend Mary Lefkowitz's *Not Out of Africa* as the most accessible and to-the-point example. Amid the predictable cries of racism and "right-wing backlash" in assorted books and articles since, none of the "Afrocentric Historians" have presented sustained factual rebuttals. This is because the facts are simply too clear to refute.

Pointedly, almost none of the "Afrocentric historians" read Latin, Ancient Greek, or Egyptian hieroglyphics, instead relying on English translations of the foundational works. This leads to misinterpretations, especially when many of the Afrocentrists' claims rely on adventurous readings of ambiguous passages. Caught up in the sociopolitical urgency that Afrocentric historians cloak themselves in, we are easily distracted from how grave it is that they cannot read in the original the texts they are referring to. We shudder, for example, to imagine a presumed Russian literature expert writing papers on Tolstoy having only read Constance Garnett translations rather than the original texts. No one addressed as "Professor" pontificates on *Madame Bovary* only to quietly reveal over dinner after the talk that actually, they do not read French.

But most "Afrocentric historians" are no more motivated by a sincere interest in "history" than Creation Scientists are by science itself. Molefi Kete Asante, Yosef ben-Jochannan, and their comrades are driven at heart by indignation that "our" history has presumably been wrested from us by a racist academic tradition.

Good intentions aside, the factual validity of an academic inquiry decreases to the extent that it is motivated more by hatred than human curiosity. Blacks of all persuasions labor under remnants of the white perception of blacks as mentally inferior. To embrace—or even let pass—a historical "framework" with no factual basis only reinforces this. How realistic is it to expect to be accepted as mental equals when blacks presenting themselves as "professors" chart our history with mythical narratives, as if we were preliterate hunter-gatherers? And how constructive is it to foist upon us a "history" that only heightens our sense of embattlement and alienation, especially when the "framework" in question is a tissue of fabrications anyway?

Then there's Kwanzaa, which presents a different kind of problem. It was created in 1966 by an Afrocentric scholar-activist at California State University, Maulana (né Ron) Karenga. It is modeled broadly on African harvest celebrations, with artifacts and ideologies named in Swahili.

Kwanzaa is beautiful in itself. It is founded upon seven principles that all the world's peoples would benefit from (the *nguzo saba*): unity (*umoja*), self-determination (*kujichagulia*), collective responsibility (*ujima*), cooperative economics (*ujamaa*), purpose (*nia*), creativity (*kuumba*), and faith (*imani*). Yet at the end of the day, after thirty-five years, relatively few black Americans practice Kwanzaa. Hallmark may now have a line of Kwanzaa cards, but I would still venture that forty-nine out of fifty blacks randomly surveyed would draw a blank on the seven principles, and Christmas remains as central to the black experience as it was in 1966.

To be sure, Karenga specifies that Kwanzaa is intended as a cultural rather than religious holiday, and is thus compatible with Christianity. Good idea: but this brings us back to the difficulties in parsing black Americans as "culturally" African. Generations of scholars have devoted themselves to unearthing the African legacies in black American culture. Yet the very fact that these traits require so much effort and training to unearth suggests that blacks in America have, to a large extent, incorporated the culture surrounding them. Calls to found our identities upon "Mother Africa" are asking us to pretend a sense of living kinship with people speaking languages we do not know, who neither move, dance, cook, sing, nor often view the world the way we do.

Besides this, we also run up again against the dangers of the monocultural conception of "Africa." Swahili is spoken in only about eight of the four dozen African nations—hardly the "pan-African" language that Karenga claims. I have a coloring book my parents gave me in the early 1970s describing how people celebrate Christmas in various nations, with each description given both in English and the national language of the country. The book nodded to black people by including Ethiopia, but translated the description into Swahili. But Swahili is alien to Ethiopia, where the national language is Amharic, a relative of Arabic and Hebrew, as unlike Swahili as English is to Japanese. The editors were on the right track in their genuflection—a coloring book about "The World" published ten years before would probably have skipped Africa entirely. But slapping Swahili on Ethiopia looks a bit dismissive of the people themselves. It's rather like describing Christmas in Brazil in Spanish instead of Portuguese because that's "close enough," or calling Russian "the language of Europe" because it is taught and often spoken in seven or eight of Russia's former satellites. Treating Swahili as "the language of Africa" smacks of the same kind of overgeneralization, whether one is black or not.

For descendants of Sierra Leoneans, Ghanaians, and Angolans to adopt Swahili and "cherry-pick" aspects of assorted African cultures as "our heritage" is analogous to a Welsh-American learning Greek and dancing Russian *trepaks* in Dutch clogs on holidays, out of a sense that after all, "Europe is Europe." Of course, since most black Americans cannot know exactly what parts of Africa they trace to, perhaps the "pan-African" conception is the best we can do. But the artificiality remains: no actual group of humans has ever lived in the pan-African "culture" Kwanzaa is based on. Culture sits in the heart. Kwanzaa, made up at someone's desk a few decades ago, cannot help but sit more in the head.

Another obstacle to Kwanzaa's wider adoption is the post–Civil

Rights sense that spiky resistance is the measure of what Malcolm X called "a real black man." Changing a culture requires focus on the young. But while Karenga constructed Kwanzaa to celebrate "family and community," today's black youth culture considers Tupac Shakur a hero—and this includes people now pushing forty who were more or less "youths" when Shakur was alive. When "fight the powers that be" becomes the *sine qua non* of "blackness," "family and community" becomes something of a formality in comparison. And besides—just which people on our planet do *not* value family and community?

The very mention of Kwanzaa often elicits a bit of a giggle among many blacks, truth be told. This is because the notion of our identifying with a people so very different from us on the sustained level of a week-long holiday cannot help but seem a tad forced. There is nothing wrong with Kwanzaa in itself. But ultimately, it will remain as formulaic and gestural for black American identity as Thanksgiving is to signaling 'American' identity.'" Kwanzaa asks the black car salesman in Chicago to celebrate the first yields of the harvest in a Ugandan village. Obviously we, as a people so deeply American, need something beyond this.

———

Black Americans would benefit more from a conception of history focusing not on Africa but on *us:* blacks *in America* speaking English, worshipping a Christian God, living (and often mating) with whites, in a post-industrial society. The reason the history of *us* has not taken true hold in black America is a matter not of *whether* it has been told but of *how* it has been told.

For example, there is no dearth of books, calendars, and audiovisual materials chronicling major figures in black history.

And surely it is important that we preserve the memory of Harriet Tubman, Frederick Douglass, Paul Laurence Dunbar, Mary McLeod Bethune, Paul Robeson, Medgar Evers, etc. However, I suspect that the big pictures of such people that festoon urban public libraries every February play about as inspirational a role in most blacks' consciousness as the figures carved on Mount Rushmore do in most whites'.

The reasons for this are local to our times. The New Double Consciousness—"I'm fine but racism pins most other black people down at the bottom of the well"—makes us see black heroes less as inspirations than as exceptions to the rule. *Overtly* one cannot help but admire a Thurgood Marshall. But that big drawing of him hanging in the library window evokes in us formal admiration rather than a burning sense of the potential within us. How can that drawing tell us "You can be like him!" when so many modern black thinkers and leaders insist that black success is merely a matter of a few tokens let through the crack in the door?

Furthermore, the sense that "real" black people define themselves against the evil oppressor blunts the inspiration that blacks once derived from figures like Marian Anderson and George Washington Carver. These people, after all, made their mark in equaling whites in a race-neutral activity. Anderson did not swing or rock, nor did she sing the blues or "God Bless the Child"—she sang classical music in trained operatic style. Carver did not fashion an "Afrocentric Science."

It is not an accident, then, that Malcolm X is the most beloved black figure of the past among young blacks. It is similarly predictable that the debate between W. E. B. Du Bois and Booker T. Washington took a central place in the collective consciousness of the black community in the late 1960s, Washington's "accommo-dationist" perspective valued as an object lesson in the "wrong" way to be black.

Within this zeitgeist, late-eighteenth-century Phillis Wheatley's ability to write classical poetry in English after having been born in Africa and taken into slavery elicits respect, perhaps, but not identification. She has even taken some potshots from black intellectuals uncomfortable at finding a lack of interest in being "black" in her work. Gwendolyn Brooks, who won a Pulitzer Prize for her poetry in 1950, found herself criticized by black radicals in the 1960s for conforming to "white" norms. Brooks, a transitional figure, fell into line, reminiscent of Adam Clayton Powell, Jr., at the same time donning "Black Power" rhetoric in the final act of his life. Since then, the aspiring black poet is unlikely to seek inspiration from someone who took her formal cue from the likes of Alexander Pope.

Certainly on a formal level blacks esteem ancestors who showed that we can do as well as whites can. But then black talk radio stations remain abuzz with the claim that "We don't know our history," despite Black History Month coming around year after year. It's not that we aren't told about these ancestors: it is, I think, that most black Americans aren't terribly moved by them. It is understandable why they aren't—but it also means that we need to approach our history with different lenses if we are to find true meaning in it.

———

It will not do, for instance, to render black history as a succession of tragedies: the horrors of slavery, Dred Scott, the quick demise of Reconstruction, *Plessy v. Ferguson*, the rise of the Ku Klux Klan, lynchings, the beatings of Civil Rights activists, Emmett Till. To not attend to such things at all would be folly, of course. But even so, a history dominated by such horrors is not one to exactly inspire us for the future.

Take, for example, Mba Mbulu's *Ten Lessons: An Introduction to Black History*. Mbulu devotes the meat of the book to chronicling slavery and segregation. There is a dollop of blacks' contributions to what is called "White History." But the main thrust is sections such as "White People's Attacks on Other People," "White Supremacy," "Back in Our Place," etc. The intent to give black students an explanation for the sadness of their history is understandable. People like Mbulu are trying to say, "Don't think that these awful things mean that you are no good." But the overall message of his book is, at the end of the day, one of perennial victimhood: we blacks are mired in a country run by evil whites—be on your guard.

This kind of history would hardly be comfort food to any group, but it is particularly damaging to blacks. For one, blacks do not have the privilege that, say, Jews do of being able to see these horrors as a "second act" after an initial period of glory. The "Mother Africa" ideal is an attempt to provide a positive "first act," but it is too abstract to be felt deeply by most. Then post–Civil Rights ideology again plays its hand on the other end. Under the mantra that racism remains as virulent as it was in the past, the "tragedy" model of black history is interpreted as evidence that racism is not only a nightmare in the present but is even more horrific in its longevity. When "Learn your history" often means "Don't get fooled by superficial changes," yesterday's Bull Connor is today's New York City Street Crimes Unit.

———

In *The Debt*, Randall Robinson surmises that deep down most black people don't like America. Given our history, it would be surprising if this were not the case. Certainly blacks have demonstrated their patriotism in innumerable instances—most recently, after the terrorist attacks of September 11, 2001, there were as many Walgreen's flags waving from blacks' car antennas as whites'. Nor have blacks as a group displayed any more substantial interest in Communism than other Americans. But all the same, it is safe to say that blacks generally feel "black" first and "American" second, in contrast to most Jews and other "hyphenated" Americans.

Whether whites or blacks are more responsible for this faint affection for our own country today is a rich issue. But what it means is that for the time being, mere narratives of the lives of the great black achievers of the past cannot speak to most black people in a meaningful way. The dominant modern conception of "cultural blackness" is focused too strongly on rebellion for Phillis Wheatley to be felt as a role model. Many of us might like it to be otherwise. But to simply state that and let it lie serves no purpose.

To do us any real good, our history books must show the positive aspects of blacks' lives here in the United States *in ways deliberately targeted at a race distracted for thirty-five years by a self-defeating ideology.* Abstract "pan-African" visions have little to do with teaching us how to make our garden grow right here, and must be marginalized. Moreover, our focus must be on the *communal* level, to show that black American achievement has not been solely a matter of lightning striking for the chosen. Here are some suggestions:

■ *Black business districts.* The "great man" model of historiography will not do when black common consensus tends to parse our heroes as a mere lucky few. For this reason, black history must revive the memory of what even ordinary blacks have achieved through mutual efforts. The thriving black business districts of the early decades of the 1900s will serve as Exhibit A.

Too often, black history between the demise of Reconstruction and the Harlem Renaissance is depicted as little but lynching, *Plessy v. Ferguson*, and a quick look at superstars Du Bois and Washington. Today's passing observer is usually unaware that this picture is incomplete, and that even in the early 1900s, when whites largely restricted blacks to employment as menials, blacks were capable of building thriving business districts of their own.

Take, for example, Henry Louis Gates, Jr.'s observation that "What really captivated me was that in the all-black world of *Amos 'n' Andy* . . . there was an all-black department store, owned and operated by black attendants for a black clientele." Ideally, more blacks would know that worlds-within-a-world like this *actually existed.*

Chicago's "Bronzeville" is a handy example. As the city industrialized after 1875, blacks occupied a three-by-fifteen block on the south side of the city, and the Great Migration from the South swelled the black population to 109,548 by 1920. Bronzeville, also known as "Black Metropolis," was home to several black newspapers. These included the *Bee*, which occupied a magnificent Art Deco building *that black people did not move into after whites had occupied it previously, but built themselves,* and the *Defender*, a publication of national influence, whose editorials urging blacks to migrate from the South were a major spur for the Great Migration itself. The literary-minded of Bronzeville also had newsmagazines available to them such as *The Half-Century* and *The Light* (which contrast sharply in gravity with today's leading black magazines such as *Ebony* and *Vibe*).

It was said that if you held up a horn at State and 35th, it would play itself because of the musical winds always blowing. Bronzeville was a leading center of innovation in jazz, nurturing Jelly Roll Morton, King Oliver, Louis Armstrong, and Earl "Fatha" Hines. Oscar Micheaux's film company, producing a pioneering oeuvre of "race movies," was based not in New York or Hollywood but Bronzeville.

But Bronzeville was by no means only a center of black journalism and entertainment. At the end of the day, the business of Bronzeville was business. There were 731 business establishments in 1917 in sixty-one different lines of work. Of several banks, the most prominent was the Binga State Bank founded in 1908, Jesse Binga having begun with a coal oil and gas wagon and parlayed this into realty investments. In this, Binga manifested Bronzeville blacks' eager purchase of real estate. They quickly went beyond renting space from whites to amassing holdings of their own totaling $100,000,000 by 1929. Bronzeville was home to several magnificent buildings besides the one housing the *Bee*, such as the Overton Hygenic, which contained a cosmetics firm, life insurance company, major bank, and drugstore; and the seven-floor Knights of Pythias building, built by one of the districts' innumerable lodges (which were the model of the Mystic Knights of the Sea on *Amos 'n' Andy*, which in its first incarnation took place in Chicago). Again, these black people built these and hundreds of other buildings themselves; they were not renting from "The Man." And there were seven insurance companies, 106 lawyers, and several hotels, including "The Finest Colored Hotel in the World," the Hotel Brookmont.

This was a thriving civic community, including a YMCA settlement house running jobs training programs, and branches of various civic organizations. There were no fewer than 192 churches in Bronzeville by 1929, the flagship being Olivet Baptist with ten thousand members. Bronzeville churches were focused on community uplift, harboring lodging facilities for new arrivals from the South and employment agencies to shunt them into the workforce. Olivet alone had fifty-three departments devoted to community programs. Bronzeville produced several political leaders, including the first black congressman since Reconstruction, Oscar DePriest. Provident was one of the top black hospitals in the country, employing many of black Chicago's (by 1929) 176 doctors. One of Provident's founders was Daniel H. Williams, the first doctor—*of any color*—in America to operate upon the human heart. The district also had a training school for nurses.

Bronzeville's leaders, then, had their eyes on community stability and self-sufficiency. As uncultivated new arrivals from the rural South flooded the city after the 1890s, the black middle class did not cherish them as more "authentic" versions of themselves—they unequivocally saw themselves as models for the new masses. Walters African Methodist Episcopal Zion Church's pastor William A. Blackwell matter-of-factly noted that the migrants, "while speaking the same language as we do, are in many cases little more accustomed to the freedom of this city, the habits and customs of our people than is the newly arrived peasant from Europe. These people must be amalgamated and assimilated." There was no question of adopting working class ambivalence toward "striving" and teaching the district's residents to distrust black successes as "selling out." Any hint of this ideology was put on the defensive. In 1929, a chronicle of Bronzeville's rise counseled that "The Old Negro teaches his children to fear an authoritative white person and to disrespect intelligent and cultured persons of their own race in the same position; The New Negro teaches his children to fear no one and to respect every one worthy of respect."

Nor was the black criminal romanticized as a martyr, despite whites' restriction of blacks to grunt work until well into the teens. Bronzeville's civic organizations agitated constantly for cleaning up seedy streets and disciplining criminals for the benefit of the community. In 2000, Jesse Jackson decried the suspension of Decatur black teenagers who had engaged in a brawl in the stands during a football game as "racist." This contrasts tellingly with Dr. George C. Hall of the Chicago National Urban League branch complaining in 1917 that "the delinquent colored boy or girl who is taken to the juvenile court is turned out again on probation to learn more." He asserted further that "if Chicago lacks the vision to see ahead it will reap the harvest of fostering a kindergarten on the streets where gamins learn crime."

Nor was Bronzeville a fluke: the all-black world now so often considered a fantasy in *Amos 'n' Andy* also existed in West Baltimore, Atlanta's Auburn Avenue district, Washington, DC's Shaw neighborhood, and elsewhere.

The districts' demise must be covered (such as the race riot that destroyed Tulsa's Greenwood district, or the Great Depression's effect on Bronzeville). But to simply treat these districts as an object lesson in white malevolence will extinguish the soul rather than ignite it. We must be shown that when blacks two generations past slavery were relegated to separate quarters of a big city, the result was not "Barrytown" and South Central. Even amid naked discrimination, the human spirit bore fruit, and ordinary black people again and again created a "Chocolate City" on the middle-class American model and could not have imagined considering otherwise. And note that these were indeed ordinary people—no one has even heard of most of them today; few were superstars. And yet looking at what they did sends shivers down our spines.

■ *Ordinary black people can excel in "white learning" and do not need big money to do it.* The modern impulse is to assume that in any black community, an educational crisis reigns. Sadly that is usually true today, but was not in Bronzeville, where truancy rates were no higher than among white students, and black students performed as well as white ones. But today's memory of the history of black education is a procession from substandard segregated schools of the South, a memory kept alive by the *Brown v. Board of Education* victory, segueing into the inner-city sinkhole schools in the headlines today.

A black history ushering blacks into a true sense as members of their country must make clear the following: the schools Jonathan Kozol describes in *Savage Inequalities* are more ideological by-products of our times than business as usual for blacks. From the late 1800s to the 1950s, several black schools were models of scholarly achievement, regularly producing Ph.D.s and other eminent figures. Students at Washington, DC's Dunbar High often outscored the city's white schools on standardized tests as early as 1899—that is, when *Plessy v. Ferguson* of 1896 was a Current Event. Schools such as Frederick Douglass in Baltimore, Booker T. Washington in Atlanta, P.S. 91 in Brooklyn, McDonough 35 in New Orleans, and many others operated at a similar level.

Dunbar alone produced Charles Drew (discoverer of blood plasma), Edward Brooke (the twentieth century's first black senator), William Hastie (the first black federal judge), and other prominent figures. As Thomas Sowell puts it, the sheer weight of accomplished black people that schools like Dunbar produced "suggests some systematic social process at work, rather than anything as geographically random as outstanding individual ability."

In an age when societal inequity is so often mistaken as destiny, the very existence of these schools in their days of glory can seem almost counterintuitive. This makes it all the more urgent that these schools be brought alive beyond the academic papers and books where they have largely been chronicled. In that light, I must note that Thomas Sowell's works have played a central role in enlightening me to this part of black history. Time passes—books go out of print, and issues of academic journals are eventually bound in fours between leather covers and stashed in university library stacks. Yet this hardly belies the infinitely wise counsel of the texts themselves, and here I hope to bring Sowell's teachings back into the light of a black America that needs them just as much as it did in the 1970s. Short of this, collective black success again gets lost between the cracks of a historiography dedicated to keeping the setbacks front and center.

One result of that leaning is the fashionable assumption that American education is natively inappropriate to the "African" soul, memorably espoused in Carter G. Woodson's *The Mis-Education of the Negro*. The influence of this notion must not be underestimated: witness the "Ebonics" philosophy of teaching black children to read, or the megahit black pop recording *The Miseducation of Lauryn Hill*'s canny channeling of Woodson's title. In this vein, it will serve us well to note that these schools did not include "Afrocentric" curricula.

Dunbar, for instance, taught Latin into the 1950s. Meanwhile, the top black colleges were also providing students with fine educations modeled directly on the mainstream curricula of the day. The student at Fisk (my mother's alma mater) was put through his or her paces in Horace and Livy, and graduate W. E. B. Du Bois went on to write his doctoral thesis in German. In 1915, a white Fisk dean's wife was aghast at the news that Talladega (my aunt's alma mater) in Alabama did *not* even require Greek and Latin for the bachelor's degree. Or may I repeat from Chapter Three: in the late 1800s, black college students were well known for often taking top honors over whites in oratory. And not in the style of the black church, or in the artful slang of what we would call "slam poetry." They were taking prizes not for showing whites blacks' "native" verbal talents, but for wielding ornate literary standard English.

Alone, a captioned photograph of black students in a school-room in 1900 with their hair parted down the middle will make little lasting impression. None of us are seriously impressed to see that black people in the old days just, well, went to school. The schools should be covered in ways that encourage thinking beyond the box that limits us today. To show the power of agency over obstacles, it must be featured that these schools operated on substandard budgets, with often creaky physical plants. And we must also counter the misimpression of many blacks of a certain age that these schools only catered to a rarefied and light-skinned crème de la crème. As such, it must be shown that many of these schools educated as many lower-income blacks as more fortunate ones.

▪ *Ease up on Booker T.* With it established that blacks have been capable of stunning successes in this country despite racism, we will be in a position to resituate the "Blacks in Wax" as figures to worship rather than merely "respect." This can begin with the debate between W. E. B. Du Bois and Booker T. Washington.

Washington's image has congealed into a bogeyman archetype of the black "sellout." He sits so readily on the tongues of so many that I am beginning to lose count of how many times I have been called "a Booker T. Washington" by my detractors. A lifetime of dedication to black uplift has been reduced to a sour parable, in which an opportunist quisling urged blacks to roll over and tolerate racism and content themselves with manual labor, and was nobly defied by the avatar of black pride, Du Bois. But this reduction of Washington to an object lesson in how not to be "black" deprives us of a role model, one in many ways more useful to us today than Du Bois.

Contrary to the fantasy nurtured by black radicals (most of whom appear never to have read more than two sentences Washington ever uttered or wrote), Washington's message was not that blacks "turn the other cheek." Two decades before Du Bois had even arisen as a critic to defend himself against, Washington was asserting as a matter of course that "there should be no unmanly cowering or stooping to satisfy unreasonable whims of the Southern white man." Washington's chariness of active protest did not stem from weakness of spirit or lack of concern for his race. He was born a slave in the Deep South, witnessing the implacable racism of the period at much closer hand than Du Bois had growing up in burgherly circumstances in Great Barrington, Massachusetts. On this basis, he advised that blacks would be better off attaining the bread-and-butter skills necessary to building an economic base than fighting a Sisyphean battle against whites' control of public offices. The legend tarring him as the antithesis of black "authenticity" has Washington's teachings simply stopping here. But in fact this was only a first step. His idea was that racism was more likely to abate when blacks had concrete accomplishments to point to than on the basis of abstract spiritual appeals.

Okay, Washington was behind the curve in some ways. His famous call to "cast down your buckets" was not, as often thought, a call to satisfy ourselves forever with lowly labor, but a call to build an economic base in the South rather than risk the uncertainties of migrating North. But obviously blacks who did make the Great Migration found rich opportunities. Meanwhile, the successes of schools like Dunbar and Howard and their graduates did not speak well for his advice that blacks postpone pursuing higher education until they had spent decades establishing themselves materially.

Yet meanwhile, Du Bois was urging blacks to dwell on a "double consciousness" founded as much in an "African" spirit as an American one. That sentiment is an apt summation of the "Souls of Black Folk" indeed, and no one before or since has rendered it as artfully as Du Bois. But in the end, this ideology, with its call to look inward and meanwhile treat our problems as those of all "brown" people throughout the world, had nothing to do with building the great black business districts from the ground up. For all its greatnesses, nothing in Du Bois's philosophy directly inspired the concrete glories of a Bronzeville.

When it came to concrete action, Du Bois was more interested in a "talented tenth" providing "guidance" for the masses, seeking public offices and articulately protesting the barriers to attaining them. For most blacks today, this approach has more gut-level appeal than Washington and his buckets, especially given that protest in Du Bois's vein eventually created the Civil Rights miracle. I myself would rather have had dinner with Du Bois than Washington.

Yet Washington's philosophy was by no means a bankrupt one. Just as he predicted, the trend was indeed for blacks to attain significant offices *after* translating the financial clout of these districts into political power. Du Bois's ideology requires a certain adjustment for us today in its unquestioned Victorian elitism, founded on an assumption that black success would be driven by superstars. Washington was trying to show how we could *all* be agents of our own success—and history has borne him out just as decisively as it has Du Bois. Washington and Du Bois ultimately pointed to different paths to the same mountaintop.

After all, deep down we all know that, despite the injustice of it, no amount of slogans and posturing can replace concrete accomplishment in inspiring respect from others. This was Booker T. Washington's message, and it must come through in how we remember him. Too often since the 1960s, blacks have been led to suppose that the main task before us is therapeutic: to bemoan whites' racist sentiments and treat them as rendering black success accidental. This philosophy had nothing to do with building the Binga Bank or Olivet Baptist, and it has roots not in Washington but Du Bois, whose primum mobile, at the end of the day, was a profound indignation that blacks were not allowed to be, essentially, white.

And he had a point—our ultimate goal indeed must be that blacks and whites learn the same things, have the same jobs, and cherish the same cultural ideals—i.e., that blacks become Americans. Fittingly, Du Bois gave Washington a run for his money. Yet at his death Washington was still a figure of massive influence, especially among the black business class, and we risk a certain smug hubris in dismissing Washington's millions of black adherents of the time as naïve. A chronicler of black Chicago got it right in 1916 in noting, "Those working for the uplifting of their race in Chicago as elsewhere may be divided roughly into two schools—one working on the plans followed by the late Booker T. Washington and the other following the theories advocated by W. E. Burghardt Du Bois of New York. Though their ideas may differ on details, both groups are striving sincerely for the advancement of their race."

Washington deserves better than to have been reduced to a mere epithet, and our new history must allow him to speak to us once more.

■ *Treat black heroes' triumphs as object lessons rather than as legends.* When we realize that untold millions of blacks have hit the bull's-eye in this land with all of its flaws, then even the individual "Blacks in Wax" will come alive in a new way. The tendency to only find visceral inspiration from black rebels like Stokely Carmichael follows from a black self-conception as expatriates from Africa, ever questioning the value of embracing the mores of a "foreign" land whose rulers allow only a token few to rise above poverty. But armed with a more accurate and uplifting sense of our scorecard in America, we are poised to recast the black heroes who embraced becoming American as business as usual, rather than as shooting stars.

For example, we often miss how inspiring the very circumstances a black hero grew up in are. The fact that a famous black did *not* grow up in poverty is usually treated as a kind of footnote except in full-length biographies. Yet just as those pre-Copernican astronomers could not see the import of the "eccentricities" in the movements of many stars, the "racism forever" paradigm deflects attention from how very many black greats did not grow up wondering where their next meal was coming from. Such people were not scions of families blessed by netherworldly good fortune. Often they grew up nurtured by black worlds-within-a-world created with meat-and-potatoes initiative and tenacity.

Thurgood Marshall did not just "grow up in Baltimore"; he went to Frederick Douglass High, another sterling all-black school that put the lie to the claim that minority schools' problems are due just to lack of funding and "Eurocentric" curricula. Gwendolyn Brooks was not just "from Southside Chicago"; she was a product of the vibrant black community I have described. She first published in the *Defender*, and was nurtured by a Bronzeville literary ferment paralleling Harlem's Black Renaissance, which included Richard Wright. With people like this "it took a village," indeed—thriving "villages" of financially stable black people looking forward rather than backward (the "New Negro"), embracing membership in this nation.

And with a revived awareness of this side of the story, we are even set to revise our conception of black heroes born in less fortunate circumstances. The leftist skepticism of individual initiative hobbles black America with the canard that history is destiny. But every time we are told that "slavery refuses to fade" (Derrick Bell), "racism continues as an ideology and a material force within the U.S., providing blacks with no ladder that reaches the top" (Robert Chrisman and Ernest Allen, Jr.), or that "slavery has hulled empty a whole race of people with inter-generational efficiency" (Randall Robinson), hundreds of blacks who rose from slavery or poverty to transform the world are reduced to statistical noise.

For example, when Frederick Douglass escaped slavery on the Underground Railroad, history was no more destiny than it was for the children of slaves who built Bronzeville. Hardly "hulled empty," Douglass instead became one of the nineteenth century's most influential thinkers on abolitionism and women's suffrage. Booker T. Washington was also born a slave, worked in mines and as a houseboy after Emancipation, and arrived at the new black college Hampton broke and dirty. No "ladder that reaches the top" was in evidence—the year after Washington graduated, the "Party of Lincoln" traded off Reconstruction for the instatement of Rutherford B. Hayes. But Washington adopted the teachings of Hampton's white principal on the value of manual labor and efficiency, and passed these on to thousands of black students as president of Tuskegee Institute. These are also *American* stories, in that whites were crucial in determining the life paths of both men, something true for countless other black figures.

To dismiss these people's stories as mere lightning striking echoes the very whites who were convinced in Douglass's and Washington's lifetimes that black people were congenitally incapable of anything but menial service. *We cannot claim that we are a strong people while also insisting that none but a few of us can be expected to thrive short of ideal conditions.* The idea that chronicling the modern underclass is *more* important than telling the stories of slaves rising to fame and fortune presumes that black people will somehow take inspiration from failure. On the contrary, we must focus on those who made the best of the worst. Otherwise, we create our own anti-black stereotype: that we are the world's only people whose evolution is Lamarckian—inheriting the traits that life stamped upon our ancestors—rather than Darwinian—where survival is all about making one's way in a competitive world by showing one's best.

▪ *Black music became America's music.* The notion that a useful black history will inspire us to become *American* will elicit discomfort in many blacks. Integration, after all, has become a dirty word, out of a fear that it signals the disappearance of black culture. As such, the new black history must attend to this fear.

As it happens, the black contribution to American music is a perfect antidote. It demonstrates that while blacks will necessarily become more "white" in an America where interracial harmony reigns, in the meantime whites have already become "blacker."

The facts here are simple: the popular music that all Americans cherish, sing, and dance to today would not exist if Africans had not been brought to this country. This started with ragtime. Ragtime is distinguished by the devilishly infectious rhythmic impulse created by syncopation, setting a steady pulse in the left hand against capriciously contrapuntal rhythmic figures in the right. Itinerant black pianists in the South forged this music by imposing African-derived rhythms upon European march forms. When they brought it north in the 1890s, it quickly took the nation by storm and became a staple element in mainstream popular music. Ragtime is most familiar to us in the form of Scott Joplin's piano pieces like "The Entertainer," but in its era, ragtime made its main impact in the form of sung ditties backed by the new catchy rhythm. Irving Berlin's "Alexander's Ragtime Band" was a particularly successful example.

Yes, this tinkly little thing was, at the time, "black" music. For instance, lost to us today is the "black" allusion in the title: "Alexander" was a standard name in jokes for a black person "putting on airs," the idea being that it was funny for a black person to have so formal a name as Alexander. The song was about a black man's band, then, and for a white person to dance to it was equivalent to a white person dancing in 1990 to MC Hammer's braggadocio in "Can't Touch This." Ragtime was America's first "crossover" music. It is seldom made clear enough that *before the 1890s, no music this uniquely catchy existed in the United States.* All Abraham Lincoln knew in terms of popular music was marches, jigs, waltzes, weepy parlor ballads, and folk tunes. Americans did not, in any sense we would recognize, "jam" before black people made them do so.

Ragtime met the other black American musical creation, the blues, and became jazz. Jazz was taken up by whites as, for one, the "swing" of the big bands, and at the same time was fashioned into the idiom of the old standards. That is, the groove of Frank Sinatra's classic cuts that we play on dive bar jukeboxes would not exist if African slaves had not been brought to this country. Then, early jazz plus the blues plus white folk country music equals rock and roll—and this is the wellspring of all of the contemporary popular music now basic to the American identity. No slaves, no Crosby, Stills and Nash, no Elvis Costello, no Melissa Etheridge, no Nine Inch Nails.

Even the way any white pop singer sings today would sound netherworldly to the Victorian. Slaves' blues singing used earthy vocal colorings unknown to an America where singing meant living room sopranos warbling in the European classical style of Jenny Lind. Ever since white "red hot mamas" of Sophie Tucker's generation aped black singing styles, blackness has been central to "white" singing in America. I urge interested readers to rent Mae West's old movie *I'm No Angel* and listen to her sing. Her black models are utterly unmistakable; there's simply nowhere else a working class white gal from Brooklyn could have learned to sing that way. Black vocal styles—blue notes, sliding up to a note instead of hitting it dead-on, sprinkling one's singing with *ain't*s and *baby*s alien to one's actual speech, etc.—have become so central to popular American singing that today few white singers are consciously aware of the roots of their singing styles.

And this must assuage our fear that we "become white" while whites just stay the way they were. If Tori Amos were transported back a hundred years, she would strike listeners as a white woman singing "like a colored girl." And yet she could not sing any other way even at gunpoint—it's her essence; she is, in her singing style, mulatto.

Thus it is not enough to note that Scott Joplin wrote some pretty music or that Duke Ellington's orchestra traveled the world. Our history must make clear the larger point: that without African slaves, there would have been no George Gershwin or Richard Rodgers to forge the American musical theater tradition; that the swing sound of Benny Goodman and Artie Shaw, sung to by Sinatra, would never have developed; that there would be no Elvis Presley, Beatles, or Rolling Stones; that the songs of Bob Dylan and Alanis Morissette and Kurt Cobain and Britney Spears would simply not exist. Without Africans, there would today be no white people "rockin'" or feeling the groove. We must be aware that if success in America requires a degree of "assimilation"—and it will for us as it has for everyone else— white Americans have become "blacker" in the meantime.

One objection one often hears is that this is just "white people stealing our musical styles." But come on—if they did not, then the same people would be saying that it was evidence that they hated us. Imitation is the sincerest form of flattery, even if it is only a first step when it comes to races coming together.

Then there is the variation: "White people are always stealing our musical styles and selling them back to us." But we underestimate ourselves here. As far back as the twenties, black people bought a lot more Bessie Smith and Louis Armstrong than imitators Bing Crosby or Bix Beiderbecke. In the 1970s, few black people were swooning to the Captain and Tennille over the Spinners. And today, Vanilla Ice and Eminem have accounted for a mere sliver of black Americans' music budgets—hip-hop has seen no "Elvis." Black people have always preferred black artists.

What is really happening is that white people are selling "our" musical styles *to each other*. Only a tiny number of white artists hewing to the white classical tradition become superstars. To really hit the big time in mainstream America requires singing and playing in a way that would be unheard of if Africans had not been brought here. To put a point on it, the mustachioed or petticoated white American of 1900 watching Aerosmith or Jewel would lean over to their companion and wonder why "those white people are up there singing like *niggers!*" A battle has been won here—we're inside of them and most of them don't even know it anymore. This is harmony in the best sense of the term.

"But it's white people who are making money off of Aerosmith and Jewel," one might respond. But this brings us back to hip-hoppers' "bling bling"—plenty of black people are raking in the bucks from pop music these days. In our moment, it is virtually expected that the young black rapper will form his own produc-tion company. Why must we dismiss ourselves by treating Russell Simmons, "P. Diddy," Jay-Z, and even Quincy Jones as "excep-tions"? And these people's life stories give no evidence that they are spectacularly gifted or unique, nor do any of their stories hinge on Horatio Alger–style "lucky breaks." They are simply hungry businessmen, who parlayed their stick-to-it-iveness into riches. Let's treat them as inspirations. We diss them and our-selves otherwise.

"But the really big recording companies are all run by white men," we may hear. But then at the end of 2001, a black man of blue-collar origins, Richard Parsons, was appointed chief execu-tive officer of AOL Time Warner. This is an important landmark—let's get it into the history books.

▪ *Temper the "stereotype" analysis of the black performance her-itage.* As I argued in Chapter Four, the New Double Conscious-ness's imperative to seek rot behind all black success has led to a tradition among black thinkers to nimbly frame all black popular performances as "stereotypes." Certainly there is some room for this argument: that much of what black performers once had to settle for was demeaning is obvious, and the eye-rolling and shuf-fling of Stephin Fetchit and Mantan Moreland will not serve as sources of pride. But since then, opportunities have opened up for blacks to express themselves in more dignified and honest performances.

But meanwhile, a tradition has frozen that reflexively con-demns almost anything any black performer ventures to do. This teaches many blacks to be ashamed of one of their people's most vibrant contributions to this country.

The saddest thing is when the "stereotype" obsession relegates valuable work to footnotes when it does not fit the program. Allen Woll's *Black Musical Theatre*, currently the only comprehensive survey of the subject, devotes loving attention to the early musicals mired in tropes a few steps beyond minstrel shows. Woll's work here is stellar. But he largely rushes through the musicals of the second half of the century, though these include Langston Hughes's gospel musicals (who knew Hughes even *wrote* musicals?) and other shows depicting blacks positively such as *Purlie* (where black ingenuity trumps white supremacy) and *The Tap Dance Kid* (the one and only Broadway musical since the 1920s about the black middle class).

In other words, the fact that Bert Williams had to wear blackface makeup cannot be seen as a more urgent message for us than that in 1957, Langston Hughes's *Simply Heavenly*, a quiet tale about simple goings-on among working-class black folk, was one of the hottest tickets in New York. One character's opinion on the "stereotype" issue bears repeating:

> Why, it's getting so colored folks can't do nothing no more without some other Negro calling you a stereotype. Stereotype, hah! If you like a little gin, you're a stereotype. You got to drink Scotch. If you wear a red dress, you're a stereotype. You got to wear beige or chartreuse. Lord have mercy, honey, do-don't like no black-eyed peas and rice! Then you're a down-home Negro for true—which I is—and proud of it!

■ *There have always been whites who supported black uplift.* Obviously white Americans will take a major beating in any sensible black history. But we cannot condemn whites for stereotyping us while letting it pass when black writers dwell in rhetoric tarring whites as innately evil to the core.

We must not forget that as early as the late 1700s, Quakers argued widely for the abolition of slavery and beckoned blacks into their churches. We must not forget that starting in the 1830s, William Lloyd Garrison and other white abolitionists often put their very lives in danger arguing against slavery. Garrison and his cohort sincerely saw slavery as incompatible with both Christian teachings and the Constitution's appeal to the rights of man. There is nothing of the canny operator in Garrison's call in the first issue of *The Liberator* that "I am in earnest—I will not excuse—I will not retreat a single inch—AND I WILL BE HEARD." Next to the numbers of slaves wrested from Africa, we must hear that many northern states abolished slavery in the late 1700s, that in 1837 Massachusetts, New York, and Ohio were together home to 633 abolitionist societies, and that the following year the American Anti-Slavery Society had 250,000 members.

And the abolitionist imperative was strong enough to help motivate the Civil War. Yes, many northerners' investment in it was pragmatic, stemming from a wariness of economic competition from the South and even a distaste for the increase in the black population that extending slavery into new territories would entail. But the formation of the Republican party was based just as much on a sense that human beings must not be in bondage, and Lincoln even flouted the Constitution more than once with this in mind. Not for nothing has the Emancipation Proclamation been called "one of the greatest confiscations of private property in Anglo-Saxon history."

To be sure, the typical Republican of the period was only disposed to take this concern so far. Republicans revealed themselves as men of their time in eventually letting Reconstruction slide when issues of power and money came to the fore. There is nothing to sing about here in itself. But it was a start, showing glimmerings of humanity whose potential was borne out later in the Civil Rights revolution when white students were among the Freedom Riders taking beatings in the South. If nineteenth-century Republicans' opposition to slavery had been purely practical, they would not have even ventured a preliminary effort to usher black men into high positions across America after the Civil War. There was, after all, not yet a substantial body of black votes to appeal to.

Nor must we allow the impression that white indignation over racial injustice was limited to people with three names frozen in daguerreotypes. The following simple fact ought to occur in any black history text: the NAACP was founded by white people. At the founding of the organization, Du Bois was nervously awaiting word as to just how he would be included, and he was *appointed* editor of the organization's house organ, *The Crisis*. And one searches in vain for any indication that founding white NAACP stalwarts like William English Walling, Joel Springarn, and Mary White Ovington were motivated by anything but a human revulsion at how blacks were treated in their time.

Black people growing up since the 1960s have seen a Civil Rights movement largely dominated by various stripes of black radical. One thing that will help blacks develop a sense of hope in their country is the knowledge that a passionate devotion to helping blacks has been one variation on "whiteness"—a minority one, but vital—since the very beginning of our republic.

■ *White charity can cripple as easily as uplift.* There is a dominant concern among many blacks that whites not be "let off the hook" in addressing the legacies of the racist past. This concern is reasonable on its face. But a useful black history will show that whites eager to show their awareness of the hook they are hanging on have done us as much damage as good.

Namely, black Americans must be regularly taught that the expansion of welfare in the late 1960s created the unique desolation of today's inner cities. Many blacks look at the inner cities and assume that "racism" trapped people there. Add to this the common reflex to see inner-city blacks as most of the race, or at least "real" blacks, and the result is a misconception that after the Civil Rights Act, whitey kept his foot on most of our necks.

Many blacks add another wrinkle to this analysis, seeing black classism as another factor leaving other blacks at the mercy of The Man. One often hears that black districts went to ruin when disloyal "bourgeois" blacks moved away as soon as they were allowed to. The idea here is that blacks without middle-class "role models" next door could not help but sink into misery. Finally, it is assumed that inner-city blacks were further done in when blue-collar jobs moved to the suburbs or disappeared. So—what created what we see when we drive through a ghetto was that, first, whites wouldn't give black people jobs, then, those few who managed to get them picked up and left, and after that, what jobs there were moved away.

But this scenario does not hold water when we widen our lens. For one thing, as I mentioned in Chapter Three, black employment was on the rise when welfare was expanded.

And then, okay, the black bourgeoisie left. But abject poverty has not led to rampant criminality, substance abuse, and illegitimacy in India. Nor did it among Lower East Side Jews of New York City in the early 1900s. Why did this district not become a violent crime zone when no one who made enough money to move uptown had any hesitation in doing so? Poor Jewish boys down on Delancey Street did not need middle-class role models living next door to keep them from knocking up women and dealing in bootleg liquor. The argument that black people were helpless after the doctors and lawyers moved away is a hollow one, which one never hears applied to anyone on earth but black people in the United States in the 1950s and 1960s.

The falsity of the poverty argument is especially clear in a look at what a black "ghetto" was like before the late 1960s. There were certainly black slums, and an example was our Bronzeville by the 1950s, after the Depression had dulled its edge. Typical lodgings for poor people were dirty, overcrowded tenement buildings subdivided into one-room "kitchenettes," where families shared hallway bathrooms. All blacks lived under a racism more overt than anything imaginable to us today. Only six out of seventy-seven hospitals in Chicago accepted blacks, and five of them enforced quotas beyond which blacks were turned away. (And remember this was Chicago, not the deep South.) Police officers routinely singled out, harassed, and beat black people, with no glossy exposés in national newspapers or antidiscrimination laws to address it.

Yet Bronzeville was no disaster zone. It was a fundamentally stable community, knit together by the churches, black-owned businesses, and widely read newspapers we have seen. Crucially, the two-parent family was still, while hardly universal, a norm; Bronzeville was not a district of single mothers and deadbeat dads. One did not tour Bronzeville shocked by a culture celebrating violence, turning a blind eye to parental neglect, and condoning dependence on the government. In his study of black Chicago in this period, Alan Ehrenhalt notes that a crucial distinction between Bronzeville and today's Chicago inner-city areas was a basic sense of posterity, a constructive, optimistic orientation toward the future—and this amid the naked racism I have mentioned.

What all of this means is that poverty alone does not create the violent cityscapes of New Jack City. We neither read nor hear of such acrid hopelessness in black communities until the late 1960s—this is not, for example, the Harlem that James Baldwin or Claude Brown depicted in their work.

There are strategies the victimhood squad have to parry facts like this, but they fail as well. We cannot claim that religion makes people in India and the Lower East Side Jews different. For one, second-generation New York Jews were, as often as not, rather secular in their religious orientation—the *Partisan Review* intellectuals and the Broadway tunesmiths like Irving Berlin were not exactly yarmulke types. And meanwhile, black people are today a fervently, unquestioningly Christian people.

Nor can we claim that it is unfair to compare ourselves to immigrants, under the idea that immigrants have a unique drive to make it. People in India are not immigrants into their own country. And again, blacks in the late 1800s and early 1900s were long-standing residents of the United States and spoke nothing but English, and yet look what they did.

Then there is the argument that black people were left bereft when factories moved to the suburbs. But it is too seldom asked why blacks did not simply move where the work was, as so many had when migrating North. In 1992, the mainstream media celebrated Nicholas Lehmann's *The Promised Land*, depicting poor blacks in the teens and twenties moving thousands of miles north for work with sacks on their back. But then five years later, the new flavor of the month was William Julius Wilson's *When Work Disappears*, depicting those blacks' grandchildren as mysteriously incapable of following work two bus rides away. Few noticed the paradox here. But peel away the leftist brainwashing, and the questions pour forth:

1. If public transit was inadequate, then *why didn't they just move?*
2. If suburban housing discrimination was the reason they did not, then why are so many cities today surrounded by a suburban "inner belt" that black people have lived in for decades, where "the culture of poverty" is nevertheless well ensconced, while whites have long since moved out to the "outer belt"? Was there really *nowhere* in the suburbs for black people to live?
3. Why didn't the blacks who did not move take the jobs remaining in the city, now easily found and often dominated by immigrants?

4. What stopped these black people from opening their own businesses as black people had sixty years before, in an America where black people couldn't even get a hotel room or try on clothes at department stores?

I do not ask these questions merely to criticize, but to lead to a point. The reason so many black people just sat on their hands and descended into slovenly dependence in the late 1960s was that the expansion of welfare deprived them of any urgent reason to do otherwise. Some people are naturally driven; just as many strive because they have to. Welfare brought out the worst in human nature in the latter group among blacks. Translated into a thesis that should inform a new black history, misguided white benevolence created the inner-city hell that our Tupac Shakurs depict.

Many blacks suppose that critics of welfare are merely "racists" rearing their ugly heads. "There are more whites on welfare than blacks" is an oft-heard factoid. But with black people accounting for less than a tenth of the population, obviously mere head counts are not the issue. What matters is the *proportion* of blacks who have been on welfare, and the extent to which they clustered in communities and drifted into living on the dole as a lifestyle.

And this traced to the New Left in the 1960s, who joined forces with new black state officials pandering for votes to expand what began as a safety net for widows into what we would today call "reparations" for blacks. A bureaucracy was created to pay unmarried black mothers to have children and spend their lives on the dole. Sure, lots of black people stepped past this. They now constitute our black middle class. But just as many did not—it is a human universal that self-discipline is unequally distributed among individuals. Expanded welfare encouraged the worst in human nature among those blacks least inclined to resist it.

Yet both the public intellectuals and the state-level bureaucrats responsible for this remain unrepentant today. Goodly white guilt teaches them that what they would condemn in their own poorest relatives is "understandable" among poor blacks. Whitey really done us wrong this time: the expansion of welfare created more black misery than any number of brutal policemen, white thugs yelling "nigger," real estate agents turning black applicants away, or white teachers not calling on black boys in school.

The facts here are not difficult, but they are virtually unknown outside of books and articles largely read by academics and the punditocracy. It also does not help that one of their most readable and closely argued presentations, *Losing Ground,* is not only long out of print, but was written by Charles Murray, who later ruined his reputation among leftists (including most blacks) with *The Bell Curve.* But Murray's claim in that later book that blacks are less intelligent than whites does not, in itself, invalidate his conclusions about the effectiveness of welfare. Few (myself included) think that welfare should be abolished completely. But Murray's basic position, that open-ended handouts do not help people, is echoed by many concerned white liberals, as well as more than a few black thinkers. I have seen the truth about welfare enlighten young black people, when presented properly, into realizing the dangers in the seductive but pernicious idea that "Civil Rights" means seeking open-ended handouts. (See the Afterword for sources on welfare in America in the 1960s.)

A useful black history must spread this message more widely. The sense that the inner cities are the fault of racism and classism is a prime factor in so many young blacks' rejection of the establishment in favor of the street. This is only logical given the narrow range of facts they are currently exposed to. A concretely uplifting black history will treat the true story of welfare as every bit as crucial a landmark in black history as *Plessy v. Ferguson*.

▪ *The African language black Americans learn should be Mende.* Finally, as a linguist I feel moved to make a suggestion that we supplement the use of Swahili as a way of getting in touch with our African past.

As things stand, thousands of black people are taking courses in a language that none of our ancestors spoke. Swahili is unknown on the west coast of Africa where slaves in America were taken from, and it is likely that not a single slave brought to this country spoke it. The *"Jambo* means *Hello"* tradition is as off-kilter as Jewish descendants of Eastern European immigrants going around saying *Bonjour!* to one another out of a sense that "many Europeans speak French."

Mende, on the other hand, is spoken in Sierra Leone. So many Mende-speaking slaves were brought to South Carolina that some older blacks there still sing songs in the language (although no longer recalling the meaning of the words). This and other cultural connections between South Carolina's Gullah Creole-speaking culture and Sierra Leone are so strong that delegations from the two areas have recently reestablished contact. Mende is thus a piece of black Americans' linguistic ancestry that still survives in traces, and is revivable with the help of actual African speakers now concretely interested in revivifying the tie. The current wars and desolation in Sierra Leone will, hopefully, lead to many of its residents moving to the United States in the near future, which will ensure a large number of people who could serve as teachers.

Like many languages spoken on Africa's upper west coast, Mende is tonal—"melody" plays as important a role in conveying specific meaning as the shapes of the words themselves. Black folk speech retains an echo of this in its "musical" intonation. While Black English is in no sense the African language with English words that some writers have claimed, Mende has a "sound" that black Americans might recognize as related to their own intonational patterns. Swahili, on the other hand, is not tonal.

Finally Mende happens to belong to a subgroup of African languages that are relatively easy as languages go. English speakers have a hard enough time dealing with European languages' division of nouns into two or three genders taking different articles and endings. But many languages our ancestors spoke, like Wolof and Kikongo, have eight or more genders. Meanwhile, the tones in languages like Yoruba and Twi are so complicated that learning such languages is as difficult for an English speaker as mastering Chinese. Like all languages, Mende is by no means "simple." Learning any foreign language takes some doing, and even Mende's tones take some practice. But there are no *amo-amas-amat* lists of conjugations, no gender on the nouns, words tend to be on the short side, and there are no sounds one essentially has to be born into to render decently.

A new black history would ideally include a revival of Mende, an interesting and accessible language still lingering in the mouths of some black Americans as I write. This connection will be much more vivid than a forced one with Swahili.

———

The need for a positive history is more urgent for black Americans than for any other American ethnic group. The misimpression that our story is simply one of whites having "hulled us empty," as Randall Robinson has it, is a prime factor in the ambivalence many blacks feel toward taking advantage of the opportunities before us.

This sense of America as what we're stuck with rather than our home too often leads us to make the worst of our history repeat itself. Chary of "whiteness," blacks today enforce the "one-drop" rule as vigilantly as white segregationists once did. Celebrating rebellion against The Man, black pop culture enshrines the very pathologies that early Civil Rights leaders decried whites for associating with us. Seeing whites' guilt as just deserts, prominent black leaders treat black progress as a dirty secret just like bigoted white officials in the old days.

A history depicting occasional superstars rising out of a vale of tears will not help get us out of this holding pattern. Ideally, these bright lights will have more meaning to blacks of the future, and we must keep their memory alive in preparation for that day. But they will only truly speak to us when we are steeped in a new paradigm—an energetic chronicle of what *ordinary* blacks have been able to accomplish in this country *communally,* and how their doing so left indelible cultural imprints upon whites. Only when resistance is not the measure of the "authenticity" of black figures will we be able to spontaneously engage with such people as humans first. Only then will Wheatley's poetry and George Washington Carver's feats with the peanut truly touch us, instead of sitting as inert symbols of people we privately feel as only dimly relevant to us today.

We first need a new series of black history textbooks, aimed at the elementary, middle, and high school levels. They must not focus on sound-bite presentations of isolated black "heroes," but on celebrating how blacks of all levels of society and accomplishment have made the most of their situation in America over the past four hundred years. The heroes must be incorporated as much as possible into this theme.

The injustices and setbacks must be given full play—it would be a crime to leave young black people naïve of what we have been through, or with a sunny 1940s history primer's view of what America means. But even here, the guiding impulse must be gut-level inspiration rather than therapy. For Mba Mbulu, the atrocities serve as a lesson in the depravity of whites, the upshot being a call for a vague "solidarity" in the future. The essence of the message is merely "Watch out." The new black history textbook's message must be "Here's how," utilizing past horrors as a tool for highlighting that we got past them and how we did it.

At present, there exist no standard black history texts distributed by the leading textbook publishers. Most black history "textbooks" are marginally distributed tracts from the Afrocentrist fringe. Typical is Jawanza Kunjufu's *Lessons from History: A Celebration in Blackness,* which "celebrates" us as "Africans" who were the first humans to develop writing and worship a single God (none of which is even true). Otherwise, we get a pageant of black

American "greats" (who we are told invented the stove, the refrigerator, soap, ink, shampoo, and the third rail), a running indictment of whites, and near the end an ominous piece of advice that "Racial unity is more important than community differences." No—the last thing a race brought here in chains needs is history books based on untruths that teach black children that they live in hell and should avoid forming their own opinions. For a race so wary of its own home, a historiography highlighting the foreign, the extraordinary, and the tragic will yield neither peace, healing, nor pride.

John Hope Franklin's sober and detailed *From Slavery to Freedom* is the most prominent exception to the usual genre, published by McGraw-Hill and periodically revised for decades. The book is useful and, within its bounds, a minor masterpiece. But it cannot inspire. It is ultimately more concerned with obstacles than victory, leaving the uninformed reader with little hope for a better future. Neither Bronzeville nor Dunbar High appears in the index. Booker T. Washington is damned with faint praise. The emergence of inner-city wastelands is blithely traced to white flight. Welfare and Affirmative Action each get a single passing mention, and blacks' contributions to the performing arts get a total of about three pages.

Obviously, then, we cannot rely on the black radical left to write the new black history. But since the 1960s, it has almost always been people of this political stripe who have been driven to write black history texts. Black scholars and thinkers of genuinely progressive ideologies—including conservative ones—currently have a new responsibility: to step up to the plate and compose accessible black history books to get black America back on the track the early Civil Rights movement set us on. Black writers outside of the Molefi Kete Asante camp must resist writing only for the literati and the converted. To do so leaves the field open to the Prodigal Sons confusing guiltmongering for uplift. And future young black history professors who can see beyond the New Double Consciousness could do their race no greater service than penning new black history textbooks that teach black children something beyond idealizations of Africa and testy vigilance.

Only the kind of new black history I have outlined can play a meaningful role in getting black America to the point where we can afford the luxury of ahistoricism. It is, for better or for worse, an American tradition to assume that it's okay to look back as long as you don't stare. Blacks' history in America makes that message especially urgent. Just now we need to stare awhile longer—but only at the things that will give us the strength to eventually face forward for good.

8

Black Academics and Doing the Right Thing

"They Don't Care What You Know Till They Know That You Care"?

■ ■ ■

This essay is an expansion of a piece I wrote for City Journal *in the wake of Cornel West's contretemps with Harvard president Lawrence Summers in early 2002. Leaving Harvard for Princeton when Summers questioned the trajectory of his career, West neatly acted out the black intellectual's rendition of the New Double Consciousness—a sense that giving the finger to the white oppressor is the very Soul of Black Folk. But that's not what Du Bois meant.* ■

Over the past year and a half, as I write this, I have tossed my hat into the public intellectual fray. I am a contributing editor for *The New Republic* and *City Journal,* am often called upon to write for other publications, and am regularly consulted by the media for my views on race issues and beyond. I also do public speaking engagements around the country, generally about once a month.

But by day I am an academic linguist. Over the past ten years I have written two academic books and about twenty-five academic articles on linguistics. I'm not bragging—this is what linguists do.

To be sure, I would not wish any of this linguistics work on anyone beyond a few hundred academics. In these books and articles I engage in an ongoing conversation about highly specific, abstract issues that only a linguist could love.

Yet as much as I relish my academic work, I have always been troubled by the hermetic nature of modern academia. Most academic books are quickly consigned to university libraries, stripped of their dust jackets, and consulted only by the occasional graduate student or professor. Academic articles sit hidden in journals unknown to the general public, the issues annually gathered between hardback covers and sent to those same dusty university library shelves.

This was not what I had in mind when, at five years old, I told my mother that I wanted to be "a book writer." Humanity would be poorer without a caste dedicated to forging new frontiers of thought, and over time, the best of such work does often penetrate the general consciousness. But I have always been driven to also write nonfiction for the general public that would actually be engaged outside of the ivory tower. In recent years I have written several books for the lay reader on both race and linguistics.

But I have taken this on as a *second* career. I still produce a linguistics article every few months. As soon as I began putting the finishing touches on this book, I started writing an academic paper examining whether the endings in language, such as the *–ed* that marks the past on words like *walked,* is innate to our species.

As I write, I am leading a graduate seminar that will produce a book-length grammatical description of a language spoken by descendants of Africans who escaped from plantations in Surinam and founded communities in the interior of the country that survive to this day. Meanwhile, my current linguistic research beyond this will culminate in a new academic book in a few years. After I chip away at the voluminous e-mail correspondence I get every day regarding public issues, I settle down to exchanges with linguists around the world on the topics that this academic book will treat. And neither that book nor the grammatical description of Saramaccan Creole will net me any talk show appearances.

And in this, I am *ordinary*. Public intellectuals with academic posts regularly produce papers for their discipline that few of us could get through at gunpoint, and this even enhances their public writings. My last book for the general public treated how languages change and mix. But it was a "translation" of years of my academic research. And even my undergraduate teaching would long ago have gone stale if I did not have new insights to bring to my lectures from my current research.

———

I find myself thinking about these things in light of Cornel West's leaving Harvard for Princeton in 2002. The new president, Lawrence Summers, in one consultation out of many he scheduled with prominent Harvard professors, suggested to West that he return to producing new original academic research. West is well known for his lucrative career as a speaker on the lecture circuit, and at the time had recently recorded a rap CD (West preferred that it be called "spoken word") and supported Al Sharpton's bid for the presidency. West widely aired that he felt "disrespected" by Summers's suggestion, and even after a second consultation where Summers apologized and then followed up by offering several more olive branches during the semester, West finally decided to pack up and leave for Princeton.

By the time you read this, the episode will be virtually forgotten. In long view it was just a minor media flap during a slow news period after Christmas. Indeed, it quickly became fashionable among more moderately minded black observers to dismiss the whole thing as "overblown" (rather like many of the same sorts were suddenly "tired" of the O.J. Simpson affair as his guilt became ever clearer). But the story had a larger import than some realized.

Many on the black left objected that West's academic *gravitas* was confirmed by his having written well over a dozen books. But really, for academics, there are books and there are books. I always cringe a bit inside, for example, when I am introduced as having written "seven books." One of them is more of a booklet for teachers, and another is an edited anthology of other scholars' papers that I gathered and checked over. It is not always clear outside of academia that when one is *editor* of a book, one is toastmaster, not author. The editor did not write what is between the covers. And if the editor contributes an "introduction," it is usually just that—a dozen or so pages of scene-setting. It presents neither original research nor, usually, particularly fresh insights. For an academic, introductions are, in a word, toss-offs. Not long from now, this book will be counted as one of my own "books," and yet I consider it more a collection of essays most of which I had already published elsewhere. And since none of these essays are intended as scholarly treatises, I will never consider this book an academic credential.

In this vein, West had certainly written some academic volumes in his field, philosophy, but he had published these a decade and more ago. West's books since he had become a media celebrity were all either edited anthologies, collections of pieces written for the media (like this book), or coauthored books for the general public. An example of the latter is West's collaboration with Henry Louis Gates, Jr., *The African-American Century*. The book itself is lovely, a coffee-table collection of mini-biographies of black heroes and heroines. I hope the book sold well. But the fact is that the biographical sketches were researched not by Gates and West but by assistants (many of them regurgitating contributions they had made to Gates's and Kwame Anthony Appiah's *Africana* encyclopedia), and the book does not present any original research.

Surely, even West's body of work is no mean feat—but these are not academic books. Certainly not all of them are puff pieces; many are on serious topics. But when I appeared on a news program debating the issue with Michael Eric Dyson, Dyson appeared to suppose that a book is "academic" as long as it has an earnest title and lots of footnotes. But this is not the standard that has long prevailed in academia. Scholars are evaluated for promotions on the basis of books written for their academic peers, and reviewed before publication by two or three such fellow scholars. A book not subject to this kind of peer review is considered a different animal. My *Losing the Race*, for example, is not an academic book despite coming in at almost three hundred pages and having a longish bibliography. It did not count in my promotion file, nor would it have even if I were a sociologist instead of a linguist. The simple fact is that serious academics have always been expected to produce a steady stream of *academic* work.

Of course West proudly identifies with the class of "scholar activists." As such, he sees it as morally urgent that he communicate steadily with the general public. And there is not a thing wrong with this. But many people in his position attempt to maintain a foothold in the academic realm.

To be sure, it's a delicate balance. Today I do not write as many linguistics articles as I used to. I even took a year's leave of absence from UC Berkeley to write a new book for the general public, couching observations on language within my sociopolitical positions. However, at the same time I continued writing the book on Saramaccan Creole, as well as other linguistics articles I had in the works. And as often as not, my academic career impinges on my public one: I turn down quite a few requests to write and speak in favor of maintaining my linguistics output. And once again, this is just par for the course for academics who double as public intellectuals. It's what we do.

In contrast Gerald Early of Washington University, among those defending West and dismissing the episode as "overblown," implied that the issue is a matter of either-or: "I think universities would prefer that people were able to do high-level, specialized scholarship while also speaking to the broader audience. Very few people can do that." But this would surprise Richard Posner, Lani Guinier, Steven Pinker, Randall Kennedy, and legions of other university intellectuals who have based their careers on switch-hitting between the academic and the popular. Stephen Jay Gould spent two decades writing a monthly column for *Natural History*, monographs for the reading public, and media commentaries crusading against creationism and scientific ignorance. But at the same time he maintained his strictly academic output on snails, and just prior to his death had produced a massive summation of his theoretical perspectives that few will take to the beach, *The Structure of Evolutionary Theory.*

Yet West felt "insulted" that anyone would ask why he had not followed a similar trajectory. Or more specifically, racially discriminated against. West was circumspect on that charge with most interviewers. But letting his hair down in an interview on National Public Radio with a fawning Tavis Smiley, he suggested that now that there were sixteen tenured black faculty at Harvard, there were "ripples among the alumni" fearing that "the Negroes are taking over," and that these white folks were just going to have to get used to a "new reality."

———

Now, at this point, one might expect that I would launch into an attack on West's academic credentials. But no—since I am not trained in philosophy or theology, I would be stepping outside of my expertise to do so. David Horowitz and Leon Wieseltier have "gone there," as they say. Some are put off by West's writing style. But West's tone—which is indeed bloviatory and self-involved as philosophical writing goes—is one part the black preaching tradition and one part showing off that a black person knows big words and has read Big Thinkers. West expects us to "get" this as a kind of cheeky performance, compensating for centuries of debasement of black intellect. Whether this routine floats your boat or not, cavils about form leave substance unaddressed. Theoretically, one could contribute eminently coherent arguments within just such "performative" phraseology.

And I have seen no criticisms of the logical foundations of West's work that might not be aimed at other eminent philosophers. There is no more requirement that his thought be impervious to question than that, say, Isaiah Berlin's be. One might quibble that West's celebrity played as large a role as his academic substance in capping him a coveted University Professor title at Harvard. Or, all right, that the celebrity played the *main* role. But then again, Isaiah Berlin got quite a bit of mileage out of being a deathlessly charming drawing room raconteur, and more than a few see his reputation as larger than his actual work deserved. Star quality plays its hand throughout life and neither academia nor "blackademia" are exceptions. More to the point, racial equality will mean not only that there will be sober, unassailably heavyweight black intellectuals toiling in obscurity, but glitzier black celebrity intellectuals as well, taking their place alongside white equivalents.

And in any case, charges that West is an utter "lightweight" cannot stand based merely on his jiving presence at the podium, and are incomplete without one's having actually plowed through his early works such as *The American Evasion of Philosophy: A Genealogy of Pragmatism* or *The Ethical Dimension of Marxist Thought* (which I most certainly have not). Nor can I join those who imply that anyone who does forty speaking engagements a year must by definition not be keeping up with his field. In my experience, one can get an awful lot of reading done on planes and in hotel rooms.

The problem with West's response to Summers was more specific. Namely, there are other responses he could have had than crying "racism." For example, he could have argued that he has decided to temporarily suspend his academic work, feeling a duty to lend his voice and pen to the urgency of the race dilemma in America. This would have been a legitimate argument, even if some may have disagreed.

But instead, West implied something different and truly disturbing: that recording a rap CD and supporting Al Sharpton were an *equal substitute* for traditional academic work. In the Smiley interview he implied that these constituted a new "visionary," "ennobling" paradigm of inquiry, and that Princeton provost Amy Gutmann was morally and intellectually superior to Summers in understanding this and seeking West's services. Toni Morrison similarly defended West as "brilliant" but "on the ground."

But to pretend that anything West puts on paper—footnotes or not—is "scholarship" is not only disingenuous, but verges on reviving racist stereotypes. No one white or black would propose that Stephen Ambrose's line of pop history texts qualifies him as a leading academic historian, and no amount of concern for racial uplift can justify evaluating black scholars any differently. The implication looms that for black scholars only, serious academic work is a kind of party trick that gets you in the door, but after that, motivational musings qualify as the highest level of thought. Surely this is not what West's patron saint W. E. B. Du Bois had in mind, supreme "activist-scholar" that he was.

Yet lurking behind West's studied sense of "insult" was a coded wink to black people that Summers's approach to him was racism on the march—"the Negroes are taking over." But I see a different subtext here: that serious academic work is optional for black intellectuals, and that to require it of a black scholar, especially after a certain point, is a racist insult.

Since the publication of *Losing the Race* a certain contingent, concentrated in the education school mill, have dismissed my claim that black American culture has a powerful anti-intellectual strain as a distortion that promulgates a "stereotype." But West's response was an eloquent demonstration of exactly what I meant. I proposed that too often, black students as well as academics quietly see intellectual endeavors as clothes rather than skin. It's not that black parents do not send their children to college, or that black culture does not *overtly* esteem scholarly accomplishment. The problem is that once "black identity" was equated in the 1960s with maintaining a wary distrust of whitey, it naturally followed that the scholarly realm, traditionally run by whites, was seen as something tangential to "blackness."

Sure, you're allowed to "fake it"—for example, you might make your mark by writing a few "Poindexter" books at first. But at the end of the day, we black people are "intuitive," "down with it." Or, the main thing about being black is that whites oppress us, and therefore the "real" black person is devoted primarily to protest—there's nothing quite as authentically black as opposition, "speaking truth to power."

Following from these tacit yet decisive sentiments is that being a brainiac is a costume—like West's trademark three-piece suit. He is well known for brandishing this garb as a gesture toward the sartorial fashion of his hero Du Bois, and is chary of the dress-down fashion among today's white academics. But still, in our era, when academics of boomer age and younger are a rather dress-down crowd, a three-piece suit on an academic is a costume—not skin. "Skin" is a rap CD where West signals his allegiance to Tupac Shakur's homies. Gimme some skin.

But can West not see that this message—that black intellect is only legitimate when wielded as a costume and purveyed into street protest—only reinforces the stereotype of black mental dimness that feeds the very racism he is so quick to sniff out? Apparently not, and it is the New Double Consciousness that obscures this for him. When one of just sixteen of the elite class of University Professors at Harvard University insists that he is exempt from regular participation in academic debate because of the color of his skin, he reveals a private sense that something besides academic credentials qualifies him for his position. Namely, a sense hangs in the air that for black academics, it is how deftly one speaks up for professional victimhood that separates the men from the boys. Here "blackademia" meets the conviction that at the end of the day, resistance to whitey is the essence of black authenticity. Jesse Jackson's status as the closest thing to black America's "leader" is obviously a parallel, and thus it was nothing less than predictable that Jackson dutifully showed up in Cambridge to lend his support to West's *cri de coeur*.

To wit: "I am lucky [West is a rich man living in luxury], but most of black America lives with the white man's boot on their necks. Thus as a moral African-American, I must engage with black people on the visceral, emotional level that desperate victims deserve [rapping to the beat], and canvass for Al Sharpton since he is America's Vice-President of Victimology. Nay, for an Authentically Black person and only for him, speechifying and putting my arm around Sharpton are a new, 'ennobling' form of intellectual engagement. It would be idle and even disloyal of me to devote more than a symbolic amount of time to spinning out carefully reasoned arguments regarding philosophy or theology in a format developed by the oppressor."

———

Certainly we need intellectuals to communicate with the general public. I have always been dismayed that so few academics feel called to do so. There is not even anything wrong with an academic recording a rap CD, especially the rather low-key, didactic one West recorded. But let's face it—"visionary" or not, rap is not Heidegger, and no amount of affection from the street corner can erase this obvious truth. Denying it smacks dangerously of embracing the old canard that black people are America's entertainers, and it is any pretense otherwise that is racist.

Then West would also seem to consider supporting Al Sharpton's presidency as a "visionary" recasting of what it means to be an intellectual. But above all, the academic is dedicated to seeking truth, and Al Sharpton is, quite simply, an inveterate liar. He leveled a rape charge at a district attorney conclusively shown to be false, but has steadfastly refused to admit the lie for fear of alienating his constituency. When a white woman was raped and beaten in Central Park in 1989 by black youths, he insisted against all evidence that her boyfriend was the culprit. Sharpton is also a shameless racist—another departure from truth—all but ringleading a race war between blacks and Jews in Crown Heights. ("If the Jews want to get it on, tell them to pin their yarmulkes back and come over to my house.")

Yet West sees nothing amiss in a University Professor at Harvard

standing publicly behind such a shamelessly mendacious charla-
tan—because, once again, Sharpton is if anything one of the kings
of victimology and thus "really black." "Brilliant" but "on the
ground," West here gives scholarly imprimatur to the illusion that
blacks' tragic history and imperfect present render us beyond serious judgment. In another development so dramatically apt that
a playwright couldn't have written it better, enter Sharpton himself, who got in his licks by threatening to sue Summers.

If over the next ten years I restricted my output to the popular
press and the lecture circuit, my department chair would certainly
call me out on the mat. And the only thing that would make her
a bigot would be not doing so.

———

Nothing better demonstrated the distorted view of what black intellect is about than that, in fact, when West was confronted by
Summers he was actually working on three academic books. This
was, on its face, staggering—the simple question is why West did
not mention this to the *New York Times* or in his interview with
"Brother Tavis." To take another "alternate universe" scenario,
when Summers suggested that West return to genuine scholarship, he would simply have responded that he was just then engaged in such work, felt this as a private triumph, and not have
alerted the media to the encounter at all.

But instead, West went public with his sense of "disrespect"
and "dishonor," played down that he was in fact engaged in exactly what Summers was asking of him, and finally left the university claiming that this was the only way he could preserve his
"dignity." This only made sense as an expression of a post–Civil

Rights sense of his role as a black academic. To wit: West felt that airing his sense of "insult" at being questioned was a more urgent message than announcing that he was writing three academic books. And more to the point, he considered it a mark of *dignity* to, of all things, turn tail. But wasn't there an alternate route to dignity? Okay, Summers is hardly the soul of tact, but then West was hardly the only Harvard professor he rubbed the wrong way on his arrival—Summers asked the Kennedy School of Government to specify just how they were preparing students for public service more effectively than the Law School or the Business School, and asked Richard Chait of the Graduate School of Education whether he thought his department was even necessary. None of these people resigned. Why, then, could West not stand his ground and show Summers that he was doing just what he was supposed to be doing, thus showing Summers's suspicions of him to be unwarranted?

Because for West, playing the victim *for the public* trumped showing us the money as an individual—the New Double Consciousness, Blackademia-style.

And the messages: (1) black scholars are too emotionally fragile to stand up to anything but the most gracious and worshipful treatment from white superiors, (2) it is racist to hold black scholars to mainstream standards of evaluation, and (3) it is "authentically black" to shout this from the rooftops. This is not what W. E. B. Du Bois meant in his analysis of the black "double consciousness," and he is turning in his grave.

9

The New Black Leadership

. . .

One of the most distracting clichés about the state of Black Amer-
ica is that black people are done in by "leaders preaching victim-
hood instead of self-reliance." This notion mistakes causes for effects.
So many black people see it as a responsibility to depict blackness as
a tragedy in public because of sociohistorical developments in the
1960s. The rabble-rousing leaders that get so much press today are
merely symptoms of those developments—if there happened to be
no Jesse Jackson types, the New Double Consciousness would have
just as strong a hold on the general population.

As such, these "official" black leaders will be irrelevant to black
progress. This essay has two goals. One is to make what I just wrote
clear, and the other is to show that there are real black leaders op-
erating behind the scenes. Contrary to what we hear so often, there
is no "crisis in black leadership." We just have to shake a habit of
assuming that the "black leader" teaches his flock how to hate
white people. ■

On a CNN special marking the tenth anniversary of the 1992 Los Angeles race riot, playwright and actress Anna Deavere Smith asked, "Why is it that there has not arisen a single young black leader in the past thirty, or even forty years?" One hears that question often in the black community. Too seldom is it realized, however, that there will never again be a "black leader" in the sense that Martin Luther King, Jr., and Malcolm X were—and that this is a heartening sign of progress.

Of course, many would consider Jesse Jackson today's "black leader." Yet so many keep asking where our black leaders are, revealing a prevalent sense that leadership has not been precisely what Jackson is about. He is surely a celebrity, but then so is Zsa Zsa Gabor.

In a hundred years, textbooks will record Adam Clayton Powell, Jr.'s pivotal role in desegregation efforts and the War on Poverty, Thurgood Marshall's performance in *Brown v. Board of Education*, and King's spearheading the outlawing of formal discrimination with the Civil Rights Act of 1964. Yet for all of his prominence, just what will Jackson be remembered as doing for the people in the black community who needed his help, as opposed to for himself?

Jackson made his earliest mark with Operation Breadbasket, a Chicago project that forced small companies to discontinue whites-only hiring policies through successful black boycotts. But before long he had transformed this into a source of patronage and personal income, always just escaping indictment when investigators began closing in. A pattern was set that continued as Operation

Breadbasket morphed into his PUSH and Rainbow Coalition, lately followed by the Wall Street Project.

Disguised with lofty-sounding mission statements appealing to "empowerment" and "fostering awareness," all of these organizations have spun variations on a Band-Aid conception of "Civil Rights." Jackson accuses an organization of racist hiring practices on thin pretenses. As payment for his holding off, he demands first that they throw business to black businessman "friends of Jesse," and second that they make a hefty payment to Jackson's Citizen's Education Fund, a branch of PUSH. Afterward, the friends of Jesse pony up with their own contributions to the CEF.

Lately Jackson's preferred strategy is to go after corporations when they announce plans for mergers, threatening to dent their profits and throw a wrench into the proceedings by tarring them as "racist" unless they pay up and throw business to Jackson's rich cronies. So before AT&T could merge with TCI in 1999, it had to donate $425,000 to the CEF, and then named Jackson's friend Ron Blaylock's investment bank as comanager of a massive bond offering.

Or when SBC Communications and Ameritech wanted to merge in 1998, Jackson came a-calling with a classist spin on the usual routine—the merger would be harmful to "low-income customers." SBC/Ameritech only came to be after a $500,000 contribution to the CEF; then when GTE bought half of Ameritech's cell phone operation, the CEF got $740,000. Finally, GTE and Bell Atlantic could only merge to become Verizon with another $800,000 to the CEF, plus a directed push to give contracts to minority-owned firms.

Sometimes Jackson varies the tune, simply milking a discrimination claim for favors to his black pals. When two black employees accused Boeing of racial discrimination in class-action lawsuits, Jackson flew in and utilized the occasion to net big bucks for the CEF plus business for investment banks owned by his friends.

Then there are times when no one profits but Jackson. When Deutsche Bank fired black broker Kevin Ingram for disastrous investments, an erratic work schedule, and cheating on his expense account, he brought Jackson in to "negotiate" a severance package estimated to be between $15 and $20 million (a source reported to Kenneth Timmerman that Jackson netted 10 percent of it.) And of course Ingram gave the CEF $50,000. Deutsche Bank, after all, was in a bind, at the time seeking a merger with Banker's Trust. Paying off America's highest-profile shakedown artist was better business than risking Jackson going public with his claim that Deutsche Bank had "other reasons" than performance in firing Ingram.

The CEF is purportedly dedicated to the seemingly well-intentioned goal of "the education of voters and the promotion of full participation in the electoral process." Yet time and again audits reveal considerable sums of money only vaguely accounted for, aside from funding Jackson's posh travel arrangements and speaking fees. In 1999, of the $10 million shaken down for the CEF from various corporations, only $553,232 went to a "Voter Registration Institute" and "youth development," while $1,346,164 went to Jackson's traveling in high style.

Jackson and his fans may see even this as some kind of

"progress"—getting black entrepreneurs their rightful share of the pie. But this would only make sense if white America remained staunchly opposed to black success, an idea compatible with Jackson's warmed-over Marxist leanings but counter to real life as the rest of us live it. In truth, Jackson's shakedown routine is Affirmative Action at its worst, denying black entrepreneurs the only way to learn to survive in the real, roustabout world—serious, no-net competition. Instead, Jackson has the companies buy their way into the game for the moment, but this just suckers these people with the temptations of the quick fix.

This is not lost on all of the friends of Jesse: a black Wall Streeter notes: "You've gotten paid, but you don't have a relationship . . . It's not as though they're going to use you the next time, unless they're forced." Another pal, Robert Knowling, was one of the "beneficiaries" of the GTE deal; his Covad Communications broadband company was going nowhere until Jackson hooked him up with Bell Atlantic. Yet Knowling himself would never dream of hiring on the basis of color. When a Fox News interviewer asked him, "Are you more inclined at Covad to hire African-Americans?" he quickly shot back, "No, I'm going to hire the best person for the job."

Knowling knows that, as they say, "Give a man a fish and he'll eat for a day, teach a man to fish and he'll eat forever." But Jackson just offers fish individually wrapped, and few are fully aware that behind the smoke and mirrors, this routine is the whole meal where he is concerned. His gestures toward any "leadership" beyond this have been token ones. Few people beyond political junkies actually know what the "Rainbow Coalition" is, and many assume from its name that it has something to do with, maybe, after-school programs for at-risk children of various races (I did for many years). But it is no such thing, nor has Jackson ever run such a thing. The "Rainbow Coalition" is, today, one of several labels for an operation whose main purpose has become to line the pockets of Jesse Jackson's rich friends, period. For all of his populist rhetoric, Jackson has left behind not a single sustained and successful project designed to improve black lives beyond the boardroom.

He is sure to pop up before the news cameras at any race-based fracas lending itself to an indignant speech: the two-year suspension of black high schoolers for brawling in the stands during an athletic event, Cornel West's indignation when Harvard president Lawrence Summers suggested that as a professor at an elite university, he go back to writing academic work, etc.

But stories are legion of Jackson's meanwhile turning down local, cash-strapped black organizations who call on him to appear on the behalf of causes just as urgent but less sensational, because such groups cannot afford his fat fees for speeches—imagine King having his aides blow off Mississippi Delta churches unless they could cough up thousands of dollars. And seeking international scope, he has forged relations with the likes of Yasser Arafat, Hafez Assad, Slobodan Milosevic, and African dictator thugs Sani Abacha, Charles Taylor, and Foday Sankoh. Jackson also ran for President a couple of times, but these were largely symbolic gestures of no meaning to black lives on the ground. And with friends abroad like his, we should be thankful that he has gotten no further in elected public office. (I derive most of these observations about Jackson from Kenneth Timmerman's *Shakedown*, which we must view not as a "black-bashing" tract but as an urgent document teaching us where we must direct our attention regarding black "leadership"—and where we must not.)

Celebrity is shallow, and Jackson will remain a rock star on sheer recognizability, combined with his oratorical knack. He has no effect on the lives of most black Americans, and as such he is nothing to worry about. But thirty-five years of his self-aggrandizing machinations confirm that one thing black Americans cannot expect from this man is leadership.

———

The reality is even clearer with Reverend Al Sharpton. Sharpton openly covets Jackson's mantle as "the" black leader in America, but where Jackson can at least coast on a certain presence in a room, Sharpton will remain an opportunistic cartoon.

Once again, after a decade and a half on the public stage, complete with an "organization," the National Action Network, as vague in mission as Rainbow/PUSH, Sharpton would be hard-pressed to point to one positive development in black New York, much less America, that he was responsible for. Congressman Charles Rangel, despite warming to Sharpton in recent years, notes that Sharpton is fond of jawing with him about politics but has never asked a thing about how things were going with a bill pertaining to blacks.

The current renaissance in Harlem, for example, is occurring despite Sharpton rather than because of him. People truly committed to change have learned to work *around* the presumed "black leader," as he and Rangel sit at the gates of Harlem like the lions at the library on Forty-second Street, more interested in try-ing to steer development efforts in the old Big City Boss style than in lifting Harlem out of its misery at all costs.

Sharpton would even rather see Harlem burn if things don't go his way. When in 1995 a Jewish store owner was accused on flimsy pretenses of driving a black store owner out of business from a vendor's market in a building on 125th Street, Sharpton speechi-fied relentlessly against the "white interloper," implying a racist plot à la 1895. Eventually a young black man aroused by his ora-tory stormed the building, guns ablaze, and gutted Freddy's Fash-ion Mart. Death toll: eight; Sharpton: unrepentant. Here was a "black leader" condoning the torching of black-owned busi-nesses, seeing this as permissible damage in the name of throw-ing yet another idle tantrum against the evil white man.

Instead, Sharpton takes a cue from the Black Power era of his youth and assumes that tearing whitey a new one at regular inter-vals is the essence of Doing the Right Thing for black America. The result is a stream of arrant lies that would make his elevation beyond his petty fiefdom an embarrassment to black America. For details, see the previous chapter.

Not exactly "I Have a Dream." But then things didn't look much better for the prospects of black leadership at the national meeting of the NAACP in 2001.

In 1910 this organization released the sixteen blazing pages of the first issue of its house organ *The Crisis*, edited by W. E. B. Du Bois. In 1930 the NAACP issued the Margold Report, which spearheaded the eventual demise of "separate but equal" legal doctrine. Fol-lowing through by backing assaults on this policy through its Legal

Defense and Educational Fund, in the early 1950s the organization accomplished the *Brown v. Board of Education* victory.

Alas, fast-forward to 2001, when Kweisi Mfume and Julian Bond are mired, like Sharpton, in the idea that what black Americans need most is to be taught how pitiable they are, and that the constructive response to this is to distrust anything the government offers to help them. Bond insisted that there were "racially motivated voter purges" in Florida in the 2000 election, while Mfume dismissed vouchers as "some slick twist of playing around with things."

Bond and Mfume see blacks' salvation in an overhaul of the very underpinnings of American society. But this melodramatic idealism is out of step with the constituency they represent: a poll by the Joint Center for Political and Economic Studies found 83 percent of blacks in favor of vouchers, for example. To be sure, Mfume spoke of a "Strategic Plan" addressing health care, voting rights, racial profiling, and education. Yet while all four of these issues have loomed large in the news since August 2001, the NAACP has not been a major player regarding any of them.

Like Jackson, Mfume instead goes for the glitz. Thus over the past two years, the NAACP has been most prominent in Mfume's excoriation of the major television networks for not having enough black actors in their new shows. But today, through cable services, the typical household gets dozens of channels beyond the networks, and at any time shows from previous seasons vastly outnumber new ones. Viewed as a whole, the full television schedule has long all but overflowed with black faces, and the all-white cast is now the exception in a television show of any ambition. Meanwhile, for most ordinary blacks, whose life circumstances have never been calibrated with just how many "people like them" they see on the boob tube, the NAACP has become an abstraction.

Wary of acknowledging progress and faintly interested in grassroots efforts, the NAACP is no longer a "progressive" organization in any serious sense. Even Bond and Mfume seemed to sense this impotence at the "do" in 2001. Bond crowed that the NAACP was "still the biggest, baddest civil rights organization in the country." But people only need to say this kind of thing when they no longer really believe it.

———

But to read all of this as "a crisis in black leadership" misanalyzes what is, in the end, an inevitable historical development. Opportunism, moral weakness, and "mission creep" have been typical of leaders since history began. But they do not prevent signature historical contributions, as witnessed by Franklin Roosevelt and Lyndon Johnson, or more to the point Booker T. Washington and Adam Clayton Powell, Jr.

So yes, then, Jesse Jackson ran into hiding from the gunshot that killed Martin Luther King but then pretended to have cradled King in his arms as he lay dying. He is a "Reverend" who has never had a congregation, never finished the work for his divinity degree, and was ordained under largely symbolic circumstances—all because he wanted the clerical credential considered essential to Civil Rights leaders in the 1960s. As is often said, Jesse is about Jesse.

But the same kind of thing was often said about black leaders who nevertheless showed us the money instead of taking it home. Powell, for instance, matched Jackson almost point for point in callow opportunism and moral lapses. Yet all the same he played a major role in desegregating the armed forces after World War II, and was central in ramming reams of legislation through Congress helping blacks as head of the Education and Labor Committee starting in 1961.

Narcissism and solid leadership, then, are not incompatible. People like Powell could split the difference before the mid-1960s because black leaders had a concrete and morally urgent cause to channel their egotism into: forcing a nation to make good on its nominal commitment to democracy and equality by freeing blacks from legalized disenfranchisement.

But once the legal work was accomplished, black America was faced with a different task: to take advantage of the new opportunities available, despite residual challenges. And this is a matter of individual initiative rather than agitating for the cameras in the streets: the "riot as power" model has no place now beyond cheap thrills. Sharpton may crow that "confrontation works," but only if he means making good agitprop theater and reinforcing white guilt. When the dust clears, the head rabble-rouser has gained some exposure and, in Jackson's case, some friends get rich. But black Americans who need help remain just where they were. Just whose life did Sharpton's Crown Heights show improve in the slightest?

To wit: the Civil Rights victory eliminated the need for a national "black leader." We needed a King to take on the government and the conscience of the nation, but that job is now long done.

Some make the mistake of thinking that this is because views in the black community are now too diverse for one person to represent. But this is a distortion of black history. If anything, more consensus reigns among the most visible black spokespeople of today than in the days of yore. A century ago, Du Bois urged blacks to agitate for high positions while Booker T. Washington called for blacks to establish themselves financially from the ground up, instead of wasting energy butting up against the naked racism of the period. The competition between these two philosophies was essentially a dead heat. Both men were tarred as "wanting to be white" by some and cherished as prophets by just as many others.

As late as 1960, as a grassroots Civil Rights movement was advancing by leaps and bounds, black bourgeois scion and University of Chicago Law School graduate Jewel Stradford Lafontant stood before the Republican convention in pearls endorsing Richard Nixon, and later served as his deputy solicitor general. Lafontant did not think of herself as a maverick: she represented a healthy contingent of similarly minded blacks. The common sense that the anti-establishment hard left is the essence of "blackness" is only a few decades old.

No, the issue is less diversity of opinion than sheer progress, and the new responsibilities it confers. The rules of the game have changed. Justifying his quest to displace Jackson, Sharpton asked a *New York Times* reporter, "Well, who else is out there?" What he doesn't realize is that Jackson has never played a role remotely comparable to King's, and that there is no longer any need for anyone to do so. Glenn Loury, in his original incarnation as a black conservative, made King's widow cry in a speech in the early 1980s when he announced that "the Civil Rights revolution is over."

But he was right, and even Jackson himself had said the same thing ten years earlier, telling an audience one hot day in 1972, "The Civil Rights movement is over; that mission is accomplished . . . We have more rights than we can use."

But what could a black man seeking King's mantle do with that realization in 1972, if infected with the self-absorption typical of leaders of any race or era, and bereft of the clear mission that guided Civil Rights leaders of the past? Enter Tawana Brawley, or Mfume ending up quietly accepting an offer from NBC last year to tape a pilot for a talk show. Or Jackson, whose main point in that 1972 speech was "our problem is economic," but whose solution became making rich black people richer through the Wall Street Project.

Powell, straddling the Civil Rights Act victory, neatly played out the problem within a single career. He was born in 1908 and became a figure of note in the 1930s. The showboating and glamour-seeking aside, the meat of his career fell in an era when there were serious battles to be won, and he more than stepped up to the plate. His legislative achievements before the mid-1960s were almost dazzling. But in the end, what really drove him was the attention, and once the main battle was won, his addiction to the theatrical remained.

Hence his Black Power poses starting in the mid-sixties, longer on rhetoric than results. Powell was even the one who coined the term "Black Power," as it happens. His turn was predictable: the Panther routine was, if anything, crackling good theater, and by the mid-sixties it was the quickest route to prime press coverage for the black spokesperson. Most saw this as a decline. But wouldn't you know, Sharpton proudly recounts taking his cue from Powell in this twilight stage.

But of course he does. The Civil Rights movement aroused white guilt toward a noble cause. But then the scene was set for a certain personality type to cherish the thrills of eliciting the guilt over attending to real people's needs. Many are perplexed that our most prominent black leaders are so furiously convinced that their job is to teach their flock of their powerlessness. Human history rarely records an elite with so glum and disempowering a message for its charges. Who else in the past or present—even under the very worst of conditions—has told the ruling class "We can do nothing without your love" and held this up as empowerment and leadership? But with so many whites chilled to their bones to be called "racists," this new "Civil Rights" message is as simple as A-B-C: it gives a black "leader" the perfect formula for placing him- or herself at the center of a melodrama with an open-ended run.

———

Thus the nation's most prominent black "leaders" are asleep at the switch on the three most urgent issues facing black Americans today: inner-city stasis, blacks and crime, and education.

On the inner cities, for instance, our "leaders" dedicate so little energy to trying to turn things around in these districts that a Martian visitor would wonder whether they even existed. The issues here are subtle and complex, and so black "leaders" seek drama while white policymakers have created all of the large-scale efforts to address inner-city blight such as enterprise zones, Senator William Proxmire's Community Reinvestment Act of

1977 requiring banks to give loans to poor neighborhood institutions before mergers, and Community Development Corporations.

Focusing on handouts rather than self-empowerment, these programs have had mixed results although they have done some good. Yet Jackson, Sharpton, and company see little problem with the handout *modus operandi* when it comes to welfare, Affirmative Action, or corporate shakedowns. Thus it is notable that they have had nothing to do with these sincere, nationally aimed efforts, in favor of running their own "organizations" of even less tangible benefit to the black community.

Healing the relationship between blacks and police forces is another pressing issue in our moment: the friction here is today the leading perpetuator of black Americans' sense of separateness from the national fabric. Obviously, any serious address of this problem will first, build bridges between blacks and police forces, and second, seek to wean these young men from falling into lives of crime. And just as obviously, a "leader" seeking photo ops and the highs of interracial confrontation will see no urgency in either task.

Jackson, then, is predictably absent on the issue. Occasional local branches of the NAACP take it on, as at recent hearings held in Oakland, but the national organization is more interested in the job prospects for black actors in Hollywood.

Sharpton, of course, has his uses for blacks and crime: to promote himself by charismatically keeping his followers alienated from "the man"—never mind that this teaches people how to disempower themselves. Even Amadou Diallo's mother came to dissociate herself from the reverend as she gleaned that his interest in her son's death was primarily about idle histrionics and self-promotion.

Then there is education, as the latest National Assessment of Educational Progress survey tells us that three in five black fourth graders read below level. The household-name black leaders' only interest in the issue is to insist that the government pour yet more money into ossified public schools. But where black schoolchildren need to be led is to small-sized, effective schools with dedicated teachers. Jackson appears to know this, having sent his own children to plush, private St. Albans in Washington, DC, and two other private finishing schools, as the Chicago public school system fell to pieces.

Of course, Jackson meanwhile founded a branch of PUSH called PUSH-Excel, supposedly dedicated to improving education for black children nationwide. He even got the federal government to cough up millions of dollars in support throughout the 1970s. But PUSH-Excel rarely amounted to much beyond Jackson's inspirational speeches to students (for which he took payment from the federal grants).

"I am somebody," Jackson had students chant, this being PUSH-Excel's motto. But this chant assumed that black students' problem was that white supremacy had deprived them of self-esteem. But by the 1970s, black students' main problem was that Black Power ideology had taught them that doing well in school was a "white" thing to do. The students needed to be told that they were strong enough to make the best of what they had, not to bolster themselves against white supremacy.

Unsurprisingly PUSH-Excel had precisely no impact on the

black education problem. But rather than recast this address of one of black America's most pressing crises, Jackson has since moved on to drumming up business for affluent black friends through the Wall Street Project.

———

Yet for all of this, there is no "crisis in black leadership." Even the most selfless, well-intentioned, aspiring black leader would end up spinning his or her wheels trying to "continue the legacy of Dr. King." But there are plenty of new black leaders today who know this. Uninterested in idle quests to patrol white Americans' racial psychology, these people are steadily rescuing the minority of African-Americans still left behind. The irony is that the more effective they are, the less likely you are to have heard of them—and this is the way it should be.

Not that they are totally obscure. Star Parker, founder of the Coalition on Urban Renewal and Education (CURE), has spoken on the conservative think tank and college circuits. She has also made the rounds of most of the national television talk shows, where she is especially effective. Black people are too often called "articulate" for just speaking standard English, but Parker genuinely is a deft communicator, combining detailed policy data one minute with good old-fashioned mother wit the next. Parker's warm yet no-nonsense presence is that rare voice among black conservatives that can change minds as well as preach to the converted.

In the photos of Parker and assorted political stars in CURE's new offices in downtown Los Angeles, it is hard not to notice that most of the people in the pictures with her are white—Newt Gingrich, Jack Kemp, etc., with Alan Keyes as one predictable exception. But this makes a sad kind of sense in light of Parker's mission: to wean poor inner-city women away from welfare and into self-sufficiency.

Obviously the better-known "black leaders" can't have this, as it implies that white racism is no longer the main cause of black failure. But Parker's key concept is empowerment, endlessly repeated in CURE's literature and Parker's speeches. The time limits imposed on welfare in 1996 have left many inner-city women faced with fending for themselves for the first time in their lives, and CURE steps in to turn them toward self-reliance instead of variations on dependence. CURE holds clinics in inner-city locations pointing such women toward job training, while teaching them about personal finance. Jackson and Sharpton seek high-profile events to speak at, but Parker cherishes college gigs. No CNN in attendance, but it is here that she can get her message to the young: the people poised to create black America's future.

Parker's aim is not to combat "racism," but to "go everywhere the NAACP goes" and "run every department of social services in the country out of business." For Parker, the only appropriate social service agency in America is the church. The church turned her away from life as a welfare mother milking the system for extra payments and doing drugs. She stresses faith as a crucial factor in turning black people toward self-sufficiency, and as true black leadership goes, this is right on the money—African-Americans, across classes and education levels, are among the most deeply Christian people in the United States.

And Parker also sees the faith angle as a path toward a larger goal. She is currently crusading against Social Security, which she sees as denying poor blacks an opportunity to invest savings more profitably for their old age and children. She opposes abortion, noting that "more African-American babies have been killed by abortion during the past twenty-seven years than the total number of African-American deaths from all other causes combined." She also dedicates CURE to advocating school choice. But instead of just talking about all of this, she is going through the churches to enlighten black Americans to what a fundamentally conservative people they are.

Parker holds conferences for black pastors, where she is slowly converting several of them to setting up anti-welfare efforts among their flock, while also urging them to expose their flock to the political positions CURE espouses. A recent success has been Bishop Charles E. Blake of the West Angeles Church of God in Christ, who first came to a Parker conference skeptical, favoring the usual government-as-savior line. Today, however, he is increasingly seeing things Parker's way. And through in-church programs and sermons, he will be in a position to wield quite a bit of influence over his nine thousand parishioners—and that's nine thousand potential votes for politicians who can see beyond the handout philosophy.

Not that we're out of the woods yet—Parker recalls more than one pastor asking before agreeing to come to one of the conferences, "Don't have any cameras there—what if Maxine Waters finds out I was there?" But Parker has no time for nurturing animosity toward Waters and her ilk. She is too busy steadily forging a proactive pathway toward the only change that matters—the kind that comes from within.

Parker's oppositional stance toward the charity model of racial uplift repeatedly reminds me of Booker T. Washington, and wouldn't you know that as I left her office suite after a visit she handed me a paperback copy of Washington's first autobiography, *Up from Slavery,* to take with me, along with a stack of CURE literature. In that book Washington notes of the late nineteenth century that "Among a large class [of blacks] there seemed to be a dependence upon the Government for every conceivable thing. The members of this class had little ambition to create a position for themselves, but wanted the Federal officials to create one for them."

Sadly the situation a century-plus later is not much different, and this is exactly what irks Parker. Just as Washington urged blacks to "cast down your buckets" and acquire skills and capital from the bottom up instead of immediately seeking public offices and higher education, Parker sees small businesses as the salvation of inner cities, and she agitates for loosening the byzantine restrictions upon small business loans and holds clinics training potential entrepreneurs in how to obtain and utilize such loans.

I might note that Parker's stance on abortion and focus on religious faith depart from my personal positions. But I write about her not to push my own particular ideas than to show what modern black leadership is—showing the people left behind how to catch up, rather than teaching them why it isn't worth even trying until life is perfect in America. This is what is key, and my personal differences in philosophy beyond it are beside the point.

Despite Anna Deavere Smith's bleak prognosis for black leadership on the tenth anniversary of the Rodney King riots, it was in the wake of that event that Parker's disparagement of the rioters brought her a public audience and led to her founding CURE in 1995. Moreover, this was only one of several conservative black organizations that arose in the wake of the same unrest. Two others were the Center for New Black Leadership and BAMPAC (Black America's Political Action Committee), while another was Operation HOPE, which black entrepreneur John Bryant founded out of dismay at seeing black people destroying their own neighborhoods.

For Bryant, the problem was less "oppressed people expressing their rage in the only way possible" than a people with too little stake in their own communities. He founded Operation HOPE to help inner-city residents in Los Angeles buy their houses instead of renting. As James Baldwin said in *The Fire Next Time*, "The most dangerous creation of any society is that who has nothing to lose," and Bryant's gloss on this is that "The best social policy is a house." People with real estate are less likely to allow their neighborhoods to go to seed, more likely to take an interest in the social and political affairs that affect their investments, and will have an automatic asset to pass on to their heirs. Bryant's organization pushes inner-city residents in this direction through programs designed for "economic empowerment through education."

On the ground this translates into the "Operation HOPE package": cybercafés in inner-city communities where people are taught how to get their finances in order and buy houses, and in-school Banking on Our Future seminars for fifth through twelfth graders, teaching young minority kids basic economic literacy.

"Who wants to have money?" Operation HOPE's Karen Clark asks a class as she starts one of these school seminars. We are at

Edison Middle School in South Central, a functioning but tatty public school with a predominantly Latino and black student body. All the eighth graders raise their hands, but the atmosphere is tentative and sullen at first. Asked what their life goals are, they are less likely to say "go to college" than "go into the Marines," "be a mechanic," or, sadly often, nothing much.

But as Clark takes them through learning what a savings account is for and how to make and follow a budget, most of the students gradually light up. This is not a language these kids hear very often—"It's a little weird," says one. But Operation HOPE is teaching it to them and classes in three hundred other schools in Los Angeles; Washington, DC; Chicago; and all five boroughs of New York City; with Oakland soon to come.

Meanwhile, Operation HOPE's Los Angeles cybercafé is deliberately located in South Central. It incorporates a Pacific Bell payment center as a "hook" to attract clients. People paying their phone bills find themselves smack in the middle of a buzzing organization offering in one wing a check cashing service charging a mere 1 percent fee, and in the other wing a bank of computers, coffee shop, and elegant lounge for meetings and contact-making, all hosted by a concierge. Artwork by Los Angeles Unified School District students decorates the walls, and on the coffee tables sit issues of not only *Ebony* but also *Fortune*—message: there is nothing "white" about financial success.

For $100 a year, members can use the center to become acquainted with the internet—inner-city blacks and Latinos who cannot afford personal Powerbooks sit surfing the web at the terminals. Meanwhile, members are offered a ten-week seminar through UCLA Extension, teaching them about budgeting, saving, and credit. After this, they can work one-on-one with Operation HOPE caseworkers who assess their finances and match them up with mortgage loans. For inner-city residents distrustful of the world outside their neighborhood and uninformed of the steps toward solvency that middle-class people learn by imitation, Operation HOPE's staff offers a precious intermediary.

To date, Operation HOPE has gotten 450 mortgages for inner-city residents, with not a single default, and one thousand more are in progress. In 1999–2000, Operation HOPE matched up more inner-city residents with incomes below $41,000 with mortgages than the top eight banks combined. The organization also provides matching funds for particularly indigent applicants, but puts the funds into escrow rather than giving them directly to the client. So far Operation HOPE has also gotten small business loans for seventy enterprises.

And the results show: the efforts of Operation HOPE and other organizations involved in related activities have created a South Central visibly less desolate than it was in 1992. A drive through the Crenshaw district reveals a neighborhood patchy but stable, in a way that it was not ten years ago. The overall impression is a neighborhood that its residents care about, and we could identify nothing that the traditional Civil Rights gang has done since 1992 that affected this transformation. This came from *real* leadership—the unglamorous work of teaching people one by one how to make the best of themselves—while Jackson wangled deals for his rich cronies, Mfume got some black people hired in Hollywood, and Sharpton fiddled while black businesses burned.

To be sure, most of the money for Operation HOPE's efforts comes from corporations, some interested in pro bono work and others investing in future profits, such as State Farm with its "We Live Where You Live" program. But Bryant channels these funds into giving, as he puts it, "a hand up, not a hand out." Jackson "leads" by giving black businesses one-off graft payments, but Bryant requires the companies he deals with to foster ongoing relationships with his organization and its efforts: he has little time for one-time gifts. For example, he has banks send representatives to conduct the Banking on Our Future seminars. This remains a less starkly self-sufficient philosophy than Star Parker's, but the two share the goal of ultimately making poor minorities the captain of their own fates: "stakeholders in our communities," as Bryant puts it.

And Bryant is no more interested in identity politics than Parker: "I'm black but I'm not black for a living," he often says, and he is well aware that today, poverty is more a class issue than a racial one. As such, Operation HOPE has as much of a presence among poor Latinos as poor blacks.

The Reverend Eugene Rivers in Boston had a rocky start like Parker. His father left the family when he was a toddler, and by his teens, he was running the streets in a gang. But Rivers always had a studious side, and spent some time at Harvard and Yale, finally getting a degree from the Eastern Baptist Theological Seminary.

Rivers has directed church efforts toward saving young black men of Boston from lives of crime and violence. In 1992, the same year Parker was galvanized by the L.A. riots, the last straw for Rivers was when a group of thugs stormed a murdered youth's funeral and stabbed and beat one of the young men attending. Rivers cofounded the Ten Point Coalition, a group of about fifty black ministers who started taking the church to the streets, counseling young black men and interfacing between them and the criminal justice system. He continues this effort today, working from the Ella J. Baker House, a restored crack house in Dorchester, a black and Latino neighborhood that is more or less Boston's Harlem. "The vast majority of these kids are just looking for parents," he told me, and Rivers's background gives him "an intuitive, existential recognition of himself in another child."

Also like Parker, he sees religion as a key factor in turning black lives around: "It's the only thing that goes deep with black people. Besides, it's the only thing left." Rivers wants to put a different face on a Christian church that has come to be "seen as the chump institution with regard to black males." Rivers recalls how when he was growing up, "the bad [as in *cool*] dudes went to the mosque."

Crucially, it has been working. It's no accident that Boston, despite a core of poor blacks typical of a large American city, has not erupted in a profiling controversy over the past several years. There were 152 murders in Boston in 1990, but only 31 in 1999. During what is now often called the "Boston Miracle," 1995 to 1998, there was not a single killing of anyone under seventeen. It was crucial that Rivers and other ministers worked to forge trust between the police and inner-city communities, with the police contributing to recreational and job-training centers for troubled youth.

Rivers is under no illusion that racism is dead in the United States, but he is well aware that this message is no longer the one that real black leadership will require. "The principal obstacles to black people's development are not primarily white supremacy or white people. If slavery could be overcome, and could not keep us down, we need to get up off the whine thing." For him, the protest strategy cherished by Jackson and Sharpton should be, at best, one card in the deck: "The black community's got to decide, at some level, whether they want to do 'protest politics' or have measurable goals and reduce crime. One does not usually lead to the other." Rivers wants to train a young African-American leadership elite to "overthrow this Kuhnian paradigm" that leads so many current prominent blacks to dwell in the victim routine. "Life is not a BET video, and it never has been."

Rivers also has no time for indulging in the idle "root causes" rhetoric that supposes that poor blacks can only be expected to take care of themselves in a perfect world. "There must be a recognition that no amount of federal, state, or municipal goodwill can serve as a substitute for effective parenting and leadership in the neighborhood." And while he initially hoped to be able to save all of his charges from prison, over the years he has come to realize that doing the best for the black community means turning some of the most hard-core criminal cases over to the law: "In order to save the masses, you have to sacrifice a few."

On politics, Rivers is not far from Parker: "It was an intellectually and politically disastrous mistake for the black community to put all of their eggs in the basket of the Democrats," since this only lets them take blacks for granted. Meanwhile, "Republicans write us off, partly because we won't give them our vote and partly because they see that we're not strategic in our voting.

"Poor people are morally obligated to fight for themselves,"

Rivers says. The issue is teaching them how to do so, and Parker, Bryant, and Rivers are pointing the way, with themselves as object lessons. And all are extending their scope. CURE has a think tank division in Washington, DC, and I noted that Operation HOPE already has programs in several cities nationwide. Rivers co-chairs the National Ten Point Leadership Foundation, whose goal is to reproduce the Ten Point Coalition strategy in forty inner-city communities across America by 2006. So far, there are branches in Gary, Memphis, Tulsa, and Indianapolis, with Buffalo and Baltimore not far behind.

People like Parker, Bryant, and Rivers, then, are exactly the new black leaders that Deavere Smith rues the absence of. The leadership they offer does not make good television: there will be no cathartic scenes of whites being brought to their knees in the sequel to the Civil Rights victory that so many see as the next step in bringing blacks to parity with whites. Spike Lee will make no movie with Angela Bassett as Parker or Denzel Washington as Rivers—or might he? It'd be a great idea. But it is these people who are leading African-Americans today in the only meaningful way—teaching them to fend for themselves in an imperfect world.

———

And that brings us to something else we must accept as ordinary in a new racial landscape. Namely, "black leadership" will no longer be restricted to blacks. Contrary to the common wisdom that whites "don't care about us," as often as not non-blacks are smoking out and addressing the remnants of race-based inequities. The lawyer who won a billion-dollar settlement for black farmers who had been discriminated against for decades in loan policies by the United States Department of Agriculture was the Hispanic-descended Alexander Pires. Pires went so far as to seek out farmers eligible for payment and debt forgiveness; the NAACP's once-famed legal team was nowhere to be found.

Two reading programs aimed at disadvantaged students that have had promising results with poor black children are Success for All, created by white Robert Slavin, and Open Court, developed by researchers at the pedagogical materials company SRA (Science Research Associates). PUSH-Excel never ventured anything of the sort. The closest equivalent from the Civil Rights squad has been sparsely distributed pamphlets teaching black students standard English through comparison with Black English, under a conviction that black students have been "denied their rights as bilinguals."

Surely, however, blacks will play the principal role in closing the remaining socioeconomic gaps between whites and blacks, and resolving the interracial tensions that bedevil us still. History records not a single group of people who insisted that they were incapable of progressing without handouts and lowered standards from the ruling class, and history will not be kind to a group that continues to insist on this when more of its families are middle class than poor.

Many object that this is too much to expect of a group with such a tragic history. But this both overestimates the obstacles and underestimates blacks' resilience. Today, black success stories tend to be almost counterintuitively mundane, based on good old-fashioned hard work, ingenuity, and inner strength rather than snatching victory out of the jaws of defeat. Blacks who have made it after the late 1960s rarely address residual racism when they first tell their stories. When inevitably asked about it by their interviewer, they recount it as a minor nuisance they overcame by keeping their eyes on the prize, not as a virulent force that occupied their every waking hour. The traditional black "leadership" waits for a revolution, but meanwhile most blacks rise and thrive *in spite of* black leftist ideology, not in response to it.

People like this—today a norm, not exceptions—need national "leaders" no more than Latinos or Asians do. Today, black achievement will come from within, as it has for human beings throughout history under circumstances unimaginably worse than any black American's today.

As such, the new black leaders will be concerned citizens working on the local level to foster change through direct interactions with individuals. This is indeed a new America. Resurrected, Du Bois, Washington, Powell, and King would find themselves with nothing to do.

A vocal fringe will insist that it is naïve or callous to put so much faith in African-American individuals to determine their own fates. But at the end of the day, who else is out there?

Afterword

Of all the points I make in these essays, the one that in my experience evokes the most bewilderment, pique, or requests for further information is that Aid to Families with Dependent Children was expanded in the 1960s with black Americans in mind.

The point is crucial enough to justify suspending my desire that this book not be "academic" in tone. As such, I refer the interested reader to some sources especially useful on this question. Four books to consult are:

Welfare As We Knew It: A Political History of the Welfare State, by Charles Noble

From Opportunity to Entitlement: The Transformation and Decline of Great Society Liberalism, by Gareth Davies

The Price of Citizenship: Redefining America's Welfare State, by Michael Katz

The Future Once Happened Here, by Fred Siegel

For those aware that a book does not automatically become "ideology" because its author writes from the right, these two will also be germane:

The Dream and Nightmare: The Sixties Legacy to the Underclass, by Myron Magnet

The Tragedy of American Compassion, by Marvin Olasky

Index

About the Author

John McWhorter is associate professor of linguistics at the University of California at Berkeley, a senior fellow at the Manhattan Institute, and a contributing editor to *City Journal* and *The New Republic*. He is the author of seven books, including the bestseller *Losing the Race*, *The Power of Babel*, and *Doing Our Own Thing*.